A Guest House Journal

A Priest's Personal Journal During Alcoholism Recovery

To Diane
Peace
Father Bill

A Guest House Journal

A Priest's Personal Journal During Alcoholism Recovery

by Father Bill Stelling

Memphis, Tennessee
Eagle Wing Books, Inc.

A Guest House Journal

Published by
    Eagle Wing Books, Inc.
    P.O. Box 9972
    Memphis, TN 38190

For information about Guest House, visit their web site:
    www.guesthouse.org

ISBN: 0940829320
Retail Price: $14.95

DEDICATION

This Guest House Journal
is dedicated to

Austin Ripley

the founder of Guest House, in grateful
acknowledgment for his vision and the values
and mission that he instilled in Guest House.

It is his vision, values, and mission
that have returned me, and untold
numbers of priests and religious
men and women, to active and
meaningful ministry.

Table of Contents

Introduction by Daniel Kidd

Preface 1

Chapter 1: Week One 3

Chapter 2: Week Two: The Journal 35

Chapter 3: Week Three 51

Chapter 4: Week Four 61

Chapter 5: Week Five 69

Chapter 6: Week Six 89

Chapter 7: Week Seven 99

Chapter 8: Week Eight 109

Chapter 9: Week Nine 117

Chapter 10: Week Ten 129

Chapter 11: Week Eleven 137

Chapter 12: Week Twelve 145

Chapter 13: Week Thirteen 153

Chapter 14: My Story 165

Chapter 15: What Happened 172

Chapter 16: What It's Like Now 173

Chapter 17: Austin (Rip) Ripley 179

INTRODUCTION
By Daniel Kidd

When Father Bill Stelling sent a copy of his manuscript for *A Guest House Journal*, I immediately went to my bookshelf to review copies of two of his other books that he had previously sent to me. In looking for them I remembered that I had given each of them to someone else who was looking for some kind of help in dealing with an alcoholism issue. The practical help provided by a book by Father Stelling is always there as he writes from his own experience.

The book is the epitome of writing from his own experience as a client at Guest House. This journal is more of a journey as we travel with Father Bill in his day-to-day thoughts which are honest and cogent on what it is like to begin one's recovery from alcoholism and pills. From his initial doubts and denial about having alcoholism to his graduation from the program, Father Bill sketches a very typical picture of a priest at Guest House. I can hardly help but think that this will be a great help to future priests in treatment, but also a help to the lay alcoholic who begins a journey of recovery.

One single day is a very important possession for each of us in making our way through this life. A journal captures the present day, and keeping a daily journal is an activity we often recommend to our priests and sisters in the Guest House treatment programs. The program in recovery is a path of progress, as seen from a macro view, and a journal helps one to capture the key insights into a program of progress. Father Bill's journal is open and candid in exploring his initial ninety days of recovery.

Father Bill, as you will read, spent Holy Week at Guest House. I think there may be something special, a blessing seemingly in disguise, about a priest, or religious spending these sacred days in a recovery center like Guest House. Bishop Thomas Daily of Brooklyn has told me that he actually envies his alcoholic priests who go to Guest House because they get to experience the Paschal mystery of Jesus' suffering, death, and resurrection in a way unique to those in an addiction. The mystery of Jesus' death and rising to new life can never be unreal to a priest at Guest House during Holy Week.

Guest House has changed a few things about its treatment program since the 1980's, but the essence of what we do remains the same. It is about reflecting the unconditional love of God for each of His human creations in the way our guests are treated. It is also about introducing them to a new way of life in following the Twelve Steps of Alcoholics Anonymous each day, steps which also reflect the Spiritual Exercises of Saint Ignatius Loyola. One of our graduates said that he believes that Guest House "loved" him into his recovery. Because of the way priests, deacons, sisters, brothers, and seminarians are treated at our facilities, we enjoy a rate of recovery that is nearly unequaled in the history of addiction treatment.

Enjoy his journal, whatever your reason for reading it, as you would enjoy an ocean voyage. The trip has occasional waves and storms, but the results are worth it.

Daniel Kidd
President and CEO, Guest House,
Lake Orion Michigan,
December 26th, 2001

A side view of the Guest House in the snow.

PREFACE

I was a guest at Guest House from March 22nd until June 18th, 1989. Guest House is an alcoholic treatment center especially for priests, deacons, religious men and women, and seminarians. Guest House is located in Lake Orion, Michigan, just outside of Detroit, on the grounds of an estate formerly owned by the Scripps family. It was founded in 1956 by Mr. Austin Ripley. Today there are two locations for Guest House. The one in Lake Orion is the headquarters and is now dedicated to the treatment of alcoholism in religious sisters. The center for men has been moved to Guest House in Rochester, Minnesota. The pictures in this book are those I took while a guest at the Guest House in Lake Orion.

In an earlier book, **"You Can Get There from Here"** I focused on my road map to recovery. I would have included much of the information that you will find in the following pages, but I had no idea where it was. I thought I had lost forever the journal I kept while at Guest House, and the letters I had received and written from there to people at the Church of the Nativity. In the Spring of 2001 I found both.

Since I left Guest House I have enjoyed continuous sobriety. As of this writing that has been over twelve years. That would not have been possible without regular attendance at AA Meetings and living a program of recovery. I thought that the journal and the letters might be helpful to people entering a road to recovery, so I have set myself to the task of putting together a book based on my journal and the letters I wrote and received while at Guest House. Since my Journal is rather sketchy, from time to time, I have filled in gaps with present memories. I have also visited Guest House to refresh my memories. In reading over my journal I have discovered that I frequently change the tense of verbs, at times in the same sentence, and at times I have made corrections, at other times I have not. I hope this does not cause the reader any confusion. I do, however, wish to express thanks and appreciation to Ann C. Caradine for proof reading and other assistance with this project.

Now and then in the journal I have added material from the present day. These additions are in *italics*. The first three, or four days were written soon after I arrived at Guest House. Most of the time in referring to various priests I do not use the title: Father. This should not be taken as a sign of disrespect. It should be taken as a sign of familiar friendship. My Journal begins now.

A view from the front —more snow.

CHAPTER ONE
WEEK ONE

THE
JOURNAL

Let me make it very clear from the beginning: I don't know how to write a journal. I've never kept a journal, or a diary before. I don't know if anyone, other than myself, will ever read this. Nevertheless it seems to me that it should be written to someone. I mean a real person. I have no idea to whom it should be written. So, I'll write it to you.

MARCH 21, 1989
Tuesday of Holy Week

It all began on Tuesday of Holy Week, March 21 ,1989. But the truth is it began a long time before that, a very long time. However, I shouldn't get behind myself, so I'll begin at this second beginning.

It was 4:30 Tuesday afternoon. Jock and I were having a drink. Jack for me, water for Jock. Jock always drinks water, you know - he's a dog, a Shetland Sheep dog. Also known as a Sheltie. He is one of my best friends. I always have Jack, Jack Daniels that is, and a little water. We were sitting on a wicker couch in what I call "The Lynchburg Room". I also have two wicker chairs and a wicker coffee table in The Lynchburg Room. All of these were white wicker, and I had picked them up on sale. This is where I like to relax. Actually it began as a screened-in porch, but I changed my mind as the house was being built and it has become a glassed in, all weather porch. If you know anything about Jack Daniels, you know why I named it "The Lynchburg Room," - that's where Jack Daniels is made, Lynchburg, Tennessee. I'm a Catholic priest, and the founding pastor of the Church of the Nativity in Bartlett, Tennessee. In a few months I will celebrate 25 years as a priest. But to return to the matter at hand. Jock and I were having a drink. It was just 4:30 p.m., and I had to leave for the Cathedral no later than 5:15 p.m., so this left plenty of time to have just one drink.

In our Diocese - The Diocese of Memphis in Tennessee - Tuesday of Holy Week is the day of the Chrism Mass. This is the Mass at which the Bishop blesses the oils to be used sacramentally throughout the diocese until next year's Chrism Mass. It's also the time the priests renew their vows. I was looking forward to renewing my vows as a diocesan priest. Diocesan priests take vows of celibacy,

3

and obedience and respect to our Bishop. Religious Order priest add a vow of poverty. This annual renewal always stirred up in my mind the reasons I had and have for being a priest. I enjoy being a priest and I've always approached this renewal with a serious joyfulness.

Since I was sure they would have something to drink at the celebration after the Chrism Mass, I was only going to limit myself to one drink. But as I searched the fridge for some chicken scraps to mix with Jock's dog food I decided to sweetened my drink, just a little. I've always thought that when I sweeten a drink, I'm still just having one drink. Jock finished his dinner just as I finished my drink. Then I brushed my teeth and rinsed with a mouthwash. I mean, well I didn't want to go to Mass smelling like a distillery.

I backed my Honda out of the garage, and turned on the CD player. I own a Honda Civic, that is the bank and I own it. It didn't come with a CD player, but I had one installed in the trunk. I like classical music and I like to listen to it when I want to listen to it. Traffic was no problem since most everyone was going home out of the city while I was going into the city.

The Cathedral is on Central. It's an old building in an architectural style that many have called Romanesque-Colonial-Spanish. Parking is always hard to come by at the Cathedral so I wanted to get there early. Besides that I had a task to accomplish. I enjoy the fellowship, the conversations, the general camaraderie, and the good natured kidding of priestly gatherings, but to be honest, which is what I suppose a Journal should be, I don't really enjoy social mixing all that much. You might say I'm an uncomfortable mixer. As for that task I had to accomplish - I was looking for two very special priests.

Although I was early there were already a number of priests vesting for the Chrism Mass in the basement of the Cathedral, which at that time was a dark and dingy place. At one time it had been an auditorium of sorts. *(This basement was later renovated into a beautiful and functional Marian Hall. The Cathedral, itself, still later was renovated and was dedicated on the feast of the Immaculate Conception, December 8th, 2001.)* After I vested I started my search. I was looking for someone to fill in for me on the weekend of our Parish Pastoral Council Retreat in April. I was also looking for someone to give the Retreat. I found Joe Tagg first. He agreed to give the retreat. There was a catch however: I had to find someone to fill in for him. Now I had to find two more "fill-ins." Ned Elliot said he might be able to fill in for Joe Tagg, and Len Oglesby might be able to fill in for me. They both said they would let me know tomorrow. In our diocese there are never enough priests, and it's always a chore, and twice that, to find another priest to fill in for a weekend.

Before I could look for a backup priest, just in case something happened, the Master of Ceremonies called for us to listen up. He gave instructions, that we only half listened to, as to how we would get to our proper places in the front of the Cathedral. The sanctuary was not built to accommodate more than a dozen, or so priests. There was talk of a future remodeling, but that was somewhere down the road. When we had concelebrated Masses, the priests remained in the first three

4

pews on both sides of the main aisle and joined the Bishop at the altar when the Eucharistic Prayer began.

The procession for the Chrism Mass formed without incident. Before I knew it we had started to move. We made our way outside the building and wound around to the front doors of the Cathedral. As we stood on the steps waiting to enter the music and the voices of the choir greeted us. I can't remember the song, but I do remember singing with enthusiasm. I enjoy singing, perhaps more than other people enjoy my singing. The Cathedral was almost filled with people and everyone seemed to be singing with a good spirit. So with song and ceremony we made our way into the first three rows of pews in the Cathedral.

Although I don't enjoy pomp and ceremony all that much, this Mass was particularly meaningful to me, I'm not sure why. Certainly the renewal of my vows of priesthood played a part, but it was more than that. I remember thinking during the Bishop's talk how much I admire, respect, and even love our Bishop. I've never found it easy to relate to Bishops socially, so this was surprising to me. We all renewed our vows, the oils were blessed, the sermon given, and the Eucharistic Prayer concluded with the great Amen. Then there was Holy Communion, and shortly after that the Mass was over.

After the Mass there was a dinner in the rectory. I entered through the back door and the kitchen. I've always found it helpful to greet the ladies working there. The table in the dinning room was crowded with food and it all looked inviting. It wasn't a sit down dinner. You grab a plate, fill it up, then you get a drink, and sit wherever you can. After filling my plate the first thing I noticed was that the only thing they had to drink was wine. Of course they had coffee and soft drinks, but no hard stuff at all. I took my plate, and a glass of wine, and went in search of a place to sit. I don't remember who I was sandwiched in between, but without the usual before dinner drink I found it difficult to carry on a conversation. The fact that I had my mouth full most of the time helped. I knew right then that I was only going to have the one glass of wine, maybe two, and then get home, and have a real drink, or two, or three. I can't explain it, but I really felt cheated that night. I felt that "they" were trying to control my drinking, and I resented it. I resented it very much.

When I finished eating I visited with Al Kirk for a while. Al is not really tall, but I guess because he is so thin he just looks tall. We've been friends since we were in the seminary. We talked about a future Bridge game, and promised to set it up some time after Easter. We talked a bit about our present assignments. He had followed me at pastor of St. Mary in Jackson. Since we had both been in our present assignment for 10 years we wondered about a change. At gatherings like this is was not unusual that the Bishop would ask a priest to "consider" this appointment, or that one. I began to look for the door.

It was right then that I saw Pete Sartain coming toward me. We talked a little bit, and then he told me that the Bishop would like to "visit" with me at 9:30 the next morning at his home. I was not thrilled, and I asked Pete if I should lose any

5

sleep over it. He was noncommittal. I wondered if I was going to be asked to accept a change of assignments.

Next I ran into the Bishop, himself. So, I asked him the same question. He just smiled and was noncommittal. It was right then that I recalled that line from Shakespeare about someone smiling, and smiling and being a villain.

I wanted to get back to my rectory for a drink, a real drink. I assumed that most of the priests there were of the same mind. The drive home was filled with confusion, and anxiety. I searched every corner of my mind trying without success to find some good reason the Bishop could have for wanting to "visit" with me. Once I got home I mixed a generous Jack and water, then I became concerned in earnest: What does he want? Does he want me to take a different parish? I'd hate to leave Nativity. Maybe Clunan is retiring, and the Bishop wants me to take his place. I remember thinking that I'd hate to try to pastor a parish that big. Perhaps he wanted to appoint me to the Presbyterial Council. I went through a dozen "Perhapses" before I mixed the second drink. Deep in my heart I knew that there was something wrong. Maybe some people had written letters, not just one letter, but many. I knew that the major thing wrong in my life was getting a handle on my drinking. I knew it, but did anyone else know it? I didn't think so. How could they know. The question gnawed at the pit of my stomach and the bottom of my heart.

I had taken a resolution to give up drinking for Lent the year before. I discarded that resolution before Lent was half was over. Somehow I had buried the guilt, and shame that came with one more failure. This year, I had sworn it would be different. Before Lent started I prayed long, and seriously, and then I made the same resolution. The morning of Ash Wednesday I felt good about giving up drinking for Lent. I put up a good fight denying the desire to have a drink all day long. I denied myself all during the normal Happy Hour, and I felt good about that. After the evening Mass, when all was said and done, the time came to relax. I guess I just got tired of fighting with that unquenchable desire to have a drink. I thought to myself that I had put up a good fight all day long, so I decided to relax with a little reward. I'd have just one little drink. As soon as I had that first drink I knew that I had failed. I hate being a failure. I ended up having three or four.

The next morning I reasoned with myself. I'd just have to find something else to give up for Lent. I knew that I could not go through Lent feeling like a failure. So I'd just find something else. I had to admit I couldn't go without Jack nor could I live with the shame of failure, so I'd just do something I could handle. I don't mind being weak. Everybody has at least one or two weaknesses, and they live with them. Jack had become a friend in need, and I needed a friend.

Nevertheless I still didn't think that I showed any of the "typical" signs that anyone else would notice. How could the Bishop know? I was also concerned about my temper, and my memory. These were probably related to drinking.

When Bruce came in, I asked him if he knew anything. He knew nothing. At least that's what he said. I don't think he would have told me if he knew anything. I've known Bruce since he entered the seminary. He was teaching at Bishop Byrne High School when he decided to apply to the Diocese as a seminarian. He lived in

6

my rectory in Jackson that summer before he left for the seminary. He called me "Father". I remember telling him, "Bruce, I'm old enough to be your father but I'm not, so please just call me Bill." I also served as his supervisor for a while during his deacon year. He even invited me to preach at his first Mass in his home town of Scranton. Now, as a priest unassigned to a parish he worked at the Chancery, and lived in the rectory at Nativity. Lately it seemed to me that things were changing between us. I decided to mix another drink and go to bed.

MARCH 22, 1989
Wednesday of Holy Week

The next day I met Bruce in the kitchen before my Mass, and again I asked if he had any idea what the Bishop wanted. The only thing he said was that I should not worry about it, and, "the Bishop is a kind person." That really did worry me. There was no particular intention for the Mass that day, so I offered it for me. After Mass I came back to the rectory for one more cup of coffee. Bruce had already gone. I read something vaguely sinister into this, though there was nothing unusual about it. I was really beginning to worry, but I knew that things were out of my control. So I just got in my car and aimed it for the Bishop's house at the corner of Poplar and Graham. The house was given to the Diocese when Dozier was here. He was the first Bishop of the diocese.

I arrived on time at the Bishop's house. I noticed that there were flowers in bloom, then I recalled that this was the first day of Spring. I thought, maybe this just might be a good sign. I didn't notice any other cars in the driveway, so I guessed that meant that it was going to be a short meeting since I assumed I would be one on one with the Bishop.

The Bishop answered the door. Another good sign. He invited me in. As I entered the living room I immediately noted the presence of Pete Sartain, Bruce Cinquegrani, and my deacon, Larry Howell. They were all seated in such a way that four chairs formed a semicircle, and all of them faced one empty chair.

I was immediately alarmed, "What's going on? Am I on trial?"

The Bishop invited me to have a seat, and told me that this was not a trial. They just wanted to share with me some of their concerns. I knew that my seat was the HOT SEAT. Somehow, or another, I knew the game was over. I knew that they knew that I had a problem with drinking. The Bishop told me, "Bill, you're a good priest, and you do good work, but you've got a problem and we want to help you with it." He assured me of their love, respect, and their concern.

Then they, each in turn, catalogued the signs of "my problem." Each one began, and continued speaking in a simple, matter of fact, tone of voice. I don't know how they did it. I began to notice something about the way they were saying things. They never once accused me of anything, so I didn't have the need to mount a defense.

The assurances of the Bishop had their intended effect. My alarm seemed to dissolve. I was not all that uncomfortable. I was embarrassed. At times I wanted to scream, "STOP IT!!" But I dared not try to stop them. I was actually afraid that I just might succeed. I had to let them continue. Something in my mind, or heart, told me that this was the help, the chance, I had been looking for. I noted once, or twice, that this, or that, was wrong, or misinterpreted, but I wasn't about to argue over inches, when they had miles of evidence.

When they finished I sensed that they were uncomfortable. I knew I was expected to say something. I guess they were waiting to see how I would react. Perhaps they were concerned about how I would react. I decided to take the Bishop at his word. I assured them that I had no argument. I actually tried to thank each one. What I really wanted to say, but was unable to was, "What took you so long?"

The Bishop told me that since I no longer had control of my life he was taking charge of it. He told me that he had made arrangements for me to go to Guest House, a treatment center for alcoholic Priests, which is just outside of Detroit, Michigan. I didn't like the term "alcoholic", but decided not to make an issue of it.

I asked if I could say something, and the Bishop said, "Of course." I asked for the meaning of the word "maudlin" and, when that was answered, I asked when I could leave for Guest House. The Bishop said that I would fly up tomorrow. I asked him if it was possible that I could leave that day. He turned to Father Sartain. The two of them conferred, and Pete left to make a phone call.

(As I review this from the vantage point of more than twelve years later I must admit that to this day I have no idea what moved me to be so cooperative. The only thing I can come up with is the grace of God.)

I assumed that since the Bishop was making arrangements that someone would take charge of my parish. Nevertheless I asked the Bishop about it. He said that Father Leonard Oglesby would fill in for me. I had known Len for a number of years. I was once his associate and we were, and are, good friends, so I was somewhat relieved.

I remember wondering aloud who would break the news to the parish, and how. The Bishop suggested that I write a letter. I agreed. I told the Bishop that I would write something like this: "Dear People of Nativity, well you have finally done it, you have driven me to drink." Everyone laughed, but I assured them all that I knew that I, alone, was responsible for my drinking.

(I wrote that letter. The treatment lasted three months, and, while in treatment, I wrote a letter to the people of Nativity almost every week. Writing a weekly letter developed into, "From the Heart and Mind of Father Bill," a weekly insert for the parish bulletin, and later into a column in the newspaper for the Catholic Diocese of Memphis, in Tennessee, now known as The West Tennessee Catholic. Some of those columns have appeared in my book, "Spiritual Reflections on Everyday Living.")

I told the Bishop that I had been concerned for some time that people had been leaving the parish, and that it was probably my fault. I told him that I would be glad to leave the parish if my presence was hurting the parish. He assured me that I was the pastor, and would remain the pastor of Nativity. He said he had confidence in me, and suggested that Larry Howell read my letter to the people.

It was then that I realized that the treatment program was to be for 90 days. My 25th anniversary would occur on May 17th and I thought out loud, "Well that celebration is out the window." The Bishop told me that one day I would think that this was the finest 25th anniversary present that he could give me. *(He was right.)*

Everything was settled, but as we started to move out Pete Sartain came in with the news that it was possible that I would be able to leave that afternoon. I said, "Fine!" I'm ready to go. He assured me that he would call me as soon as possible with the final arrangements.

Bruce and I drove back to the rectory. When we were almost there I remembered that I had to pick up my income tax papers, so I made a side trip to Jim Liles' office.

When I finally got home there was a message that said I would be able to leave that afternoon at 3:00 p.m. At that point things really started to move rapidly. I had so little time, and so much to do, but as far as I was concerned there was no turning back. I had to make sure that Bruce knew how to take care of my dog, Jock, a Sheltie. I had to stop by the vet's to get some things. I had to pack. That was a problem: "What should I take?" This was the first day of Spring, but what was Spring like in Detroit?

Bruce fixed lunch while I went to talk to my staff. They knew that I knew that they had played some part in the intervention. I assured them that I was not angry. I told them that I was confident that they would be able to carry on. I got one member of the staff aside, and tried to point out that he/she had my full confidence, but to avoid undue criticism she/he would do well to let the Deacon, Larry Howell, have the spotlight. *(I choose not to identify that person by name or gender.)*

Victor, my neighboring pastor, and an old, and good friend, came over and offered to take care of Jock if needed. I didn't think that it would be necessary. *(As it turns out it was, and Victor did take care of Jock.)*

I said, "I think I'll have a drink", meaning club soda. Someone said, "Go ahead, you deserve a last drink." I knew what I wanted, and it was not alcohol. I really hoped that I could do something about my problem with alcohol. Greg, a seminarian in residence at Nativity, returned with Bruce's car. Bruce had left his car with Greg so I would not see it at the Bishop's house. I was uncomfortable around him because I didn't think he could possibly understand my disgrace.

In the midst of all those unusual things, ordinary things continued to happen. Rick came by for spiritual direction. Someone called seeking information about T-ball. I didn't know whether to laugh, or cry. Steve Miller called, and was very supportive.

Somehow, or another, I got everything packed, the letter to the people written, and I had some time left over. I sat in the living room in my easy chair with Jock. How could I tell him what was about to happen? I held him close as I thought of how much he would hurt, and how much of that was my fault, and the fact that there was just no way for him to understand. There was no way I could write a letter that he could read. It was then that the tears came. They were silent tears, and there was no way to stop them.

Greg was leaving on the same plane as I to visit his family in Detroit. Bruce took us both to the airport. What a ride. I had tears inside, and outside. I tried to talk to Greg. To tell him how ashamed I was, and that I hoped it did not turn him off to the priesthood. Both he and Bruce assured me that was not what was going on. They both told me that Greg, who was a West Point graduate, and had served in the army, had a more mature understanding of alcoholism. I was still uncomfortable, and almost totally defeated. We finally got to the airport. I had my ticket in hand but still had to check in. I found that Ernie Magree, a parishioner, was behind the ticket counter. I simply told him that I was flying up to Detroit for a visit.

We boarded the plane, but because my plans were made in such a rush Greg and I didn't get seats together. There was some delay, and we just sat there. Finally the announcement came that the flight would be delayed for two hours. Everybody got off the plane. I wandered aimlessly. Finally I saw a hotdog stand. I had been too nervous to eat much lunch so I got a hot dog. All they had to drink was coke, and I didn't care for one. I went into the nearest bar for something to drink. It was a club soda with a slice of lime. I'll always be grateful to Greg for not following me to see if I got something alcoholic to drink. I didn't really want anything alcoholic to drink. The plane finally took off, two and a half hours late.

We landed in Detroit about 9:30 p.m. I met Greg's father. I don't remember much about him because I was dead tired. Also almost immediately I met the two people from Guest House, John M. and Bob, the driver. There was much confusion about the baggage. It took over a half an hour to get the luggage, and John seemed to be more upset than I was. Then I realized that they have been waiting in the airport for over two hours. It turns out that they had been waiting for over three hours.

We traveled from the airport to the treatment center in the Guest House van. Bob really knew how to miss every light. The traffic moved swiftly, however it still seemed like a long way to Guest House. I was past caring. John didn't seem inclined to conversation, which was just as well because I was worn out.

Abruptly Bob turned and said, "Guest House coming up." As we drove through the gates of Guest House a bright light flashed. John told me that I had just had my picture taken. I thought he was serious, but he wasn't. The flash was a warning to the night man at the desk that someone was coming through the gate.

It was about 10:30 p.m., yet the office was not deserted. Jackie, the nurse, was there, and she checked me in. There was not much that could be done that late at night. I had a vicious headache, and a pain in the neck that was more than I thought I could bear. Jackie told me that much of that may have been due to the fact that I hadn't eaten. I agreed since there had been no scheduled meal on the plane, but then the plane hadn't kept its schedule. She told me that I could get a sandwich, a few cookies, and something to drink in the basement. She advised that I should not eat anything in the morning because I was scheduled to have some blood work done, and that I should meet the driver out front at 7:00 a.m. Then she looked at me with a smile, a big, beautiful, and sincere smile, and she also told me that I should expect a miracle. She was serious, but I didn't know it then. I thought that was just something she was supposed to say.

John M. led me down a narrow stairway to the basement, and food. I was greeted by a few of the guys in treatment. I'm always nervous meeting new people, and I knew that I would not remember their names in the morning. There were the usual questions: Name? Parish? Diocese? When was my last drink? I ate two sandwiches quickly. I looked around and jokingly said, "What! No wine?" I was joking, but a glass of chilled white wine sure would have tasted good. I told them that I was so accustomed to wine with a meal that I automatically ask about it. With mock anger I said, "It's savage to dine without wine." They all laughed. They knew, or hoped that I was kidding. They had all been there. They knew what I was going through, better than I did.

John had disappeared so someone else helped me with my luggage, and led me up some stairs, and then down a short narrow hallway to a place called "Hogan's Alley." My escort *(I'm sure he told me his name, but I have never remembered it.)* told me that the rooms in this hallway were reserved for all newcomers. The hall was named after a guest named Hogan. It seems that while he had been a guest he decided to spend the entire three months there and for that reason it became known as "Hogan's Alley". There was even a plaque over the entryway that bore the legend, "Hogan's Alley". He also told me that the rooms along this hallway had been used by "live in servants" in the days that people had "live in servants."

What a day: I celebrated Mass at Nativity at 8:00 a.m., and now hours , and hundreds of miles later, I went to bed in "Hogan's Alley" at Guest House at 11:15 p.m., March 22nd, 1989. It was certainly "one of those days." It was a day I'll never forget.

MARCH 23, 1989
Holy Thursday

I needed no help to be up early. Actually someone did knock on my door at 6:30 a.m. Since I was to have some blood work done I had no breakfast, not even coffee. I glanced at the newspaper, but had no idea what I was reading. Finally Davie, the driver, arrived, and we went to the lab. The trip took about 20 minutes. Davie told me a little about himself. He surprised me with what I thought should be personal information. Davie is an alcoholic, and he was very open with me about how he handles it. I found this surprising, but very encouraging.

I was more surprised that there were patches of snow here and there, and it was cold. It only took a few minutes to take the blood. I do have a concern about what the lab results might show. It has been 8 years since I had that slip. What the hell, since I am being honest I might as well face it all, I'm tired of hiding from things.

After the blood work I asked Davie to stop for a cup of coffee, he did, but he shouldn't have, it was awful. I had a fantastic cup of coffee years ago and that's what keeps me coming back for more. I know there's a mate to that cup of coffee out there somewhere. I haven't found it yet, but "hope springs eternal." When someone makes coffee to taste as good as it smells that person will make a fortune.

We got back in time for breakfast, and some good coffee. I am surprised by how good the food is. I should say the food is great, and it's served with style. I re-met some of the guys I met last night. I told them that I have a memory problem. They told me that memory is part of the alcoholic condition. Its called CRS: "Can't Remember Stuff." Except they didn't say, "Stuff."

After breakfast I finished "Intake" with Jackie, and had my first session with Jack Gregory at 10:00 a.m. Jack is different. He is a psychologist. I cannot tell if he is serious, or not. He gives me a picture of some geometrical figures, and tells me to draw them. Well I do my best, which turns out to be pretty good. When I finish he tells me it's a test for the DT's, which I don't have. Next he gives me a concentration test. Starting at 100, I am to count backward subtracting 7 each time. Math never was my strong suit. I'm glad this was not a speed test. We talk for a while. I tell him that he doesn't have to persuade me to do anything. Just tell me, and I will give him my full cooperation, I just want to get started so I can get back to my parish. He seems to be at pains to put me at ease. Well I am fully at ease, I think. I just want to get started.

11:00 a.m. – I see Doctor Lyons. He is an older man, and much like I recall the G.P.'s of the past. He has my immediate confidence. He speaks in a soft but compelling voice. He tells me about Alcoholism. According to him it has a genetic factor that most people call the "X" factor. Not everyone has it. According to some people it is commonly, but perhaps not scientifically, associated with, but not limited to, certain national and racial groups. It manifests itself differently in each person, and once it is triggered there is no way that person can ever drink normally again. I believe him, that is I believe that he believes what he is telling me, but I'm not totally convinced.

He gave me a complete physical. I was somewhat surprised that I weigh only 137 and $3/_4$, about 10 pounds less than I thought. I'm happy about that. I mention to him my drunken escapade of about 8 years ago, and my worry about the results from the blood test. He doesn't think I have much to worry about. He'll let me know when the lab results come back. I am somewhat relieved, but not fully.

At lunch I meet again my team leader, my sponsor, my guru, John M. It's his job to make sure that I find my way around, and get acquainted with people, and the schedule. I don't think he's all that interested. I'm lost most of the time, but I got to remember that this is still my first day. Maybe I'm in too much of a hurry. I'm confused, and I'm not yet ready to be patient and let things work themselves out.

I find an unexpected help in Don K. He is a religious Brother. I forget which order. I think he will be a good unofficial guru. Don is a man somewhat younger than I. He seems to be filled laughter and life. I find it difficult to believe that he has gone through the doubts, the fears, the failures, the tears that I have. I can see that he has something I want. We hit it off right from the start and he is very willing to share with me whatever he knows about Guest House, and about the treatment program.

The dining room is magnificent. The walls are all hand carved wood paneling, the ceiling is leather, at least that's what I'm told. I'm the type to take what people tell me as the truth. The ceiling might well be leather, but it looks like someone has painted it. There are four windows of leaded glass with a stained glass picture in each. The stained glass pictures depict: Guests Arriving; A Wine Steward; A Cheese and Fruit Steward; and The Host Greeting His Guests.

There is a smaller dining room for more intimate meals. This is where the professional staff eats. I am told this is one of the Scripps homes. In fact, I'm told, this house was built as the Summer House for his daughter. Like some of those homes in Newport, Rhode Island, this is just one of the great homes built before the days of income tax.

I have another surprise after lunch. There is a van leaving for K-Mart. The guys tell me that I should take every opportunity I have to get away from the house. Although I've never been accused of being conservative, I wonder at this liberal attitude. Won't people stop at the first liquor store for a fifth of this or that? But then it's really none of my business. This will certainly be a different way of living: A shopping trip to K-Mart as the high point of my week. I remember the movie, "One Flew Over the Cuckoo's Nest" when Jack Nicholson took the residents of a mental hospital on a trip. Now I'm one of the inmates. I'm able to laugh about it.

After the trip to K-Mart there are more Office details to take care of: Pictures are taken for the Staff; forms are filled out; authorizations are signed; etc. These authorizations are important. I'm told that I can identify by name just who I will receive phone calls from. About the pictures, I asked them if they were going to have me hold my name and some numbers in front of me. They thought I was serious.

I am given an "Overview of Clinical Experience." This tells me briefly what will be happening to me over the next thirteen weeks. I skim to the last week and find that there is a "Departure Mass" and a "Recognition Luncheon." Well, that's a long way off, but I can dream, can't I?

I'm also given a page of "General Information." It tells me when Mass is and when meals are. Hey they even got people to clean my room, and a laundry service. And then there's that mention of "Self-shopping trips" this is really surprising to me.

After the office stuff I can go and meet some of the guys, but the last thing I want to do is meet more people, so I head for "Hogan's Ally" and a nap. No sooner had I settled down for a nap than I realized that today is Holy Thursday. It is 4:30 p.m. and time for Mass. I rush to the chapel area in time to vest for Mass. What an absolute jumble, and conflict of emotions. We're all vested, just standing around waiting in the Hall for things to begin. Nobody seems to know what we are waiting for, at least I don't. As far as I can tell it is like the military: Hurry up and Wait.

I think of my people, the people of Nativity. God, how I miss being with them. What will they think of me when they find out as Larry reads that letter? When will he read it? Is Holy Thursday the right time? Should he wait for Easter Sunday?

These are all the wrong things for me to be thinking about. Right here, and right now, these are not the thoughts I should be concerned with. But I do miss them. Someone else has to do my job - all because of my failure, the people deserve better.

I suddenly realize that all I'm doing is thinking about how bad I feel. How sad I am. How much I'm hurting. There I am standing with a bunch of priests, vested for Mass, about to celebrate the Holy Mysteries of God's love, and all I'm really doing is thinking about me. I tell myself: STOP THINKING SO MUCH OF YOURSELF. I almost say it out loud.

My job now is to get well, at least that's what the Bishop told me when he said I shouldn't worry about the parish. He said that alcoholism is a disease, and that the program at Guest House would help me to get well. I don't really know if "well" is the right word. Doctor Lyons, and the guys here tell me alcoholism is a disease, and I want to believe them. It's both easy, and difficult to believe. I'm not fully convinced.

As Mass begins so do my tears. I'm sure everyone must be looking at me. Perhaps they think I'm saintly, perhaps they think I'm nuts. Perhaps they think this, or that about me. There I go again: All my thoughts are on ME. If Doctor Lyons is right about this "X" factor, and it means that I wouldn't be guilty about the drinking, at least I can be guilty of being self-centered. *(Later I find that this doesn't mean I should be relieved of all responsibility for my drinking.)*

Why is it so important that I be, or feel guilty? So I can be forgiven? This is too much for me, and I have no idea how to sort it out. I do miss my people , and the support, and love I get from them. I am so choked up I can't even sing.

The sermon begins. Marcel is preaching, he speaks of Marsalis, who said to him at dinner last week, "You know this is the first time in 47 years I've not been in my parish for Holy Week." Right then I realized that everyone is feeling exactly what I'm feeling, some even more so. I also realized that there were tears, and sniffles here, and there. Few of us were willing to look the other in the eye. I take this as a gesture of kindness that granted each person his own privacy. I dreaded the sign of Peace, but when it came somehow my tears were not important.

The 10th Station came to my mind - "He stood exposed to the jeers of others, STRIPPED OF EVERYTHING." Of course the big difference is that HE was innocent. Communion came, and I wondered about drinking from the Chalice. I had determined that I would not receive from the Chalice, but all the others were, so, I thought it must be alright. Nonetheless I simply let the Precious Blood touch my lips. I do not want to ever take another drink of alcohol, until I get this problem under control, and even though it is the Precious Blood of Jesus Christ, it's still alcoholic. I promise myself that I will be open to all they have to offer here, and to learn how to live a new way.

14

After Mass, at dinner, I meet Don K. again, he seems to know just the right thing to say to help a guy. Meal time is a very important time. It's a time for socializing, sharing, and caring among peers. I find out that seats are assigned, and they change each week. This helps people to get to know each other, and to help each other. Don tells me that alcoholics do start getting well here, with the counseling and lectures, but it is important for the alcoholics themselves to work on, and with each other.

MARCH 24, 1989
Good Friday

What a night, hardly slept at all. The room that has been assigned to me is not much bigger than a monk's cell. I almost said a prison cell. There is closet to hang things in, a chest of drawers to put things in, a chair and small desk. Of course there is a bed, and a window with a view of the parking lot.

I lay awake for what seemed like half the night wondering: "Did I make a mistake by agreeing so quickly to come to Guest House?" Was there a message in that two and a half hour delay at the air port? Do I really belong here? There was no loud, or quiet sobbing, but I could not stop the tears. Finally I realized that, mistake, or not, I was here, so I might as well make the best of it. I don't know for sure if I am an alcoholic, but I do know that I have a problem controlling my drinking. Maybe they can help me with that. I hope so. If I can get a handle on that perhaps it will be worth it. I finally got to sleep, but then, too soon it was 8:15 a.m. I take my first shower here. The bathroom is down the hall. Yesterday I was in too much of a hurry because of the blood work, and finishing up all the intake procedures. The whole day was filled with too many confusing things. Boy did I need a shower. I don't know how to explain it but it turned out to somehow be a Spiritual Act. A washing away of the past, a rebirth, a baptism. Whatever it was I see it as the beginning of a new life. I pray that I will be able to live it out.

At breakfast, since I don't yet have an assigned seat, I sit at a table with an empty seat. Marcel is at this table, and I thank him for last night's sermon. He tells me that Marsalis is 72 years old. The thought occurs to me, "Why put a man of his age through all that I think will be required by a change in life style.

(Later, much later, I find there is a very good reason, but I'll tell you about that later. See 'My Story, What It Is Like Now,' chapter 16, page 177.)

I also find that Marcel, and I are celebrating our 25th anniversary of ordination this year, he May 16th, and I May 17th.

After breakfast I find a place to walk, and pray the Office of Readings and Morning Prayer. I struggle with feelings of failure, guilt, shame, uncertainty. I know there is life after this, but I don't look forward to the labor pains. People here are telling me about some of the "classic" signs of alcoholism. I begin to recall some things in my own experience that relate: pouring a drink only many minutes after, or even hours after arguing with myself about whether, or not I should have a drink. Then pouring the drink all the while knowing I didn't really want to have

15

one; hiding my glass when someone would come to the door; making sure that Bruce was in his room before mixing my second, or third, or fourth night cap; and asking myself WHY? And getting no satisfactory answer. Oh yes, I was ready for Guest House. I just didn't know how to ask for help. I was afraid to ask for help. I'm glad, very glad to be here. I'm a little confused about what is going to be expected of me. In fact, I'm very confused. I'll tell you just how confused I am. Last night I was almost convinced that I should not be here. Now I'm convinced that I should be here. Tomorrow I'll probably change my mind again.

I'm also confused about how the people back home will understand why I am not there. How they will accept it? I'm devastated about hurting so many people, and my dog , Jock, who only knows that I am not there. Strong guilt feelings about what I have done. How could I have so selfishly hurt so many people? A lot of this is selfishness itself. I trust, that here, they will show me, and help me to deal with this in a truthful, and healthy way. What I'm doing now just ain't real healthy.

At lunch I thought I noticed that Don had been crying so I ask him if he would walk with me. I was mistaken, at least he says so, but he walks and talks with me. He's good, and easy to talk to. He has only been here four weeks. I hope I can be as supportive when I am here four weeks. I try to explain my feelings to Don: I want to go back to Nativity, but know that I can't go back 'til June, so I'll stay the course. I'm afraid to go back even then. Don says most people will "take their hat off to me." I want to believe him but I realize that's the way a novel ends, and this is not a novel.

I take time to write to the Bishop, Bruce, Peter and Larry. They were my inter-veners. I want to thank them for a tough job. I also write to my Staff. I try to encourage them to carry on. I need their support. I know my notes are dripping with self-pity, but that's how I feel as I write.

At the Good Friday Services I have feelings of profound unworthiness. I would very much like to be in my parish but where would I get the strength to be Pastor? I realize that the strength to pastor is from the Lord, or it's no strength at all. My mind goes back to the 10th Station - "Stripped of Everything." I'm stripped alright, but that's where the comparison ends. Perhaps I should sing "O Happy Fault," from the Easter Vigil. Yeah, but I ain't happy right now.

I've been here a full day and a half, and although I've never been to an AA meeting I've heard the guys here talking about them. A strange thought just hit me: A week ago I think I might have been able to have walked into an AA meeting with a drink in my hand just to show them that I was not like them, that I'm still in charge - even though in the secret of my heart I would have known otherwise. Somehow, or another, I don't really trust this treatment program, I don't think that it will work. But I'm willing to try. Something has to work.

After supper I need some time to think, I need a walk. The food is good and a guy could get fat up here. Mood swings are still part of my life. From acceptance of myself, to a necessity to think of anything else, to wishing I was dead. I've been told that nothing will happen to me, or for me, as far as this program goes 'til after Easter.

I was in such a rush to get here, and now because it's Holy Week, not much is getting done. I continue to think now and then that I have made a mistake by agreeing to come up here so easily and so quickly. I have begun to think that the major delay with the plane may have been a message that I should not have come up here. I was supposed to see my counselor yesterday, but I was in a state of total confusion about where I should be, and who I should be with. I missed that appointment.

Ed B. (a priest) returns from TL (Therapeutic Leave) . I remember that one summer he worked in my parish while he was a seminarian, but that was a few years ago. I call him, and he is coming down from the Villa. We talk for a while, I'm somewhat depressed. Ed has almost finished his three months, and I thought it would be good to talk to him. But something is wrong, maybe it's because he seems so healthy, and I don't. Maybe that was it. After he leaves I am totally depressed. Not suicidal, but sometimes I do wish I were dead. A lot of crying tonight. The coffee (and stress) with Ed give me very painful gas, so I take two Tylenol #3. I try to read a little, and try to lay perfectly still so the gas will pass off. Gas has always been very painful for me. Sleep comes late. I stay awake thinking about my disaster. I recall what an old drinking buddy used to say, "Life goes on."

Can I ever play the part I feel called to play, live the life I think I'm called to live? Can I ever be a good priest again? Have I totally messed things up? Why do I write all this stuff? I really don't know. I'm trying to be honest, but I'm so used to not really being honest with, and about myself - I wonder what value this writing will have. I hope that it has some value, at least for me. I've always heard that keeping a journal is therapeutic. I sure hope so.

MARCH 25, 1989
Holy Saturday

After breakfast I walk with Frank O. Walking is one of my favorite things. It makes no difference whether I have company, or not. I like to take my dog, Jock for walks. Even when I have no one to walk with I've always known that God is with me. That may sound overly pious, but it is the way I feel. When I was in the seminary I learned to walk and read at the same time and that is what I continue to do, especially with the priestly Office.

To get back to Frank. He has recently quit smoking, and is facing an operation to remove a tumor in his lung. He told me that for him it is much harder to quit smoking than it is to quit drinking. I quit smoking about ten years before I got here. He looks at the coming operation as a gift from God. "If I had not come to Guest House for alcoholism, I might well have died of lung cancer. The doctor discovered my cancer in a routine physical when I checked in here."

On a lighter note Frank tells me about one of the AA meetings he has been to outside of Guest House. He tells me that people come to pick us up to take us to various AA meetings. He had tried several meetings, and didn't really feel at home until one night he heard this guy say, "My name is John, an I'm an alkeyhalic."

17

Frank told me that he knew right away that the guy was from his home state. Frank was right, and he continues to go to that meeting.

I've been here three days, and today I take my first picture. For many years I have enjoyed photography as a hobby. In fact for a number of years I have been working on a book involving my pictures. The plan of the book is to take a picture - mostly nature pictures - and then write a brief meditation, about 500 words, to match the picture. I would include some appropriate scripture. I have to acknowledge now that I've been working on this book for about 15 years, and I have only a dozen meditations written. I begin to wonder if alcohol has been a major road block. Sure it has.

There is a discussion in the Music Room, a room now used for newspaper reading, smoking, and bull sessions. The discussion is about the Liturgy. It becomes a little heated, I stay out of it. I hear expressions like, "I HAVE TO" go out for Mass, "I'VE GOT TO" do this, or that. I just note it, say nothing. As I write this I wonder if this is evidence of my superior attitude. Whatever it is, I do try to get people in the parish, myself included, to use the expression "I GET TO" instead of "I HAVE TO" and "I'VE GOT TO." It's all a matter of attitude. It reminds me of the PRIVILEGE I have when it comes to the Liturgy.

I have a dry throat, persistent cough, and headache which reminds me that the results of the blood work will be back Tuesday. I hope that they will not reveal what I fear they will reveal. So you want to know what I fear. Well I'll not tell you, that's between me and my counselor, I mean my confessor.

Ed reminds me of two weddings I am supposed to have in April, and I remember a marriage case I was working on. Well those are things that Fr. Oglesby is going to have to take care of.

On my walk, and Office of Readings and Morning Prayer I discovered this reading from Hosea 5:15ff. *"Thus says the Lord: In their affliction, they shall look for me: 'Come, let us return to the Lord, for it is he who has rent, but he will heal us; he has struck us, but he will bind our wounds. He will revive us after two days; on the third day he will raise us up, to live in his presence.'"* I find this meaningful. Not that I blame the Lord for my condition, but I find confidence that with His hand I will be healed.

On the grounds of Guest House there is a rather large outdoor mosaic depicting Tobit and the Archangel Raphael. The scene is from the 12th chapter of the Book of Tobit. Would you believe that I don't have my Bible with me. I had to borrow a Bible and look it up. Verse seventeen says, *"No need to fear; you are safe."* I'm sure this expresses the mission and ministry of Guest House.

A strange thought occurs to me, am I ready for people to forgive me? To understand? Do I need to cry? Do I want to cry? Is this wallowing in SELF-PITY? I've heard it said, and I reckon it's true, "Too much introspection will drive you (to drink) crazy."

Sometimes as I write this journal it seems like I am writing to a person I know. Actually I have no idea who will ever read this, other than me. I do hope that if anyone reads it they will find hope, and help here. I just know that I have to write it, and it seems to be helping me. I guess the professional would call it therapy.

I began to write in my Meditation Book today. It feels good. I begin to feel more at ease with myself. I wrote to Philip O., and Helen H. today. *(Philip is an older teen and Helen is a widow. I had been friends with Helen and her husband, Don, for many years. I buried her husband and we have remained good friends.)* Tomorrow is Easter - I celebrate the Lord's Resurrection, and look forward to my new life in the world in three months.

I'm eating better, and more. The food is really good. My bowel movements are better and regular. I was beginning to worry about that. My throat is still sore, and headaches continue. It occurs to me that at home I am not usually around so many people who smoke. I wonder if this is working on my throat and head.

After the Easter Vigil there is a reception - a nonalcoholic one. The first I can remember ENJOYING. I used to refer to this type of reception as a Baptist Reception. At the parties where I was drinking in the last 5 to 1 0 years I would never (I better say "seldom") get drunk. However, I would always leave early to go home and get quietly high, or at least enjoy a few drinks without everybody around. Tonight I actually listened to, and talked to people. This is progress, I think.

If I left here now I would be drinking without control very soon. I have absolutely no doubt about that. But even if I didn't, there would be something wrong. I heard a new term tonight, "DRY DRUNK," and this is what would be wrong. It refers to that time a guy does not drink, days, weeks, months, even years, but retains an alcoholic's mind set. I'm not exactly certain what that means but I have my suspicions.

I am still uncomfortable so I leave the party early, not to drink though. The party food begins to give me gas, and the forecast is painful so I take 2 Tylenol #3. I must tell the doctor about this practice because I took two last night. *(I did talk to the doctor, and turned the pills over to him.)*

MARCH 26, 1989
Easter Sunday

It is foggy and cold, and would you believe it - traces of snow are still on the ground from the last snowfall!! It took a while to get to sleep last night, after midnight, but I slept 'til 7:50 a.m. Don K. tells me that alcohol has a cumulative effect on the body. It does more than just get you high.

Too cold for much of a morning walk. I take time for a Rosary walk, but not the Office. Mass is at 10:00 a.m. Mass was really different. The celebrant - Zeke - sang everything, the Offering prayers were in Hebrew. I participated from the balcony - too confused to be part of the congregation. Am I losing my identity as a priest? Why do I even ask that?

After Mass I go to the second non-alcoholic reception. I am just going to have to get used to this change. I meet Dick K. He is Executive Director of the place, and has been for 25 years. He is easy to talk to, and seems to be genuinely interested in me. I am surprised at how people seem to want to know me, are willing to listen to me, will talk to me.

It finally warms up, and I can take a walk around the grounds. I find a "landing" opening to a place to launch small boats. It is built of stone, but is overgrown with weeds, last year's weeds are about 2 or 3 feet tall. It must have been something very nice once. The weeds have grown up through the cracks in the stone floor. While walking I'm listening to a Richard Rohr tape, "The Spirituality of Subtraction" - the Landing could be a great "graphic" for this talk. I take some pictures, then head back to "Hogan's Alley" for a nap.

Dinner is at 2:00 p.m. There will be an In-House AA meeting tonight at 6:30. I am not looking forward to it.

The Meeting was good, better than I thought. I have trouble identifying as an actual alcoholic, so when it comes my turn I say, "My name is Bill, and I have a problem with alcohol". I'm told that AA meetings that are not all priests and brothers are somewhat different. There is more action in them, whatever that means.

There is a movie, a video, tonight, "The Ten Commandments." It is too long so I go to write a few letters. I get a phone call from Greg, the seminarian, who flew up here with me so he could visit his parents. He wanted to know if I needed anything from Bruce and wanted to know how I'm doing. He is returning to Memphis tomorrow. I give him a list, we talk awhile, he really sounded down. What a very thoughtful guy. After I hang up I worry about him, make a more complete list and call him back. I also give him my address, and toll free number, and tell him that to me he sounded really down. I also tell him that if he ever needs someone just to talk to he can give me a call, or write anytime, besides it would help me. He sounded happy about that. I really think he must be going through a rough time.

I wrote several cards and letters today: Bob Ewing; Steve & Mary Miller; The Ladies of the Legion; Bob & Kathy Trainor; and Harry & Mary Alice Sullivan. *(These are all friends both in and outside of the parish. Unfortunately I have no copies of some of these letters.)*

MARCH 27, 1989
Monday

I slept 'til 7:30 a.m. Breakfast is good. I still don't have a designated place at any table so I sit wherever there is an empty place. I don't think it makes much difference at breakfast. My walk takes me from the residence building to the Office Headquarters. It is a winding blacktop and I guess it might be a mile - round trip. Whatever it is, I am able to pray the Office of Readings and Morning Prayer. It is still cold, with patches of snow here and there. I'm beginning to wonder when Spring arrives in this part of the country.

9:00 a.m. – The lecture is "The Challenge of Recovery and the Twelve Tools." It seems that the 12 Steps of AA can be divided:

1 - 3 are healing and relate to God;

4 - 7 deal with self;

8 - 9 with others;

10 -12 long term maintenance.

Recovery is not a part-time job. I hear conflicting views: AA is a ME program; AA is a WE program. One thing for sure, AA is a confusing program, at least it is now. I've got to stop, and remember that I've been here less than a week. That takes patience. I wonder if the program is going to tell me that I have to be patient. Now this is something I'll have to talk to Len (my Counselor) about. One thing that is recommended is a daily meditation book. Something called "Touch Stones," or something like that, is mentioned. I think to myself: Now why on earth would a priest need another kind of meditation book. I don't know. Something else to ask Len.

10:00 a.m. – I take a walk and pray the Rosary. The Rosary I'm using was a gift from a person I've never met. He, or she, made some rosaries especially for priests - I think. Each Rosary has a cross attached with the name of the priest to whom it has been sent. The beads are something special. They are called "Job's Tears". The more the Rosary is used, the more each bead changes color. Right now I can relate to Job with all the suffering he endured. Except for the fact that his suffering was imposed on him, mine is self-inflicted. I don't really think I am as bad off as Job was, but sometimes I just feel sorry for myself. This is my first real day here and I am anxious to get started on this program.

11:00 a.m. – I meet with Len, my Counselor. It's a good meeting. We get to know each other. I trust him immediately. I want him to help me. I tell him I need him. I did not tell him I'm tired of lying to myself, tired of fighting battles that are not really battles, tired working hard to avoid facing the unpleasant side of me, the side I don't like. I hope we get into that sometime. I hope he will help me bring it up. He gives me my first reading assignment: 100 pages in "I'll Quit Tomorrow," and some in the AA Big Book. I remember that someone gave me, "The Big Book" and, "I'll Quit Tomorrow" several months ago. It might even have been a year ago. I don't remember who gave them to me, or why. I wonder if they knew more than I did about my problem with alcohol. At any rate, both books ended up on the shelf unread. Naturally I forgot to ask Len about AA and whether it is a ME, or WE, program. I forgot about the meditation book. I told you I got memory problems.

After lunch I start "I'll Quit Tomorrow." Then a session with the intake person. Then a session with Counselor's Secretary, Nova. After that the weather had warmed up a little. I went outside to do a little reading in, "I'll Quit Tomorrow." There seems to be a community of squirrels around here. I was soon distracted from the reading. Since I had my camera with me I started taking a few pictures.

I'm beginning to be at peace with myself. I'm still very uneasy about how the people at home feel. From the few phone calls I've had, and what fellow inmates tell me, people are generally supportive. That's general, Nativity is particular. I've got to stop referring to myself as an inmate. I'm a patient, at least that's what everyone here says.

Mail for the first time today. It is very heartening. I have a card from the Bishop, and notes from Jim & Gina McGee, notes from Barbara Bozzell, Ken & Sue DeWitt, Frs. Bill Davis & Bob Wiseman. There is no way on God's green earth I can tell you what that mail meant to me. I'm way above cloud nine.

MARCH 28, 1989
Tuesday

I had a very bad time last night. I have this persistent cough, it kept me up 'til about 2:30 a.m. I slept late so I have breakfast at 8:00 a.m., and then a walk, with the Office of Readings and Morning Prayer.

9:00 a.m. – video on the 12 Steps - I enjoyed it.

10:00 a.m. – I met with Dr. Lyons. I'm really impressed with him. He is everything MY doctor should be. Kind, gentle, qualified, good old country doctor. He takes his time to explain my blood work. I ask him if I made the team. He doesn't know what I mean. I tell him that the way the guys talk, if the blood says you are an alcoholic, then you have made the team. He confirms that my blood qualifies me for the team, first string. I'm a little cynical and I ask him, "Well doesn't every one make the team?" He says, "No." This surprises me, and it gives me confidence in Guest House. My cholesterol is a little high, and the blood pressure is too, and these will bear watching. He tells me that I may well be off the blood pressure medicine by the time I leave here. *(He was right. I had been taking blood pressure medicine for many months, but when I stopped drinking it went back to normal and has stayed there.)* The doctor does not have the results of the one test I am most concerned about. I explain to him why I am concerned. He doesn't think I have anything to worry about.

11:00 a.m. – Group with Len. There is a confrontation between Len and Zeke. It seems to me that Len sets up the confrontation but since I don't know the method, or motive of "Group" I can't really say. What I think is happening is that Len is trying to draw Zeke from behind his defenses so he will see they are not needed, or to use his word, "not appropriate". I was very uncomfortable. It has (I think) something to do with appropriate ways of making a point, dealing with a situation. I did this by drinking, by not getting into, but avoiding arguments with expressions like: "You're in charge." "Whatever you say." "It's not important."

At lunch I begin to understand more of what went on in Group, at least I think I do.

1:00 p.m. – Jack's Group. My first group session with a psychologist. He is interesting, gets us interacting well, discovers some complaints. Later I'm told he is very good - he observes, and picks up well on what is going on in each person.

2:15 p.m. – I met with Diane, (Clinical Secretary). I take all sorts of tests for about an hour.

22

After Mass, and Supper a group goes out to movies. I'm not sure if they went to a video store, or to a theater. I have letters to write, and besides I don't enjoy movies. I'm sure I need my glasses changed because movies always give me a headache, no matter where I sit. I write seven brief letters. Take a walk and listen to Richard Rohr tapes: <u>The Spirituality of Subtraction</u>.

I'm beginning to like the way I feel. I said today in group that I am glad that Dr. Lyons confirmed that I am an alcoholic. I'm glad I'm an alcoholic - because if that's not the cause of my behavior then I am back to square one and in real trouble. *(Later, much later, I have begun to realize that alcohol is not the cause of my behavior. My behavior is the cause of my alcoholism.)*

This is part of the beautiful dining room.

The Office Mail Box covered in snow.

THE LETTERS

MARCH 22, 1989
Wednesday of Holy Week

To All the People of Nativity,

By the time this is read to you I will have gone to Guest House for about three months. Guest House is a place for Priests, Religious Brothers, and Seminarians who have a problem with alcohol. While I am away I will still be your pastor, but Father Oglesby will be here to serve your needs. Please be kind to him.

Now, about my problem: I have known for some time that I have a problem with alcohol, but I hoped that I could control it. I do not really drink all that much, and I seldom get drunk. Alcohol does cause rather noticeable mood changes for me that I am often unaware of, but are hurtful to those around me. I surmise that this has been the reason that many have had for leaving the parish.

The gifts with which God has blessed me: myself; my priesthood; this parish; and my friends mean too much to me to damage by continued drinking. I do find it difficult, perhaps impossible, not to drink. So with the help, and understanding of our Bishop, good friends, and the staff of Nativity, arrangements have been made for me to get the help I need. I am indeed thankful for this help and understanding, and very grateful that this is out in the open.

Some will look on this as a moral weakness. That is a problem they will have to handle. As for me, I have a problem, and I am going to do something about it.

As I said, I am, and remain, your pastor. We have problems together, both spiritually and financially. Once I get my problem under control I will be back to work with you in solving our problems. It is difficult for me to speak to you about my problem, even through the medium of this letter. It is, perhaps, difficult for you to deal with my problem, but these are difficulties we can surmount with Grace and understanding. It is difficult for me to leave you, even for a while, but you will be in good hands. It is difficult for me to leave my little dog, Jock. He has no way of understanding this. As I have often said to you, now I say to me, "Pain can be redemptive."

So as we celebrate Holy Week apart let us look forward to the Resurrection together.

God's Peace, and my love,
Father Bill
Pastor

(I include letters written to and about me)

24

March 23, 1989

Dear Brother Priests,

Yesterday afternoon Fr. Bill Stelling flew to Detroit to begin the 90 - day treatment program for alcoholism at Guest House. A group of us met with him in the morning to discuss our concern about his drinking, and he readily agreed that treatment was in order. Needless to say, I was grateful that he was so cooperative and understanding of his need for help. Bill is a fine priest, and the wonderful program at Guest House will enable him to return to Nativity refreshed and at peace. I have appointed Fr. Leonard Oglesby Administrator of the Church of the Nativity for the 90 days of Bill's absence; Bill remains Pastor.

I'm sure Bill would appreciate hearing from you while at Guest House. His address:

> Guest House
> 1840 West Scripps Road
> P.O. Box 68
> Lake Orion, MI 48035

As I said, I was very impressed with Bill's reaction to our conversation, and I'm convinced his stay at Guest House will be very fruitful for him.

Enclosed you will find a statement I will read at a press conference this morning, announcing a public celebration of the 150th Anniversary of the first regularly scheduled Mass in Memphis and my 25th Ordination anniversary, to be attended by Mother Teresa. The statement explains the plans as they have developed thus far. As a result of this celebration, I have canceled my jubilee Mass which had been scheduled for May 7 and combined it with the June 4 celebration.

I had wanted to inform you of this event before it became public, but the arrangements happened very fast after I spoke with Mother Teresa on the telephone yesterday. I will be in touch with you in coming weeks to discuss ways we can make this a true diocesan-wide celebration; I will need your help to insure the greatest possible turnout of people from across the diocese. The event will be especially blessed by Mother Teresa's presence.

Be assured of my prayers during this very busy week!

Sincerely in Christ,
Daniel M. Buechlein, O.S.B., D.D.
Bishop of Memphis in Tennessee

DIOCESE OF MEMPHIS
1325 Jefferson Avenue
P.O. Box 41679
Memphis, TN 38174-1679

March 23, 1989

Dear People of Church of the Nativity,

As you now know, yesterday Fr. Bill Stelling flew to Detroit to begin a 90 - day program at Guest House for priests and Brothers who suffer from alcoholism. When I expressed my concern to Fr. Bill about his drinking, he readily agreed that such a program would be of real help to him. I am very happy that he is now part of the Guest House community, which is internationally known for its wonderful program.

I want to be very clear with you about two important points. First, I do not see alcoholism as a moral failure or weakness on Fr. Bill's part. It is a disease which responds to proper treatment. In fact, many of you have probably been touched by the disease of alcoholism in your own families. I have every confidence that Fr. Bill will do very well in the Guest House program, especially since his attitude is so open and ready for help. He is a fine priest and a good pastor.

Second, although I have appointed Fr. Leonard Oglesby Administrator of your parish for the 90 - day period, Fr. Bill remains your pastor and will return to your parish as pastor when the program is completed, toward the end of June. I'm sure he looks forward to his return to you, refreshed and at peace.

In the meantime, I ask that you give Fr. Oglesby your full cooperation and support. Many of you already know him, since he was pastor of St. Ann parish for many years and is highly respected in the diocese. I am deeply grateful to him for so generously agreeing to guide your parish in the next three months.

Finally, I know that Fr. Bill would appreciate any words of support you might care to write him. I have asked Deacon Larry Howell to make his address available to you all. Keep Fr. Bill in your prayers! I fully support this courageous step he is taking, and we all look forward to his return.

Sincerely in Christ

(Signed)

Daniel M. Buechlein, O.S.B., D.D.
Bishop of Memphis in Tennessee

March 28, 1989

Dear Peg *et. al.*,
(Peg is my sister-in-law. She is also a widow. The "et. al." are her grown children and their families.)

Sorry to have to tell you this. It has been a long time coming. The return address on the envelope is an Alcoholic Rehabilitation Center for Priests, Brothers & Seminarians. I have been here since Wednesday of Holy Week. I never did get falling down drunk, with a few major exceptions. I just drank regular, and heavy every day. It finally began to get out of control. I guess I should say that I finally realized that I was out of control. The Bishop offered me a chance to recover my health, my sanity, my priesthood, and everything. I jumped at the chance. This is a 90 day program with several follow up days for aftercare. I will write more later when I feel up to it. For now it means **no** 25th anniversary party.

I am sorry to have let so many people down including you. My phone # is toll free and we are on Eastern time 1-800-xxx-xxxx. Please share this news with anyone you think would like to know.

Peace,
Bill

March 28, 1989

Dear Bill,
(This is Fr. Bill Davis a priest of the Memphis diocese)

Thank you for writing and being so understanding. I am so glad to be here, and so sad to be away. Your thoughtfulness is a great help. I am still oppressed by and obsessed with feelings of guilt & failure, but am learning how to deal with that. Keep me in your prayers. My phone number is 1-800-xxx-xxxx.

Peace,
FatherBill

March 28, 1989

Dear Gay and Bill,
(This is my secretary and her husband.)

I know your understanding of my weakness has been great and I thank you for that. Now I take courage in hand and ask: Did all of those preparing in the RCIA follow through? Did I scandalize any of them? Whatever the Lawrences and the Domans did, tell them that they are in my prayers. Did Larry read my letter? Did you post copies of it? Have any more people left the parish? Bill, I am sorry I let you & the Finance Council down. My phone number is 1-800-xxx-xxxx.

Peace,
Father Bill

27

March 28, 1989

Dear Ken and Sue,

(This is Ken and Sue DeWitt. Close friends and in charge of planning my 25th anniversary celebration)

Sorry to have let you down. Did I scandalize Bob & Eide? *(They were in the RCIA Class.)* Did they follow through? Thank you so very much for the Easter Card, and note. This is a good program, just what I need - be assured that I will & want to use it. It is painful now & then. I guess we had better cancel my 25th party - even to have it late - it would just hurt too much to invite so many & have so few show up. Please follow through on the Parish 10th Party, and work on next year's RCIA schedule.

God's Peace and my love,
Father Bill

―――――――――――――――――――――――――――――――

Good Friday

Dear Larry,

I know I said, "Thank You" on Wednesday. But thanks again. I am so glad "it" is over. I really had no idea of how to ask for help. I am embarrassed and ashamed. I know this will heal and I will work at it. It is so difficult to be away from the parish especially at Easter. I am blessed that you are my friend. I cry often. Please write.

Please help the people understand. It is **I** who have made a mess of things. Help them to forgive me for I will need them now, and when I return. Please read my letter to them. Make copies and post them. Send a copy to the Bishop and one to me. I know that I can never drink again, but I will have to do that one day at a time.

Peace,
Father Bill

―――――――――――――――――――――――――――――――

Good Friday

Dear Staff including Billy and John,

Sorry to have let you down. How can I ask you to understand something I don't understand? I am in the right place - I'm glad (if not happy) that I'm here. I miss you all so very much. Take care of Jock *(my dog)*. I will write to the Youth Group when I know what to say. Ask Larry Howell to share his card.

Peace,
Father Bill

Dear Bishop,

I hope I thanked you Wednesday morning. I intended to. I was waiting to be "caught". I knew that I could not stop drinking. I didn't know how to ask for help, I was too ashamed. I know you love me. I'm sorry I have been such a burden. I know I am in the right place. They have my complete cooperation. You have my obedience, my respect, and my love.

Peace,
Bill

Dear Vic,

(Father Victor, a close friend. He also took care of Jock for me.)

Thanks for coming over. Please help the people understand. I blame no one but me. I am not angry with anyone, on the contrary I am very grateful. I was waiting to be "caught". I didn't know how to stop, or to ask for help. You may have differences with "B", but what he did took courage. He is a friend. I know that I have embarrassed and let down a lot of good priests. All I can do about that is be here and be open to all they can do for me. I cry a lot. Some of it is self-pity. I am a priest, and in spite of drinking and a few other things, I think I am a good one. I have not been much of a pastor of late. I hope I get a chance to change that with the people I hurt. I dare not call you on the phone yet. I would just cry.

Please write. Take care of Jock. If he needs a doctor take him to Chuck Galena at Expressway Animal Clinic. My new black Bible is in my study. I could use it. I would enjoy using my coffee mug. It has "Bill" on it, and it gives the meaning for that name. It is white and blue. I'm going to make it, thanks to you and others.

Peace,
Bill

P.S. Best cancel plans for my 25th. It would hurt too much to invite a lot of people and have no one show up. Besides how dare I ask the parish to pay for my party??

Dear Bruce,

(Father Bruce Cinquegrani. He was in residence at Nativity and was part of the Intervention Team, and a good friend.)

Thank you. You are a friend and a good one. I am in the right place. I was waiting to be "caught". I could not stop. I didn't know how to ask for help. I was too ashamed. Please be kind to Jock. Vic knows who his doctor is. You did the right thing. Now please help the people understand. Bruce sometimes I just want to die. What a mess. Please write.

Peace,
Bill

<hr>

Good Friday

Dear Pete,
(Father Pete Sartain, now Bishop Sartain of Little Rock.)
    If I did not say, "Thank You" Wednesday I say it now. How tough it must be for you both as Chancellor and friend. I do count you as a friend. Sorry I caused you a problem. Ask Bruce to show you the card I wrote to him. It hurts too much to say what's in my heart. Thanks for taking care of Holy Week at Nativity. Please help the people understand, and perhaps forgive me.

Peace,
Bill

<hr>

Holy Saturday

Dear Helen,
(Helen is a dear friend. She had a great difficulty accepting the reality that I am an alcoholic)
    By now you know that with the help of the Bishop I am taking three months off to learn how to deal with my problem of alcoholism. It was not an easy thing to accept but I have been trying for a long time to come to grips with it. The Bishop met with me Wednesday morning (at his order) and by 3:00 p.m. I was at the airport. I am in the right place for me and I am glad, (if not happy) to be here. Hope everything goes well tonight. You are such an understanding person that I hope you will be able to understand this. I had no time to call anyone. Although I am glad to be here, and should be here, I am having a difficult time dealing with feelings of failure, of letting people down, of worthlessness, so it has taken me a day or two to write. I know this will be difficult for people to understand, especially the children. Jock will have no way of understanding. I miss you all so very much. I miss Jock, but I know I must endure. I will, of course, return in three months, or so, and that will be most difficult.
    Your prayers and love please. If you don't want to write I will understand.

Peace,
Father Bill

30

Dear Philip,

(Philip is a teenager in the parish. I thought he might have a vocation to the priesthood.)

I don't know what to say to you - but I must say something. I have encouraged you to listen to the Lord to see if he is calling you to the Priesthood. I feel now I have let you down. Be assured that all priests are not like me. I love you so very much, and that love will encourage me to remain here for a while and work hard on my problem. It would be so kind of you to write - but if you don't I will understand.

Peace,
Father Bill

Easter Sunday

Dear Steve & Mary,

Thank you both for the help and friendship you have given me, even before this. Mary - give way to Larry Howell. I think he is very sensitive and very important to the parish and the people. You know how I feel about you and how important you are to the parish & people. Some will argue - but I think you can moderate that by playing up Larry's role. Perhaps Father Oglesby will have some ideas on Music. I don't know what to say to the youth, or even how to say it. I think it best to wait awhile and get some advice from you and the other Youth Group people. Do assure them of my love, my sense of failure, and guilt in my service to them.

I will enter willingly and whole heartedly into everything they have to offer that I may once again fulfill my role of priest & pastor.

Steve - call Jim Harpster and let him know what is going on & why the Poker games are off for a while. If your kids, or any others ask, "Why?" Tell them I don't know either.

Peace,
Father Bill
P.S. Share this card with anyone you want to. It is so hard to write.

Easter Sunday

Dear Margretta, & Legion Ladies,

(Letter to the Ladies of the Legion of Mary)

Sorry I was unable to go to court with you. I left town in a hurry Wednesday afternoon. So many people could tell I had a drinking problem. I suspected it but could not acknowledge it, or quit. The Bishop forced me to acknowledge it, and offered me a chance to get help. I jumped at the chance. I know I have hurt and failed the Legion & and the parish. Remember me in your Rosary & I will do the same.

Love,
Father Bill

31

Easter Sunday

Dear Bob & Kathy,

I have been staring at this blank card for some time. What can I say? "I'm sorry I let you down." But after that - what? You offered me love, friendship, and membership in your family. I have failed you and scandalized your children. How can I ask you & them to understand what I do not understand? About forgiveness - I'm sure it is too early for that, and I don't know if I will ever be able to be forgiven - not because of pride, but because it hurts so much. Please share this card with the Touchetts and anyone else you want to.

Peace,
Father Bill

Easter Sunday

Dear Bob,

(Bob is a fellow priest and a recovering alcoholic.)

Where you once were I am now, where you are now I hope to be. I think I can depend on your help and understanding, at least I hope I can. I am so glad I am here, so glad I was discovered. I suspected I was "out of control," but could not ask for help - even from you. Things are different now - but I have only started back. I need your help. I have no right to it but I don't think that matters with you. Share this card with anyone you want to. It sure is different now: I am one of those people at whom others point and say, "There, but for the Grace of God go I." I used to think I knew what that meant - but now I see it in a far different light. I am going to enclose some cards with an 800 number on them. Please give them to whoever would use it. I'm taking a chance I know - what if nobody calls? I have written to Vic, Bruce, Peter & the Bishop, but I didn't know about these cards at the time.

Peace,
Bill

Easter Sunday

Dear Harry & Mary Alice,

(These are friends from the time I was at Holy Rosary in Nashville.)

I asked Fr. Bruce to call you with this bit of news, but with Holy Week, etc., he might not have. I was planning to come to Nashville after Easter to visit you and the Carters but I am at Guest House, an alcoholic rehabilitation center for Priests, Brothers and Seminarians. Of course this has been a long standing problem. I thought that I just enjoyed drinking on a daily basis, but I am an alcoholic, and I am in the right place, and I am glad (if not happy) about it. I know that I will never be able to drink again and I will just have to learn how to do that. I expect I will - but not without pain. When you hurt others they can just write you off - When you hurt yourself you have to do something about it.

Please share this with Harvey. It is not easy for me to write about it. I know Marge *(Harvey's wife - was seriously ill)* could die. Even in that event I don't know if I could interrupt this program, that is, if they would let me. What a mess I have made of things. If I have not turned you completely off please do write, or call & share my address & phone # with Harvey. Assure him of my prayers for Marge. The Guest House number is 1-800-xxx-xxxx.

Peace,
Father Bill

The card from the Bishop was an Easter card but he took the time to write: *Bill, Peace! Just a note to let you know you are loved and I keep you in my prayer - I know your program will not be easy - (signed) Bishop Daniel.*

Easter Monday

Dear Len,
(This is Father Leonard Oglesby)

Thank you for administering my parish for me. I know you must be disappointed in me - for I have long considered you one of my teachers and a good friend. I'm sorry Len. I don't fully understand how it happened yet. I will do my best to use this time well. I know you don't like dogs inside but please bear with it - it's not Jock's fault, it's mine. Thanks again & I'm sorry to disappoint you.

Peace,
Bill
(The way it turned out - Len was unable to put up with Jock in the house and Vic took care of Jock at St. Ann.)

Members of the professional staff at Guest House.

I spotted a groundhog on
one of my walks.

The secretaries feeding an
orphaned squirrel.

CHAPTER TWO
WEEK TWO
THE JOURNAL

MARCH 29, 1989
Wednesday

I slept well. After breakfast I take my walk, and pray the Office of Readings and Morning Prayer. Since I do the same thing each morning I wonder if I should abbreviate it as BWO. Perhaps it would make more sense as BOW. Nah, I'll just stick to what I been doing. I don't hear you complaining.

9:00 a.m. – The video is "Getting Familiar With Guest House." Now I know where a few things are. No Group today because of the Departure Mass for Ed B. and John M.

I liked John's sermon at Mass. He used the example of the moon. "Everything falls into decay. For example, the moon, once a great symbol for lovers, is now just another abandoned airport, but your priesthood, it goes on forever," (He was referring to the moon landings and the fact that we haven't been back). I thought that was more than just clever. It said a lot to me about how this program can help me return to ministry. It seems to have worked for him.

Ed talks at dinner. He used the story : "The Old Violin and the Touch of the Master." I had heard it before, but hearing Ed tell it packed a good punch. It is the story of how, with the touch of the Master, an old, broken violin can produce great music. I have an old violin at home. I found it in a garage someplace. I think I'll give it to Ed.

These guys have finished the course, and I am happy for them. I've been here one week - twelve more to go. I hope I make it. Someone pointed out to me that they have not finished the course - they are just getting started.

This afternoon there was a shopping trip to a large mall. I take the trip to to buy shirts, and a sweater. I was going to buy a scarf, but Ron gave me his. Well he didn't actually give it to me, he loaned it to me. Ron works here. He is in charge of Housekeeping. He asked me if I needed anything and I told him that I had not expected it to be so cold, and I could use a scarf. The next day he brought me his. It is from the University of Michigan. I am really overwhelmed by this gift. Actually it isn't a gift - it is a loan. Because of the sentiment it has for Ron, he asked me to return it when I leave. At the mall I notice a liquor store but I don't even think about going in. I buy a Walkman, mine is malfunctioning.

I like to listen to Richard Rohr tapes. This one is: "The Spirituality of Subtraction." He asks the question: "What does, 'Take up your cross and follow Me' mean for middle class affluent America?" Putting up with a broken air conditioner, suffering a hangnail, etc., offering it up? It is okay to begin there, but Richard says that taking up your cross is, "that suffering which comes with any decision that is made for the Kingdom of God."

I discover my new mail box. The other one was temporary because I was new. Today there are many letters in it. Part of the news is that Father O. has put my name in the Eucharistic Prayer, I am touched. I decide to write a regular letter to the parish. I call Gay, my secretary. She tells me that everything is going well. She tells me that she is learning to deal with "Sarge." "Sarge" is the nickname that someone has given Father Oglesby. I chose not to ask any questions about why. Bruce Cinquegrani calls, and, Bob Ewing calls but I am out. I should call Father Oglesby about that marriage case I was working on.

I went to my first AA meeting outside the House and was impressed. It is nothing like I expected. It is not a bunch of guys telling sad tales, sitting around feeling sorry for themselves because they can't drink. In fact there is a lot of laughter. A guy named Duncan says: "There is a little man inside of me (the real me) fighting to get out." Ned adds: "I admitted that I am powerless - but how often I want to take that back."

Len, my counselor, wants me to fill out a Sexual Survey. I'm supposed to go back to the time I was in the Air Force in Japan during the Korean War, and even to when I was a kid. I don't like this, but he says it's necessary if I want to "get well". I do want to, and I guess I need to, get well. I have not fully accepted this idea that alcoholism is a disease. I take the forms into the chapel and take a couple of hours to fill it out in front of the Blessed Sacrament - asking God to help me be honest about it.

MARCH 30, 1989
Thursday

I got to bed late. After the sexual survey I discovered the pool table in the basement and I enjoyed several relaxing games of pool. I'm not the best pool player, but some people have told me that the way I play is evidence of a misspent youth. I take that as a compliment. I slept well, and until 7:30 a.m. I have breakfast, take my regular walk, and pray the Office.

9:00 a.m. – The video is on the founding of AA. Don't get the idea that Guest House has formal classrooms. This used to be someone's house. A rich man's house. It has plenty of rooms and Guest House makes use of all of them. Some of the rooms are quite fancy and are somewhat at odds with their present use.

There is a funeral Mass for a priest who died of Spinal Meningitis. He was from Africa. His sister, a nun, Sister Maria, has been staying here waiting for his death. Some from the house go to the funeral. Since I don't know him, I think it is more important for me to get into this program. I read more of "I'll Quit Tomorrow." I remember that I have this book at home. It is sitting on one of my shelves - unread. I wonder why.

I find more mail in my box and I am overwhelmed. I recall that back in the 1950's when I was in the Air Force mail meant a lot to me. Today it means much, much more.

MARCH 31, 1989
Friday

Another good night's sleep. I woke up without an alarm about 7:30. I enjoy a good breakfast, but no walk. It is just too cold. I wonder if it will ever get warm up here. I pray the Office in the Chapel.

9:00 a.m. – The lecture by Tom is "Introduction to Group." I find that group is a time to open up about my feelings and problems. It is a time to get feedback and advice. From what I have seen of Group so far, it seems that a guy could get hurt by all that honesty. I really don't think that I could benefit a great deal by feedback and advice. Len gave me eight typewritten pages on what Group is supposed to be all about. I dare not let these pages just sit on a shelf unread.

Between the lecture and Group I pray the Rosary and do a little reading in chapel - it's just too cold to go outside. When will Spring get here?

Group at 11:00 a.m. We are each given 3 cards, told to choose one and complete the sentence. I choose, "I only have a short time to live..." I complete by saying, "so I will do my best to stay sober, that is, not to drink." This does not satisfy anyone. On being pressed I would also finish building the Church (*I am the founding pastor of the Church of the Nativity*), and write my book. It occurs to me that I have been working on this book for more than a few years. (*But more about that later.*) Just as I suspected: Group is not an easy place to live.

I meet with Len, one-on-one, at 1:00 p.m. We have a good talk. For some reason I am in a hurry to get my life straightened out so I can start living again. The thought just occurs to me, "What if that card is right?" I'd be the luckiest person in the world to have this opportunity to get my life in order. Len and I talk about other addictions - it surprises me how easily I would be able to fall into several different addictions. It also surprises me that I am able to talk so freely. I am filled with a growing hope. How I wish that this could have happened years ago, but it would be a waste of time to worry about that now.

Len gives me a copy of what is called the *Master Treatment Plan* for me. It lists a Problem - Plan, or Progress - Goal:

PHYSICAL - CLASS II - 16

Problem	Plan
Alcoholism	Guest House Treatment
History of Hypertension	On medication. Blood pressure 134/80
Epidermal horn - left cheek	Removed by dermatologist (Dr. L.)

PSYCHOLOGICAL - CLASS III 13

Progress: Says he is glad to be in treatment. Initial testing done.

Goal: Understand disease concept

Problem: Mild toxicity. Ignorant of disease concept.   (JHG)

Plan: Group Therapy

SOCIAL - CLASS II - 14

Progress: Seeks out others in house for conversation & fellowship.

Goal: Share more deeply

Problem: Need to risk more self-disclosure. (LEB)

Plan: Group counseling

VOCATIONAL - CLASS III - 13

Progress: Speaks highly of his priestly ministry.

Goal: Renewed ministry

Problem: No problems yet identified. (LEB)

Plan: Begin "supply work" on weekends

ALCOHOLISM - CLASS III - 13

Progress: Asks questions. Appears eager to master the principles of sobriety.

Goal: Understand disease concept

Problem: Minimizes extent of disease. (LEB)

Plan: Group therapy

I called Nativity, and talked with Gay, Eva, & Fr. Oglesby. *(Gay is my secretary, Eva works in the office keeping records and answering the phone.)* It seems that there has been some stress between staff members. There's nothing I can do about that, but it does cause me to wonder. No one said anything, but I got hints from what each person said. I wish I knew what the problem is and who is causing it.

I ask Gay to see if she can have my computer sent up here. It will be an expense but it will be worth it. I think if I am going to restart my writing, not only this journal but also my meditation book, the computer will be a big help. There is a typewriter in the Library and I am free to use it, but I am surprised to discover

38

there is a world of difference between a typewriter and a computer. *(When my computer arrived I put everything that I had been typing on a typewriter, and writing on legal pads, into the computer.)*

I learned the difference between Feedback and Advice, at least I think I did. Feedback is not advice, but sometimes advice is feedback. When a person is giving me feedback in group they are simply sharing their personal experience. If I can relate fine, if not that's fine too. Advice is just that, advice. I don't think I will like advice as much as I will feedback. Seems to me that the person giving advice always expects me to follow it and gets all upset if I don't. Sometimes it's about as annoying as bystanders at a game of chess.

I write a letter to the people of the parish. It's a way of saying, "Thank you," and telling them what is happening to me. The writing causes me to forget about Mass. This is the first time that I have missed a daily Mass in a long time. In the evening more reading and prayer. I also make use of the pool table in the basement. It is not in the best of shape, but I like it.

I have made my commitment to trust in God about my alcoholic addiction and the possibility of slipping into other addictions. Self-assurance is going, but my self-image improving. I don't know if that makes sense to anyone. To some that may sound like a contradiction, but for me it's not. I'm beginning to know what "One Day At A Time" means: I know I could drink tomorrow, but I will not drink today with HIS help. I am beginning to look for the many different ways that HIS help comes to me.

APRIL 1, 1989
Saturday

April Fool's Day. Saturday is a different kind of day, no real schedule. I take my usual walk after breakfast. Judy, in the Office, asks me to take outside supply for a parish. *(This means that someone would come to take me to one of the surrounding parishes to be the celebrant for one, or two Masses.)* She says Len, my counselor, recommends it. I agree with pleasure. I am somewhat surprised that Len would recommend me. He had mentioned it, but I didn't think it would come up so soon. I don't think I've been at Guest House long enough. But who am I to argue with the pros. I write notes for sermon, and read a lot.

Harry Sullivan calls with news about Harvey Carter- his wife is dying. It upsets me that I cannot be there, and I get all sorts of guilty feelings about it. Sue DeWitt calls. Although some of these calls do bother me, I am grateful for them all. I would hate to learn all the bad news only after I get home.

APRIL 2, 1989
Sunday

We lose an hour, but I'm up early. I'm excited about being able to go out to a parish for a Mass. It's not so much getting away from Guest House. I take it as a

39

compliment - I'm ready to be trusted in a parish setting. I'm up before seven and look over my notes for the sermon. The driver picks me up at 8:15 a.m. He is a real easygoing guy. I'm not sure what he thinks of me. I don't mean as an alcoholic. I mean as a plus-fifty man being as excited as a teenager on his first date. I celebrate, and preach at two Masses. It feels great. The altar boy is so enthusiastic that he serves both Masses. He says he wants to be a priest. I hope so. A strange thing happened at the second Mass: By accident I was presented with alcoholic wine by the server. I didn't notice until it came time to drink from the chalice. I could smell the alcohol as I lifted the chalice to my mouth. I was really stumped for just a minute. Since, as the celebrant, it was necessary that I receive from the chalice I decided to just let the Precious Blood just touch my tongue, and then have one of the Lay Ministers of the Eucharist consume the rest. I mentioned the mistake to one of the men after Mass. He was very apologetic, and assured me that it would not happen again. I did not mention this to the Guest House people when I got back around noon. Perhaps I should have. I was not afraid of what they would do or think. I just thought the problem had been taken care of.

I didn't get my morning walk in so I have long walk with John K. We have a good talk. John has recently had a knee replacement and he is supposed to walk a lot. So it seems that I will have a walking buddy in the afternoons - John does not walk in the morning. After the walk it's nap time.

Helen H. calls - she wants to deny that I am an alcoholic. I suspect it's because she thinks that she might be an alcoholic. I wonder if I'm beginning to think that everyone who drinks is an alcoholic. I hope not. Billy Jolly calls. Harvey Carter calls, his wife, Marge, is dying of Lou Gehrig's disease. Barbara Bozzel calls to tell me about her brother's funeral, Fr. Oglesby had the funeral. Louise Smith also died last week. Again I begin to fight with guilt feelings because I'm not able to be there. Damn, I know I should be there and yet I know why I can't be there. I know it's very, in fact most important, that I stay here. There's an Open AA meeting here tonight, about 100 people attend. When an AA meeting is Open it means that some of the people attending are not alcoholics.

APRIL 3, 1989
Monday

Back to my regular schedule: Breakfast, Walk, and pray the Office. The weather is getting somewhat better. Nothing like Tennessee, but better than it was.

9:00 a.m. –The lecture is by Dr. Ken Adams dealing with sexuality, and sexual addictions. It was very interesting. I meet with Ken later to talk about and clear up a few things. I congratulate him on being able to talk so freely about a subject that most people don't want to talk freely about.

Mail brings extra clothing and many letters. Now long walks will be better because I'll have some heavier clothes. Today the walk is long and I continue to listen to Richard Rohr's tapes on The Spirituality of Subtraction. It's a funny way of approaching Spiritual Growth. It seems that when I grow I want to add things, but Richard says a lot of spiritual growth is accomplished by taking things away. As I look at the reason that I'm here I can agree.

Ken DeWitt calls, and we talk about a Town Meeting we had planned to schedule. He also wants to go ahead with plans for celebrating my 25th anniversary of ordination. I encourage the first and discourage the second. In the afternoon I find time to write a letter to the Confirmation Class.

AA meeting tonight at Beaumont. I had heard a lot about this meeting and was anxious to go. It was okay, but not really any better than other meetings I've been to. Jack Donnelly, a dear friend, calls. He is very supportive, and very man to man.

April 4, 1989
Tuesday

I overslept this morning. I got out of bed at 8:10 a.m. No time for walk this morning. There is just enough time for breakfast.

9:00 a.m. – There is a video, but I do not recall what it was about. That is kinda strange - not being able to recall what this morning's video was about. I guess it is going to take awhile for my memory to get better.

11:00 a.m. – Group with Len was good. I am beginning to understand what "Group" is about. I just about wrote "all about," but I have not finished reading all those pages Len gave me to read about Group. I just don't have the time, at least that's what I keep saying. If I'd just sit out one game of pool I could have them read. There's still something going on between Len and Zeke. Zeke is one of the guests here. He is very different, and very likeable. But I don't know if he is willing to let the program work for him. I think he is ready to work the program "his" way, but I'm not sure that will work. I'm new at this, so what do I know.

1:00 p.m. – I met with Jack Gregory, and his group. He fascinates me. I go along with him, thinking he is playing a joke, telling a story, and all of the sudden he is serious, and he's got me just where he wants me. He makes me think. Today Jack had this crazy discussion: If there was some way to determine at birth if a person has the "X" factor should we mark that person with an "X" on the forehead. About 3/4 the way through I suspect he is playing a game - a serious game - but a game nonetheless. I feel used and resentful, but this is tempered with a knowledge that he is doing something serious. Perhaps I should tell him how I feel.

I wrote a note to those at Nativity who entered the Church on Holy Saturday, at the Easter Vigil. *(This note is lost.)*

I called the Office and spoke to Mary. She is the Liturgy Committee and Youth person. I also talked to Gay. She says that my computer is being shipped tomorrow. Last week I asked her to send me some grits. People up here have never heard of them. The cook says he will fix me some if I get them for him. Would you believe it. The stores up here don't have any. Yankees!! They just don't know what they're missing. Gay tells me that the grits are on the way.

I returned Sterling McGuire's call. Sterling is a priest friend of mine in the Nashville Diocese. He knows a lot about recovery and called to wish me "God Speed" in my recovery. I'm not at all sure how he found out, but I'm glad he did, and I'm glad he called.

I'm the celebrant at our 4:30 p.m. Mass. The wine we use is non-alcoholic. Any alcoholic priest can receive permission to use it, and I think everyone should. There I go again making rules, - suggestions - for everyone. Well that's what Guest House recommends.

In the talks I've heard, and discussions I've had with the guys, I think there may be issues in my childhood that I have not dealt with. I'm not one to think that I can blame my present situation on events of the past. I think that I can be a beneficiary, or a victim of past events, and that for the most part the choice is up to me. At least that is what I have always thought. Hearing some of the talks and conversations I begin to wonder if the Orphanage Experience, and the death of Mother had an effect on me that I never dealt with.

(When I was young there was a lot of sickness in my family. The family consisted of parents, six boys, and four girls. I had a sister and brother younger than I. Mother was an asthmatic, and Dad had several heart attacks. As a result of this I, and two of my sisters were placed in a Catholic Orphanage for two or three years. My Mother died a year, or so after we were reunited as a family.)

As an adult, I came to realize that the first was necessary and the second unfortunate. Dad was strict, and tough, sometimes I thought too tough. As an adult, I came to realize WHY. He was a single parent trying to raise a rather large family. I just assumed that I had dealt with the fact that I thought I didn't like my Dad as a child. Perhaps I should discuss this with Len.

I moved out of Hogan's Alley today. I have no intention of staying there for the full three months, like Hogan did. The new room is somewhat larger and it shares a bath with a neighboring room. Brother Mo is my neighbor. In "Hogan's Alley" the bath was down the hall.

The Hogan's Alley
entrance.

THE LETTERS

Dear People of Nativity,

Thank you so very much for your wonderful letters of encouragement and your support. Without them I would go completely out of my mind instead of just halfway.

I have been here just over a week now. I knew it would be difficult being away from you for Holy Week, and Easter. I had no idea how difficult it would be. I have cried often at the sadness of our being apart.

My treatment, so far, consists of a complete physical. I'm in fairly good health, but could stand some improvement. They tell me that, as a result of not drinking, rest and peace of mind, I probably will not have a blood pressure problem when I leave here. I take vitamins pills twice a day at meals. I enjoy meals that someone else cooks, and I never have to worry about the dishes. *(I often run into people that are surprised that I cook my meals, wash my dishes and try to keep the house fairly straight. I do have someone come in once a week to really clean the house and do the laundry. My Dad was a man well ahead of his time. In our house there was no such thing as boys jobs and girls jobs. We all learned to do it all. Dad was a good cook and we grew up knowing how to cook. What surprises me is that some rectories have a cook, and a few even have a housekeeper.)*

There is a lot of reading to do, individual counseling, and group therapy. A lot of help, and hope comes from just listening to, and sharing with, the guys in the House. There are about 20, or so, guests. The oldest is in his 70's and the youngest in his early 30's. All are Priests, or Brothers.

I am beginning to find, and face, things about me that I didn't know. Some I like, some I don't - but I am learning to cope with them. I have been to two AA Meetings. I am truly impressed, and humbled. "Humbled" is a word that gets used a lot, but in this case it is more than appropriate.

I am so grateful that I have a dependable staff: Larry, our Deacon - more than a symbol of unity, and always a source of strength for me. Mary with the Youth and Liturgy - I am so proud of our Youth Group and Confirmation Class. I so wish I could be there for Confirmation. It's good to have someone who knows, and looks after all the details of Liturgy - especially when a visiting priest comes into a parish. Betty in PRE *(Parish Religious Education)* - First Communion, oh how I miss that - but Betty will see that everything runs well in all the classes; Eva - busy keeping records and answering the phone; Billy working so hard to keep the place clean. What a personal interest he gives to the job. John who makes sure the grounds are beautiful. There is something I did not get done: making sure we had a Grounds Crew Chairman. John can do a lot so please help him. And, of course, Gay - I was careful to hire a secretary - not an office manager, but now Gay must manage - I know I can count on her, and I know that I can count on you to make her life as pleasant as possible. I am grateful to you - what a great Staff I have. Thank you. May God bless you.

While I am a guest at Guest House, Father Oglesby is a guest in our house. He, of course, is more than a guest. He is a friend, a brother, a fellow laborer for the Kingdom. I thank him.

I thank all of you for your very kind letters. You'll never know how helpful they are to me. My heart is saddened at the news of the deaths of Louise Smith and Roy Wilson. You all remember Louise. Roy Wilson was Barbara Bozzle's brother. I know I shouldn't, but I do feel guilty about not being there for the funerals.

There are many things that I wished I could have solved before I left so abruptly: Finances, Building Fund, Sacrificial Giving, the Bishop's Annual Appeal, the music - its organization and schedule; the Grounds Crew, the list gets longer. There is a lesson there; Do what you can while you can - things change abruptly. I'm working on only one problem now. With the help of Guest House, God's Grace, and your encouragement I'll come back to you a better person.

God's Peace and my love,

Father Bill
Pastor

An Easter Card
From Bishop Daniel

The printed message on the card said:

He Has Given Us New Life
For whosoever findeth me
findeth life
Proverbs 8:35
Through His resurrection,
He has given us new hope.
Through His love,
He has given us new life.

HAVE A BLESSED EASTER

The hand written note read:

Bill, Peace! Just a note to let you know you are loved
and I keep you in my prayer -
I know your program will not be easy.
Bishop Daniel

44

April 1, 1989

Dear Rosa and Sid,
(Rosa and Sid McDonald are friends from Jackson, TN from the time I was pastor there.)
I ask Father Bruce to call and tell you where I am. In case he did not, I am at Guest House until late June. This is a treatment center for alcoholism. The Bishop made arrangements for me to be here and I am very glad. I have asked Fr. Bruce to take care of that "thing" you gave me to have re-silvered. He is on retreat now, but I'm sure he will not fail you. Do not worry about me, but please do write. Fr. Kirk *(their pastor)* may help you understand.

Peace,

Father Bill

April 1, 1989

Dear Harvey,
(Harvey Carter, his wife Marge, and their daughter Dawn have been friends for many years.)
Sorry to add to your burden of sorrow. *(Marge has a terminal illness)* My prayers go out to you, Marge, & Dawn. I had planned to visit this week, but this trip to Guest House came up. I am not sure that I have the freedom to travel. How I would love to just be with you. To be here is a decision I have made in the Kingdom of God - the pain that comes from that decision is what Fr. Rohr calls taking up the cross. I love you and your family. Your prayers and mine are one.

Peace,

Bill

April 3, 1989

Dear Bishop,
It is about 11:20 p.m. Monday night. Tomorrow night at this time it will be two weeks since my last drink. Not much of a record, but it's a start.

I appreciate very much the letter you wrote to the people of Nativity, my people. I hope Larry Howell has sent you a copy of the letter I wrote to them.

Let me tell you why I agreed so readily and quickly to accept your arrangements: I had known for a long time that I have a problem with alcohol. It was rapidly becoming the center of my life. It was keeping me from doing many of the things that I enjoy. I had not done any serious photography in two years, and I had not done anything on the book I started writing a long time ago. I knew that something was wrong and getting "wronger." I tried, but could do nothing about it, and I was ashamed to acknowledge that. So I could not ask for help. At the confrontation *(intervention)* I knew all this, but all of that is not the reason I did not argue. Was I just too weak, too chicken to stand up to you? Perhaps. Many of the people here tell me they argued, and even put off treatment for days, or weeks, or even months. I like to think that my promise of respect and obedience had something to do with it. I hope that it did.

I think that I am doing well. I have, for the most part, gotten over self-pity. I continue to be supported by many letters of love, and encouragement from my people, my brother priests, and my Bishop. I cannot tell you how much this means to me. Without this support I would go all the way out of my mind. I have written my people a letter of appreciation and given them a general idea of my treatment. I told them I would give them a progress report at the end of April and May. Would you be so kind to let the priests of the Diocese know that I am supported, and encouraged by their cards and letters.

You will be at Nativity soon for Confirmation. It grieves me to miss that. I have written a letter to those students - I enclose a copy for you. Bishop, one of the things that weighs heavily on me is the scandal I have given to the young people. Any advice, or feedback you have would be gratefully accepted. I know that you are busy so do not concern yourself about writing letters to me. My purpose in writing is to let you know that I appreciate your support, encouragement and love.

God's Peace, and my love,

Bill

April 3, 1989
Guest House

Dear Members of the Confirmation Class of Nativity,

I will certainly miss being with you for Confirmation. I will miss presenting you to the Bishop, and testifying on your behalf. My prayers are with you, and my hopes are high for you.

Now let's face squarely the reason I am not with you: I am receiving and working with a 90-day program of treatment for alcoholism. The Doctors say this is a disease - the Bishop says that it is not a moral failure. Neither of these relieves me of the responsibility for my own sobriety. But being absolutely honest with you I gotta' tell you that neither what the doctors say, nor the Bishop says, has done much to relieve me of feelings of shame, failure and guilt. I am learning to accept what I cannot change, I will learn to change what I can change (I suspect this will take the rest of my life), and I ask God to help me in this, and to help me to know the difference between the two.

What do I have to say to you as you are about to be Confirmed? When you accept Confirmation you are publicly saying that you want to, and will try to, "Take up your cross and follow Christ." Do not trifle, and do be aware that this can be

46

very serious. Father Richard Rohr tells me what it means. It may include putting up with hot or cold weather; a broken air conditioner; a flat tire, and so on - or as the saying goes, "Offering it Up." But when you get to the bottom, this is what it means: "Accepting the pain and suffering that comes from making a decision for the Kingdom of God." Now my decision to drink was not one of those decisions, and I am not proud of it. My decision to obey the Bishop, to accept help for my drinking problem, known as alcoholism, was a decision made for the Kingdom of God. There has been pain and suffering as a result of that decision. I did not measure the pain and suffering and say, "I'll do it." Fortunately I did not know just how much pain and suffering there would be. My decision has caused others to suffer, it has caused me to be away from you at this time, to be away at Holy Week, to have to acknowledge my weakness, my problem, publicly, the list goes on. I still believe that it was a decision for the Kingdom of God.

It may seem easy to say, "Yes" to Confirmation, to Marriage, to Ordination - these are decisions for the Kingdom. You will in many ways, great and small, be shown throughout life how serious, "Yes" to the Kingdom can be. I was certain that by saying "Yes" to admitting my problem, and "Yes" to accepting treatment that I might lose the love, and respect of most of the parish and of my Bishop - but I was wrong. There was pain and suffering but not abandonment. Surely there are many who are still confused, hurt, and even bitter - but God, in His mercy, will help all of us through that as long as we keep making decisions for the Kingdom.

I am proud of you as you say, "Yes" to Confirmation. I want to encourage you with the hope I have in my own life - given me by our Christian Community. I want to support you with my prayers, and my love - Even as I am now being supported by the love and prayers of the Christian Community. I want to be very clear: the "Yes" you say to Confirmation is very serious and surely it will involve, at various times in the future, happiness and joy, pain and suffering, but bring all of these to the Christian Community, and you will be blessed with God's gift of Peace which often comes in unexpected ways.

God's Peace and my love,

Father Bill
Pastor

April 4, 1989
Tuesday 1:00 p.m.

Dear Bill,
(Father Oglesby sent me a series of letters letting me know what was going on in the parish. I guess he didn't want me to worry. All of his letters were hand written. I think it was very kind of him.)

At last I am getting around to a letter for you. Am sitting at the half circle table in the kitchen area. I eat here and often work from this spot. I find it convenient for

47

me. I am so reminded of the three months you took care of St. Ann, Bartlett when I was in Canada in 1973, and later at Mother's house recovering from surgery. I still have the beautiful letter you wrote Mother and me while we were in Montreal. It is difficult to realize that it was almost 16 years ago when that took place. I guess you know by now that "Jock" is at Victor's and thoroughly enjoying it. The rectory is wonderful. You did a beautiful job on it. *(Victor and I worked together on the plan for the rectory.)* Best living situation I have ever had. Estelle Coleman came over yesterday and we did a little straightening up: NO CHANGES - So don't worry about that. Bruce is on retreat this week - somewhere - I do not know where!!! Saturday night late I did some shopping at Krogers and saw Mary, his mother there.

We made it through Holy Week and Easter with no difficulty. I enjoyed the ceremonies. All went well thanks to Larry Howell and Mary Miller and Gay. I am sure it was an adjustment for them (and still is) getting used to me. Nice group of ladies come to daily Mass, and I enjoy a congregation again. I do let the ladies serve as lector at daily Mass. I am fast learning the names of ones I did not know from previous associations. The area is surely still building. I assure you that you will find everything in tact when you return. It will begin to go fast for you.

We **shall not** cancel your 25th celebration - just delay/postpone it until you return and you can agree on a date. You deserve that. You have worked hard and you are a good pastoral priest. The people love you and they understand!

I am not disappointed in you, I am proud of you. It takes courage, patience and determination to do what you are doing. You are and will be admired for it. Patience may be the hardest at this time. I am reminded of Angelo L. I have always admired him for his handling of the same problem. Throw away the guilt feelings. Let us rejoice!! You will have a much better handle on things when you return - might even play a better game of bridge! Ha! Ha!

I am mailing your Mug this afternoon. Marcel is coming tomorrow (Wednesday 4/5) to see about mailing/shipping your computer to you. We will hold magazines here for you unless you instruct otherwise. Your check on 15th of each month will be deposited to your account by Bill Brigance. Diocese is paying me for my time here. When I accepted the assignment here on Wednesday/Thursday, March 22/23 I had four weekend commitments which I cannot change, so Bishop agreed that Sartain would arrange to have them covered. They are: April 8/9; April 29/30; June 10/11; and June 17/18. Otherwise I will remain close and do my best to take care of things for you. I will enjoy it, but I, like the people, will be glad when you return.

I had also promised help at Our Lady of Sorrows, Holy Spirit, and St. Ann Bartlett, but those men said they would make other arrangements.

The funerals for Louise Smith and Roy Wilson went ok. I enjoyed the reception of Catechumens and Candidates at the Vigil Service. I will enjoy working with a Legion of Mary again, if only for a few months. The parish Council retreat was scheduled for April 29/30. We have postponed it until after you get back since it was also on one of the weekends that I was committed elsewhere. They are holding the $200.00 deposit and will credit it as deposit for the retreat when rescheduled. We probably will go ahead with Parish Picnic/Garden Mass, etc. The stipend I will get for the four weekends I will be away I will donate to Nativity unless it is needed for whoever takes my place on those weekends. I will let Peter Sartain decide about that.

Jimmy LaHue called to tell you that a business associate of his and friend of yours in Jackson, TN is ill - Hollis Moody (Rocky).

Was just interrupted by a phone call from Pastor of St. John in Oxford, Mississippi. His trip has been canceled. He will not need me this coming weekend. I know Peter Sartain will be glad!

Bill - people here love you and do understand and are extremely supportive of you. I hope you realize that. I must close and head out to Lakeside. Harrell B., a friend of mine, was committed there over the weekend for alcoholism. He is not cooperating and is angry at his wife and children for putting him there. I would like to share your letter to the parishioners with him in hopes it will help him admit that he needs help. Hope that is ok. Your letter to the people of the parish was beautiful, well done and so sincere.

Well, will keep up the good work. Pray for me! Pray for the people of Nativity as we pray for and with you!

Sincerely,
Leonard

P.S. Don't hesitate to give me any special instructions that you may have for me. Phone line in your bedroom does not work. No special problem for me, but has it been that way?? I am sure I will think of something else after I have posted this.

Fr. Bill trying to get around the eight ball.

49

Spring arrived and I enjoyed scripture in the Courtyard.

I enjoyed the company of Canadian Geese on my walks.

CHAPTER THREE
WEEK THREE

APRIL 5, 1989
Wednesday

Mo uses the bathroom between 7:00 a.m. and 7:30 a.m. This is late for me, but he was there before I was, so I either have to be early, or late. It's really no big deal. At least I will have time for my morning walk if I get up early.

9:00 a.m. – The video features the "Fr. Joe Martin's Chalk Talk." It's very good, but the sound track is poor. He has an interesting story, and I like the way he describes things, "I was down so low I had to jump up to touch bottom."

11:00 a.m. – Group is good today, no arguments between Len and Zeke.

Today was a day for shopping at the Mall. I walked over to Service Merchandise to get a beard trimmer. Next I went to Sears to get a surge protector for my computer. It should be in tomorrow. I stopped to get Cappuccino, (I have never had one) but the milk taste is too strong. Milk and I don't get along. I'm still amazed by the freedom we have on these shopping trips. I mean anyone could stop at any one of several liquor stores. I asked one of the guys about it, and he told me, "Hey, we're here to get well, or at least to get started getting well. If I start drinking here I know damn well I ain't gonna make it, and I want to make it."

Mike Touchet calls. He tells me about his family. His wife worked as my secretary for a while. Mary Miller calls and says Marcel will ship computer tomorrow.

Supper is a special treat. Joe Paolozzi, from Memphis is visiting and he, Ed B. and, I go out to a restaurant. We talk at supper, and carry the conversation on 'til 9:00 p.m. This kind of socializing is difficult for me. I guess this is why 90% of my social drinking was done alone. I guess I was able to socialize with greater ease at some time in my life. I don't remember being a loner when I was young, or in the service. I have to say I have lost my easy familiarity with socializing. I want to get it back even if it means just sitting there listening. I tell them I have a problem with Will C., and they say bring it up in group.

Back at Guest House I get into a game of pool. I learned to play pool while in the Air Force, and I still enjoy it. It was also a very popular game while I was in the seminary. Then before I go to bed I read the Big Book up to page 150.

APRIL 6, 1989
Thursday

I wake up early, 6:40 a.m., so I get bathroom first. It is cold again so I pray the Office in the chapel before Breakfast.

9:00 a.m. – The video is, "I thought it was my friend." That is, he thought alcohol was his friend.

11:00 a.m. – At Group I bring up my problem with Will C. I'm beginning to understand Group better. There are just some people that I am not going to get along with. It doesn't mean that the world is falling apart.

More mail today. A letter from Philip Offerle. I am very relieved to hear from him. I had talked often with him about priesthood. It turns out that I have not turned him off. He may, or may not consider the priesthood, but he is still close to the Lord, whether or not he becomes a priest is secondary.

The weather warmed up some so I had good walk, and then a nap. When I nap it is usually for about a half hour. After the nap I read more of "I'll Quit Tomorrow". The driver for AA does not show up, so there is no AA Meeting tonight.

John Tindle calls and we have a good talk. He tells me of this or that problem in the parish, or he hints at them. I must write Len Oglesby so he doesn't think I am trying to run the parish from here. Victor calls. He tells me that he is taking care of Jock because Len couldn't handle it. I ask Vic to put the phone to Jock's ear and then I use the special whistle I use to call him. He hears it, and remembers it. I can hear him bark and that is good.

A Bar of Soap - Sister Somebody very carefully wrapped bars of soap for each of the Guests here. We find them in our mail boxes. How very thoughtful. I recall the ladies of Nativity, and other parishes preparing "gifts" for the less fortunate. Now I am one of the "less fortunate." Something else about that bar of soap: I always wondered how the people who received gifts like this bar of soap felt. Well I'll tell you how I feel. I feel very grateful. I don't know this Sister, and she doesn't know me, but she cares, and that feels good. I'm reminded of that commercial for the greeting card company: "She cared enough to send the very best."

APRIL 7, 1989
Friday

I slept late again today, 'til 7:00 a.m. I join Ed B. & Joe Paolozzi for a special breakfast. They are returning to Memphis today. I'm glad to see Ed returning to the active ministry, but in another way I'm sad to see them go. They are a little bit of home. Ah! One day I, too, will be going home.

It is still cold up here, so I pray the Office in Chapel. Won't it ever get warm up here? This means that I didn't get my morning walk in.

9:00 a.m. – The talk is by Dave. He tells his story. It was interesting, but I want to hear a story that I can identify with. I didn't have too much heavy drinking. I mean I seldom got falling down, staggering drunk. I just couldn't stop regular drinking. I suppose there are some, perhaps many who would disagree with that. Maybe I just have what people up here are calling "Selective Memory." Of this much I'm sure: With me there was a gradual loss of awareness, and effectiveness. Then one day, I guess it was about two years ago I realized that I had more and more difficulty saying, "No" to the next drink.

11:00 a.m. – Group is "so-so." I guess this is because Len is out of town.

Harry Sullivan calls at lunch time. I request a "Remember Leo" type of prayer from Harry.

(I guess I had better explain the "Remember Leo Prayer." Leo is one of the sons of Harry and Mary Alice. I was having dinner with the family while Leo was in the army and overseas. Harry led the prayer of blessing before we ate. I thought he had finished and started to dig in when Harry added, "Let's remember Leo," we paused for a while in silence, then he concluded the prayer. Harry told me that Leo had made a deal with the family that each time he sat down to a meal he would remember them, and he asked that the family remember him when they sat down for a meal.)

Today is another trip to K-Mart. This is not the big Mall. It's the quick trip for a hair cut and some time in K-Mart. I'm told that men don't enjoy shopping. Well I get a kick out of K-Mart.

I write to Father Oglesby and Philip Offerle . More reading of the Big Book of Alcoholics Anonymous. There is a trip planned for tomorrow to Frankenmuth. They tell me that it's a touristy town with German accents. I'm part German, so I look forward to it. The weather forecast is for SNOW tomorrow.

APRIL 8, 1989
Saturday

I had some time on my hands before the trip to Frankenmuth and for some reason I reviewed the Sorrowful Mysteries in light of my drinking. This is what I came up with:

THE AGONY IN THE GARDEN: Looking at the past - my weaknesses, sins, relationships, seeking approval by letting others walk all over me, and hating them, and me, for it. This has been my Agony in the Garden.

THE SCOURGING AT THE PILLAR: Bringing those feelings up with a Counselor, or at Group, seeing myself as I really am. This will be my Scourging at the Pillar.

THE CROWNING WITH THORNS: Learning to let go. Actually it's more than letting go, it is the pain of holding on to what I should let go of.

THE CARRYING OF THE CROSS: Taking all things to the Lord, learning to walk with, and trust Him. The Lord fell three times. I can't begin to count the number of times I've fallen.

THE CRUCIFIXION: Letting go. As I see it this is the ultimate in letting go. Into Thy Hands I commit myself just as I am.

The trip to Frankenmuth was fun, sight-seeing, places for arts and crafts, and window shopping. A German Village, very touristy. They claim "World Famous Chicken Dinners." I am not impressed with the food. I am sort of startled by the fact that almost everyone around us is drinking beer. I guess I'm looking for "protection". They had a store that had nothing but Christmas things in it. They claim over 50,000 items, but I didn't count them. We also stop at a Discount Shopping Mall. The prices are not discount. This reminds me of what my brother-in-law told me years ago: "Window shopping is the only free recreation left to mankind." The window shopping was fun.

APRIL 9, 1989
Sunday

Would you believe it snowed again today!!

I was the celebrant at Mass today. I told them about "Poor George."

("Poor George" is a meditation I wrote some years ago. It is in that book of pictures and meditations that I have yet to finish. I add it here so you will know what I am talking about. I think the point I was trying to make is that we all have a responsibility for each other. Sometimes that responsibility is left unfulfilled and enabling is the result. The Meditation begins with a picture of two men walking in a woods, and scripture from James 5:19 -20.)

POOR GEORGE

Poor George is dead, died last night. Seems odd he should die, wasn't really sick, just had a cold, a cold in the head. Least that's what he said.

I 'member when he got it, way back last summer. Just a few sniffles and a sneeze, or two.

George wasn't worried. He was healthy as a horse. Never been sick a day in his life. Oh, he'd had a cold, or two, and a smoker's cough, but that wasn't sick, not really.

When summer turned to fall, and the cold stayed with him, some began to worry and offered their best - Hot chicken soup or, "You better get some rest."

But most everyone said, "Oh, it's just a cold George, a cold in the head, everybody gets 'em, they're common as sin."

But people who had kids told 'em not to get too close. You know how easy kids catch things. As for themselves, they weren't worried, and they told old

54

George, *"Don't you worry George, you're not sick, you just got a cold, a cold in the head. What you got everybody gets. You're as well as any one of us."*

Winter came on and the cold was still there. Some suggested a doctor, but George said, "NO!!" He wasn't sick, he just had a cold, a cold in the head. Besides, he didn't trust doctors. They'd say he was sick, give him a shot, and put him to bed, and send him a bill. You can count on that.

The doctors, they couldn't understand that he wasn't really sick. He just had a cold, a cold in the head. All his friends agreed, "George, you're not sick, you just got a cold, a cold in the head. Everybody gets 'em, they're common as sin."

Well, poor George is dead. Died last night. Doc says it's a shame. He'd be alive today, if he'd just known that he was really sick. But we told him, "No, you're not really sick. You just got a cold, a cold in the head. You're just like us, and we're not sick, not sick at all, ARE WE???"

NOW WHAT DOES IT MEAN?

Poor George could be anyone, and everyone. The cold he has could be sin, or a bad habit, or an addiction. The difficulty he has is admitting that he's sick, or he has sinned, or is trapped in an addiction. Unless George is able to admit that he is really sick, then he's going to get worse.

George doesn't get much help from his friends. They accept his sickness as health and, for the most part, encourage him to do nothing about it. Why?? Well if they admit that George is sick they'll have to admit that they're sick too. For example, let's say that George drinks too much, or cheats on his wife. If his friends tell him that he is sick, that is, his drinking, or cheating is causing problems, then they'll have to look at their own problems. So, they don't tell George that he is sick. He just has a cold, a cold in the head, everybody gets 'em they're as common as sin.

The doctors in the story are any true friends, or spiritual guides. George didn't want to face them, because they'd call on him to face himself. So he makes up all kinds of excuses for not seeing a doctor. And, of course, he dies.

AS A RESPONSE TO THIS MEDITATION PLEASE READ Ezekiel 3:17-21 The passage from Ezekiel tells of God telling him that He has appointed him Watchman, and that he must tell the people when they are doing something wrong. It is easy for me to see that the story is all about enabling.

It snowed off and on all day. Not much accumulation, perhaps 1 inch. I spent most of the day reading Jack Higgins' book, "The Night of the Fox."

The AA meeting was in house, and very good. I brought up my problem: My story does not match - that is, it does not come up to anything that I have heard. Jim McD. gives this feedback: On a baseball team not everyone plays right field, but if you are on the team you wear the uniform, even if you're just the Bat Boy. The pros, Medical, Psychological, etc., all say I am first string, so I wear the uniform. Others give feedback too, and I think I will be able to deal with the temptation of: "Well I'm not really an alcoholic" and then go back to drinking.

APRIL 10, 1989
Monday

Grits for breakfast. I share them with a few of the Southerners. The other guys want to put milk and sugar on them, so they don't get any.

9:00 a.m. – The lecture is on Sexuality by Dr. Ken Adams. It's very interesting, and informative. It helps me understand my celibacy better.

Loads of mail. Without mail I think I would really be tempted to just give up.

There is about an inch of snow on the ground. I take lots of pictures.

It is too cold to walk, so I pray the Office in the chapel. I continue my reading of, "I'll Quit Tomorrow."

The AA meeting is at Valley Woods Hospital. It's good. It is a non-smoking meeting. This is what I hear: "I used to think, If I can't do this by myself, I'm not much of a man, now I think just the opposite." I always feel hesitant about AA meetings. I would prefer not to go, yet each time I go I enjoy it. I learn something, and in a strange way feel right at home. That is, I feel like this I where I belong. It's clear tonight that these people really want to give help, and to get help.

After the meeting there is excitement among some of the guys in the house. Seems somebody has returned. He was unable to follow the program. He was found by one of the priests in the rectory, on the floor bleeding. It seems that his continued drinking had caused some kind of hemorrhage in his throat. He could have died. I recall a friend of mine who did die because of his drinking. When he died he was alone in a motel and his body was not discovered for a week. This sure calls on me to realize just how serious I should be about recovery.

APRIL 11, 1989
Tuesday

9:00 a.m. – The lecture, a class on Basics, is good. My temptations are so crazy: "All of this stuff they tell us is a line of bunk, - there is no "X" factor. It seems so clear to me. What they are presenting is simply a case of, 'You lie, and I'll swear to it.'" "Am I the only one who sees all this? Is everyone else being taken for a ride?" I just read what I wrote last night. Boy I sure do go back and forth, or up and down. I hear people talking about being restored to sanity. I wonder when I will be restored. I sure sound very crazy to me. I want to believe all these things they tell us. It would take away so much guilt. But for some reason I want to, I need to, hold on to this guilt.

1:00 p.m. – At Jack Gregory's Group I bring up my problem with guilt. I don't really get a much better understanding. I must present this to God. I'm not totally convinced about being powerless over alcohol, but I really am powerless over this guilt, and it is making my life unmanageable.

Harvey Carter calls, Marge, his wife, is not doing very well. Billy *(the janitor at Nativity)* calls, seems there is some confusion about shipping my computer. I know I'll get it. It is just a matter of when. I think it will be so much easier to keep a journal on a computer than it is to keep it with a typewriter, or a legal pad. I keep writing things down at odd times. Most of the time it is at night, but sometimes I take a great notion to write a little bit wherever I am.

THE LETTERS

April 7, 1989

Dear Philip,

I was really encouraged by your letter. I have long admired the Grace of God at work in you. You have a way of bringing the best out of people. This may be a gift, but you cooperate, and work with it so well.

God is calling each of us to Himself, and He calls each one of us in a special way. Does He call you to priesthood, to married life, to music? Who knows? You will know in God's good time. I do think that the Lord is calling you to be of good & joyful service to others - just how - well I don't know.

Thank you for the picture - I'll bet the dance was fun. A trophy from a Jazz Festival - fantastic. I do enjoy Jazz.

About my treatment here. Well it started with a physical. I thought I weighed 147, but it was only 138. My blood pressure was a little high. The liver was a bit fatty, cholesterol was too high, everything else was within normal limits. There was a malformation in the red blood cells which, I am told, is typical of the disease of alcoholism. According to these people some people can drink and not get alcoholism, some people drink and get it. Why? Well according to them the people who get alcoholism have a genetic factor that enables them, if they drink, to become an alcoholic at some point in their drinking life. Apparently it does not matter how much one drinks. Also that "point in their drinking life" is different for each person. There is the case of the little ole lady who drank only a little sherry each day when the school bus came by. Finally the "X" factor clicked in, and she was hooked - addicted. Once the addiction clicks in there is no cure - the body craves more and more. If a person continues to drink the body will deteriorate, fall prey to a host of illnesses and death results. There is no cure. The only thing that arrests the disease is to stop drinking. With an addiction that is not easy - especially since we live in a culture that takes drinking for granted. How does one stop drinking and stay stopped? Well that is what I am learning.

First we take care of the physical health, but at the same time the mental & spiritual health is rebuilt, reinforced and so on. One thing that is absolutely necessary is a <u>constant</u> support group, and that is where family, friends and AA (Alcoholics Anonymous) come in. I will tell you more about AA in other letters. I will also share with you what alcohol <u>will</u> do to anyone who drinks and also has the genetic "X" factor, and why it is almost impossible for a person in the early stages of alcoholism to recognize what is happening. I think alcoholism has been discovered in me fairly early - although I have been drinking for many years and heavily for several of the last few years.

I'm not absolutely convinced about the "X" factor - but these people are experts & use experts. So since I want to quit drinking I'll do it their way. My way didn't work at all.

Well Philip, I hope I have not confused you. I love you very much - I'll tell you what I know, how I feel - when I have doubts, and when I'm confused. I know this much: I meant what I said in my letter to the people - I need help to quit drinking - I'm going to do it their way. I know my way does not work.

God's Peace and my love,

Father Bill

P.S. It is impossible to answer each letter I get, so please do not noise it around that I answered your letters - if you wish you share this with other teenagers.

(A Card from Bishop Daniel)

April 6, 1989

Bill, Peace!

You are often on my mind and always in my prayers - fondly.

I hope the program is not too rigorous and painful. Your card meant so very much to me. What we did was indeed done because we love you.

I look forward to your return!

Bishop Daniel

Fri. April 7, 1989

Dear Fr. Bill,

(This is a letter that I received. I did not enjoy it. It claims a knowledge of my condition for several years, yet the writer had been in the parish for only about 18 months.)

Sorry for the delay in this letter. We were enjoying the Florida sun the week after Easter & I just returned last Monday.

Praise God, Fr. Bill, that you have taken that courageous <u>first</u> step of admitting you were powerless over alcohol & that your life had become unmanageable. Thank

You Lord. Thank You Jesus! I read your beautiful letter. You are right the Lord is going to greatly humble you in the next 3 months. Isn't it wonderful though that you are with other men who are just like you & have the same problem? I've always thought that group sharing sessions were (are) extremely beneficial & much spiritual & emotional growth come from not only bearing your heart & soul but listening to others. I am very familiar with the 12 step program. Overeaters Anonymous works on the same plan & principles.

Fr. Bill, I'm so very proud of you for your candor & honesty with the people of Nativity. I also appreciated the Bishop's straight forwardness. I miss your humor & your cynicism. Yes, you have given me a hard way to go often but I think I've handled it pretty well most of the time! Fr. Oglesby also likes to kid & have fun but when he's joking with you a person knows, with you, I never know if you're teasing me, or you are serious. Know that I love you. Fr. Bill, I have been praying for you for several years that you would recognize your alcohol abuse problem & want to help yourself. I have known for many years but always kept it to myself & did not tell anyone. I am so happy for you Fr. Bill. I know you will return to us changed, refreshed, & renewed. Each day at Mass I silently remember You. Facing this problem, I know has got to be one of the hardest problems you've ever had to deal with.

Fr. Bill, Our Lord, right now is inviting you to join Him in a deeper realm & relationship to be in intimacy with Him. You have answered the call to God's challenge in your life. Praise God. Praise His name!

May God grant you much peace, joy, happiness, & rest.
Know I pray for you daily & I also pray for the other men at Guest House also.

Fr. Bill, I've told you before, but I'll tell you again you helped me personally to seek a deeper relationship with Our Lord & His Blessed Mother. I have grown spiritually since I've known you. I thank you so much for what you have given me. I miss you. I miss Jock too. Things are not, will not, & cannot be the same without you. You are truly unique. Thanks.
In Christ's Everlasting Peace & Light,

xxxxxxxxx
(I have left the name off on purpose. I am always somewhat uncomfortable with Charismatics, but I do recognize that they have unique gifts.)

April 9, 1989

Dear Helen,
     Sunday - 1:00 p.m., would you believe it is snowing? Well it is. The weather is very depressing. The natives tell me the difference between Spring and Fall up here is some day in June - That is the day of the Picnic *(At Nativity)*. I'm beginning to think the sun will never shine again. I'm told that you are having a lot of rain down there.

Are the Gold Finches still there? I told John Tindle, when he called the other day, to make sure he put the humming bird feeders up.

Make no mistake about it, Helen, I am an alcoholic. There is no cure so I just have to learn to live without it. That, of course, will be one day at a time. Everyone up here tells me that I will enjoy life a great deal more. They are probably right, at least I am going to find out.

I am settling into the routine and have gotten over feeling sorry for myself. I find the opportunities for spiritual and emotional growth abundant. The food ain't bad either. They just don't serve wine with meals and the wine at the altar is non-alcoholic, too.

I begin to understand how you and others feel - you who depend on others for transportation. I never thought that the highlight of my week would be a trip to K-Mart. The day is full - lectures, videos, one on one counseling sessions, books to read, personal prayer, walks, my daily writing - but it is great to be able to get out of the house - off the grounds. Oh, there are no bars on the windows, the gates are not locked and one can walk off the grounds, but it is too cold.

See you in June, God Bless & keep warm

Father Bill

A Canadian Momma Goose
with her goslings.

This was one
of my favorite
outdoor places
of prayer.

CHAPTER FOUR
WEEK FOUR

APRIL 12, 1989
Wednesday

9:00 a.m. –Relaxation Techniques. Christian Yoga, very interesting. It does relieve stress. We get some handouts on it, I will have to save them and put them to good use.

That letter from Xxxxx is still eating at me. The letter says, "I have been praying for you for SEVERAL YEARS, that you would recognize your alcohol abuse problem, and WANT to help yourself. I have known for MANY YEARS, but always kept it to myself and did not tell anyone." *(Caps are mine.)* The person is full of it. That person has only known me for 18 months at the most. The person has a real problem of needing to be important. I have got to talk to Len about this. *(I go to great pains not to identify that person either by name or gender.)*

Departure Mass is for 5 people. Frank O. thinks the Msgr. will be back. I enjoyed Eric's reading of John Paul II's policy on clerical dress. I appreciated his reading from Austin Ripley. I asked for a copy of both. Hope he comes through.

Weather is still cold. With the cold weather I am beginning to enjoy hot chocolate instead of coffee. I am beginning to read a story, or two in the Big Book that I can identify with. Did you see what I did just now? I said "identify with" instead of "relate to." Len keeps telling me that it is better to relate than to identify.

I have some ideas about taking some pictures in chapel tomorrow. I think I will use different lens, telephoto, close up, and a few others.

The AA driver canceled for tonight. I will go tomorrow. I'm less hesitant about going to meetings now, because I know I will enjoy them once I'm there. I think AA is going to be important, and perhaps necessary for me.

APRIL 13, 1989
Thursday

Bad night for sleeping. A bit of lower bowel upset and minor runs.

9:00 a.m. – This is a session called Bridge. It is not the card game. Seven, or eight people who have completed the course here return for what is called After-care. They share their experience and answer questions. Now this is something that I think I can use. These guys have "been there, done that." I find it interesting, informative and encouraging. Everyone of them speaks of two things that help them: AA Meetings and a Sponsor. I think that I will ask Jim (the guy from the parish who wrote to me and told me his story) to be my sponsor.

11:00 a.m. – Group. Tom W. is really suffering with scruples. Can he ever be forgiven? I offer the story about the evil Hitler throwing himself on the mercy of God and that gets him into heaven. He says he gets my point, and that it helps now, but tomorrow he thinks he will be right back where he is today. I bring up my problem about that letter. The person who has known for years that I have an alcoholic problem, and yet we've only known each other for 18 months. Best comment is: "Yeah, well wait 'til you get home, that person will take all the credit for your cure."

The sun was out late today, and I had a good walk. The morning overcast was no good for pictures in the chapel. I especially wanted to take pictures of the statue of Blessed Virgin Mary.

No AA tonight, and I'm glad. Not because I didn't want to go, because I've still got a bit of the runs.

I am becoming more and more convinced that I am an alcoholic. That I am powerless, and my life was, and could be again, unmanageable. I am absolutely convinced that this is true at least in potential. I talked this over with Len a few days ago. He came right out and asked me if I was powerless over alcohol. I told him that I had started a new parish beginning with only a list of names and a vacant lot. I got the first building up, and the Rectory. Since I was able to do all that it just didn't seem to me that I am powerless. That's why I have to add "at least in potential." Then he asked me how many times I had tried to stop. I started counting, but finally gave up. I guess I got a little upset. That didn't seem to upset Len at all. He said, "Father, being powerless over alcohol doesn't mean that you are powerless over everything, - just alcohol." I got a little distracted when he used my title. It seems that all the people up here are very careful about that. At any rate I'm more, and more willing to come around to being powerless over alcohol.

Something else happened after I met with Len. I was talking to one of the guys about powerlessness. I told him I was not totally convinced. He asked me, "Have you ever canceled something, an appointment, a dinner, an outing, because of alcohol?" I thought for a minute and, bingo - there it was. One time a year or so ago someone had invited me to be a chaplain on a pilgrimage to one of the Shrines of Our Lady in Europe - all expenses paid. I turned it down because I didn't know if I could get Jack Daniels over there. Actually, it wasn't just Jack Daniels. I didn't know if I would be able to drink because I was the Chaplain. I also recalled that I would not eat dinner in a place that didn't serve alcohol. In the last year whenever I went to a movie I always took a miniature Jack Daniels with me. I recalled the many times, too numerous to count, that I had fought the desire to have a drink, and finally gave in. I'm not sure if that meant that I was powerless, but it sure meant that alcohol had a strong power over me.

I got picture of John K. in Chapel. I hope it turns out as good as I think it will.

9:00 a.m. – A class about Calix. This is an association of Catholic Alcoholics. The guy - I forget his name - presented it as something that may have value for priests. His presentation was very long and rambling. He does express his point on patience very well. Recovering alcoholics cannot expect to change right away. Give it a YEAR OR TWO. The man presenting the lecture - now I remember his name - is Fr. Mark. He is 76 years old. It blows my mind that recovery will take one to two years.

At 10:00 a.m. – I met with Len. We discussed sex. He encourages me to write a history of my sexual experiences in addition to the sexual survey I had already filled out.

11:00 a.m. – Group is good. Don C. is present. I'm impressed by him and his honesty.

I spent the afternoon writing my sexual history. WOW.

Mail is plentiful and good. I have a letter from Jeff Marx.

Jim McD. has the Mass. It is meaningful. I have misplaced my rosary. I will go out to an out of town parish for Mass this weekend. I will leave Saturday at 9:30 a.m. and return Sunday afternoon.

The Crucifix behind the altar in the chapel at Guest House.

63

APRIL 15, 1989
Saturday

The people from the parish came by to pick me up at 9:30 a.m. I meet the priest, Fr. Jim, who is filling in for the pastor. I hear confessions at 11:00 a.m. Fr. Jim and I get to talk a bit. He is familiar with the problems of alcoholics. In fact he tells me of his rescue, and free treatment at Guest House. He actually lived under a bridge. I am amazed by the willingness of people who are alcoholic to share their experience with me. Jim tells me that one of the things that keeps him sober is sharing his experiences with other people who have the problem.

I spend the afternoon writing my sermon. I guess I have almost always written my sermons. If I don't I tend to go on, and on, and on. I have the 5:00 p.m. Mass, and I am more nervous than usual. We have dinner at a local restaurant with a bar. I'm not bothered. I am a bit nervous, with headache and gas. We stop at Drug Store for aspirin and digel. Jim drives through the neighborhood, and shows me the homes of some members of the parish. When we return we watch a little TV. Then I have a cup of hot coco, and then to bed.

APRIL 16, 1989
Sunday

(I made the above notes Saturday evening while in the parish, all the rest was written after I returned to Guest House.)

I discover that I am nervous at Mass, and wonder why. The Mass and sermon go okay, but toward the end, at Communion I get chest pains, really just a tightness in the chest. Then I get short of breath. I finish Mass and go to lay down. The people come to take me back to Guest House, but I ask them to give me time to rest. I tell them that I just don't feel well. Fr. Jim comes by to look in on me. I am very nervous and actually fearful. I tell Jim that I have this tightness in my chest. At that point the people who were going to take me to Guest House take me to St. Joseph Hospital.

I remember very clearly being taken to the hospital. I was very scared, and yet very peaceful. I remember thinking: Well here I am about to die, a thousand miles from home and friends, but at least I'm going to die sober. I didn't know it then, but I was not having a heart attack, and I was nowhere near death. However I thought things were much more serious.

APRIL 17, 1989
Monday

I spent the rest of Sunday and all of Monday in St. Joseph Hospital. Fr. Jim dropped by with flowers. Other members of the parish dropped by, I was touched. I felt great, and I was beginning to wonder what happened. If it wasn't my heart, what was it? The doctor is at a loss. He says it could have been some sort of spasm in my chest muscles, or stress, but it was not my heart. I feel rather foolish.

APRIL 18, 1989
Tuesday

I return to Guest House from St. Joseph Hospital at noon. I tell my story to Dr. Lyons, he thinks stress has a lot to do with it. I perceive a negative attitude in Dr. Lyons which I find surprising. Later I get a better understanding: Dr. Lyons uses the word hyperventilation which I thought was always induced voluntarily, so I though he was saying that I brought all this on myself to draw attention to myself. I also discovered that some alcoholics are subject to what is known as "panic attacks". This side trip to the hospital also causes some additional paper work for insurance forms. It seems that I was under insurance coverage at Guest House, and the trip to the hospital caused some confusion.

At 5:00 p.m. I get gas pains, and request Tylenol #3. I am given Maalox. The gas continues til 1:30 a.m. I call Jackie, and get Tylenol #3. Get to sleep about 2:30. I hope they don't think I was just trying to force the issue. *[I'm not sure what I was trying to say here, except that I have suffered from extreme gas pains for most of my life and no one has ever taken them seriously.]*

THE LETTERS

April 11, 1989

Dear Bill,

(This is Fr. Oglesby's second report. All of his letters were hand written.)

Appreciated your note that arrived yesterday. I am enjoying the rectory but will be ready to turn it over to you when you return. I assure you I am not making any changes; just trying to protect the budget. Don't worry. You know I am not a big spender, in fact - tend to be a little close with the people's money. Everything seems to be going ok; I have asked the staff not to order any new material (educational etc.) until after you return - so you can approve. There would still be plenty of time to get material for the fall programs.

A plating company called and said that the "thing" is ready. Bruce says he will take care of it. *(This was something that I had re-plated for Rosa.)*

I have talked to Ken DeWitt, Pastoral Council, Barbara, & Vic about your celebration. We (they) all want to have one. I think you must!! We all agreed that it would be like September or October and that you should select the date after you return. *(This is about the celebration for my 25th anniversary.)*

I am not touching all the electronic equipment in the house & office - too complicated for the "old" pastor, retired / administrator. I did figure out how to get channels 3, 5, 10, 13 on the Sony in your study for 10:00 p.m. news. Haven't had time for much else. Staff is working me too hard but I am enjoying it. I'll have plenty of time to fish after July 1st and maybe we can get in some bridge games after that. Also, I want you to see my place at Enid. You never have!

65

I plan to prepare a crappie fish fillet dinner for the Bishop Saturday after Confirmation, if he will stay and eat.

I may run up to Louisville and Nazareth next week for a couple of days. Sister Constance had a complete knee replacement recently. She also has Parkinson's Disease. Had dinner at Picadilly on Stage Rd. with Estelle & Jim Coleman after last Saturday night's Mass. Am trying to figure out the thermostat. I think I have mastered it with Larry Harmon's help. Your car is at Larry's warehouse. Hope that is ok. He has promised that it is safe and well cared for. Phone that is in your bedroom (phone does not work) is no problem for me. I use the cordless at night as you suggested. Dan Richardson is celebrating his Golden Jubilee tomorrow night - but I don't plan to attend - we (Mary & I) are having Confirmation practice tomorrow night. The Legion of Mary ladies come on Friday to clean the house and change bed linens. Weather has been too cold to suit me. I wonder what it is like there?

I am leaving everything in your bedroom and study as is (exactly the way you left it.) I don't need much space for my clothes. I go to the lake once a week to get my mail and pick up any clothes I think I need.

Cold weather is slowing down John Tindle's work in gardens.

My last year and a half of retirement prepared me for doing my own laundry and meals - so that is no problem at all. The rectory is most comfortable - I am enjoying the daily Mass - not having had any congregation for so long. Everyone on staff stays busy looking after things as you would want.

So much for the present - Keep in touch and do take care of yourself and full advantage of the program. I, and all of us are proud of you.

Sincerely,

Leonard

April 13, 1989

Dear Steve,

Thank you so very much for your very warm letter.

When I arrived here it was with a feeling of absolute failure, a feeling of having let everyone down, and having been the cause of pain and suffering for many, including my dog.

A lot has changed since then. It was a grand occasion to feel sorry for myself. I soon over came that. My counselor told me to be careful about that "poor me stuff" because it could soon turn into: "Poor me, poor me, pour me a drink." The letters, cards, phone calls from so many people are a great help. The prayers & love even more. The people of Nativity helped me to hang in there.

Deep in my heart, my head, myself I knew there had to be another answer. The counselors and the other guests at Guest House have helped me know the answer. True, I drank too much, and too often, but the reason for this was not my moral weakness - my evil nature - the reason was the nature of the disease of alcoholism.

I did not know this then. By the time I was drinking too much I just assumed it was my moral weakness, and was just too ashamed to ask for help. I did not think I ever got drunk so I never thought of it as a sin, so it never came up in confession. The nature of the disease is that one becomes more and more secretive, and more of a loner. I was both of those and I was becoming very paranoid.

I have been told up here, and I believe it, (at least I want to believe it) that some people are born with a genetic X factor. That means if that person drinks enough they will become an alcoholic. The amount varies. Ethnic heritage plays a part. There is a lot of alcoholism in my family. I am told that I have a very high risk because of that and the fact that I am 3/4 Irish. There is no cure. The only way to arrest it is not to drink. The most effective way known to man not to drink is the 12 Steps of A.A.

Here at Guest House we have an opportunity to learn how to undo the dishonest defense mechanisms we developed while drinking. We are urged to look at ourselves, warts and all, and learn to accept ourselves. Each person has something unique to learn. AA is a Spiritual program and at Guest House we make the most of that.

One of things that I have such a difficult time understanding is the contradictions that come into my life. I consider myself an honest person - yet I have to acknowledge that when it came to drinking I was not. When I was drinking if someone came in I might "innocently" conceal my drink. I would never think of trying to conceal a cup of coffee, or a coke. So even though I did not drink as much as some people, I did not drink normally. What a contradiction. I was aware of it - but denied it even to myself. Boy am I glad that is over.

Steve it is so wonderful to have friends, and I'm glad you are one of them. I will be writing to the parish and repeat some of the things I have told you, but you heard it first. I did hear from Jim Harpster. He said it was just a sneaky way to get a vacation and get out of losing at poker. *(Jim was an old and dear friend from another parish. He was part of our little poker club.)*

Peace & love,

Father Bill

A tapestry based on the Book of Tobias hanging in the chapel at Guest House.

67

This is 'The Villa' with a view of a small lake, also known as the 'Sharecropper's Shack' across from the mosquito pond.

The administration Building at Guest House. My daily walk took me from the residence to this building and back. The walk was a little over a mile.

CHAPTER FIVE
WEEK FIVE

APRIL 19, 1989
Wednesday

I am up early today, early enough to get the bathroom first. My morning walk is very good. The weather is finally warming up. Thank goodness I don't have any gas, but I can tell it is lurking there.

9:00 a.m. – Ed Higgins has class on "Soil of Addiction." I see myself there frequently.

My bout with gas last night urges me to nap from 10:00am to 11:00am.

11:00 a.m. – Group is good. I am beginning to be able to share more of the things that worry me, and I'm beginning to feel at peace with the world.

I am still tired from last night. I get in another nap after lunch. My stomach is finally at peace so I get another walk in after the nap. After that I have time for a couple of letters, one to the Parish and one to Barbara.

Mass is at 4:30 p.m., and Will C. is celebrant for the first time that he is here. He has been here longer than I have, and I wonder why I got to be the celebrant before he did. At first I wonder what his problem is, and then I wonder what my problem is. There could be any number of reasons, and besides it is none of my business. Why do I hold on to things like this?

The AA driver is a no show, so I do not go to a meeting. I am disappointed and this tells me that I was really looking forward to meetings. I'm happy about that feeling. I use the time to write letters. Then I feel the gas coming back. I hope it'll not be as bad as last night. I am on daily Prune Juice now. I don't know if that will make any difference - I'm not constipated.

For some reason I think a walk through the building will help. The halls are deserted and it is very quiet. It is a comfortable kind of quiet. I'm surprised to hear music coming from the Music Room. It is very relaxing, but I have never heard anyone playing the piano in the Music Room before.

I am beginning to acknowledge that stress is real, and there are ways of dealing with it. I must discover what that method is. Maybe my gas is due to stress. My usual way of dealing with stress has been to deny it. That never worked, but it takes me a while to learn. We had a class on Christian Yoga, maybe I should look more seriously at it.

I called the parish earlier today, and found they are disturbed by incomplete information on my hospitalization. I promise to write explaining everything. My computer is on the way, perhaps tomorrow, or tomorrow, or tomorrow.

11:00 p.m. — To bed with the Rosary.

APRIL 20, 1989
Thursday

A good morning walk. I pray the Office, and see another rabbit. No deer, but I do see several squirrels.

9:00 a.m. – Jackie gives the talk. She mentions doing away with the habits accompanying drinking. She used to drink Jack Daniels from Waterford Crystal, now she never uses the Waterford Crystal. She will not use an alcohol substitute, i.e. non-alcoholic wine, or non-alcoholic beer. This starts me thinking. I have belt buckles, cuff links, patches, poker chips, poker cards, and a whole lot of other stuff, all with the Jack Daniels logo on them. I think I'll get rid of all that stuff. I also think I will follow her example about non-alcoholic wines, or beers, except, of course for the non-alcoholic Mass wine.

11:00 a.m. – The Group Session with Len wanders all over the place, and I don't get much out of it. Others say it was great. This reminds me of what Len tells me about AA Meetings: "Going is more important than Content." This AA program has a lot of sayings. I guess they are okay for some people, but I don't think they will have much value for me, and I kinda' resent them.

I wrote to Ken DeWitt yesterday about my 25th celebration. The Committee wants to do away with all alcohol at the party. I don't think that's a good idea, it sends the wrong message: "Father has to be watched." Or "When Father doesn't drink nobody drinks." I suggest we ALSO have non-alcoholic champagne and wine. I know this sounds like a contradiction, but just mark it down to the fact that right now I don't know my own mind.

Gordon is helping me make a chalice. I forgot to tell you about Gordon. He knows a lot about ceramics. Gordon comes to Guest House to hold classes for anyone interested in ceramics. The classes are held in what looks like a boiler room. There is at least one oven for firing the things we make. I'll have to take a better look, because I think there are two ovens. I'll look next time I'm down there. I don't think I will ever be real good at ceramics, but it is interesting and creative. I will always be able to use the chalice. It will help me to remember where I have been and where I am going. I still have to fire it, and paint it, and fire it again. It will be blue and white when I finish it. I associate these colors with Mary. *(I still have that chalice and I use it from time to time.)*

I have been worried about going out to help in neighboring parishes since my stay in the hospital so I asked Dr. Lyons about it. He told me that it's up to me. He assured me that he thinks I know what the score is. I thought it over for a while and decided that I would not go this weekend. Dr. Lyons is okay with it, but I'm a little nervous. I do sign up for a trip to Greek Town. This should be a fun trip. Len is absent, so I miss my appointment. I get no explanation. I feel devalued.

APRIL 21, 1989
Friday

9:00 a.m. –Len is back. We have a good video. I identify with denial and hyperventilation. The hyperventilation part puts me more at ease with my weekend "heart attack," and trip to St. Joseph Hospital. I reschedule my one on one with Len for 3:00 p.m.

11:00 a.m. – In Group the talk is about the importance of Affirmation. My contribution is: "If you have to ask for affirmation, it comes across as patronizing." For some reason nobody else sees this. I guess it all depends on how I ask for affirmation. A lot of things happen here that I just don't understand, and someone keeps saying, "There is more to be revealed." Another one of those "sayings" that I don't like.

For some reason the Greek Town trip is canceled. There is no explanation and this annoys me.

My computer is here so I use it to fill out Alcoholic Questionnaire on the computer.

NAME: William F. Stelling

ALCOHOLISM QUESTIONNAIRE
POWERLESSNESS

1.   HOW HAS ALCOHOL AND/OR OTHER DRUGS PLACED YOUR LIFE OR LIVES OF OTHERS IN JEOPARDY?
   1. Drinking and driving
   2.
   3.
   4.
   5.

2.   HOW HAVE YOU LOST SELF-RESPECT DUE TO YOUR USE OF ALCOHOL AND/OR OTHER DRUGS?
   1. My inability to quit.
   2. My insensitivity to my staff.
   3. The scandal I gave to youth.

3.   WHAT IS IT ABOUT YOUR BEHAVIOR THAT YOUR SUPERIOR, CON-
FEREES, FAMILY OR FRIENDS OBJECT TO MOST?
   1. My mood swings
   2. It is killing me.
   3. Forgetfulness.
   4. Inappropriate behavior, i.e. visiting hospitals while drinking.

4.   HAVE YOU TRIED TO CONTROL YOUR USE OF ALCOHOL AND/OR
OTHER DRUGS?
   1. Gave it up for Lent 1988. (About half way successful)
   2. Could not give it up for Lent 1989.
   3. Wishful thinking.

5.   GIVE FIVE (5) EXAMPLES OF HOW POWERLESSNESS (LOSS OF CON-
TROL) HAS REVEALED ITSELF IN YOUR OWN PERSONAL EXPERIENCE.
   1. Forgetting appointments, promises, etc.
   2. Lying about FORGETTING, a powerlessness to maintain my values.
   3. Could not be my easy going self in administrative matters with my staff.
   4.
   5.

6.   WHAT TYPE OF PHYSICAL ABUSE HAS HAPPENED TO YOU OR OTH-
ERS AS A RESULT OF YOUR ALCOHOL AND/OR DRUG USE?
   1. Decline of health.
   2. Sore fingers or toes from punching or kicking things when angry and drinking.
   3.

7. WHAT IS YOUR CURRENT PHYSICAL CONDITION?
   Good, but could be better.

8. WHAT IS THE DIFFERENCE BETWEEN "ADMITTANCE" AND "ACCEP-
TANCE"?
   For me when I ADMIT something it is for others.
   When I ACCEPT something it is for me.

   8a. ARE YOU "ADMITTING" OR "ACCEPTING"?
      I am ACCEPTING and ADMITTING.

8b. DEFINE HOW YOU ARE "ADMITTING" OR "ACCEPTING" THROUGH
YOUR BEHAVIOR.
   In my letter to the people of the parish, by coming here, by thanking the people
who intervened me, by not drinking, and by going to AA meetings I am ADMIT-
TING my alcoholic problem.

By being open to the treatment here, by listening to, and struggling with the feedback of peers, by trying to look honestly into my self, by prayer, by not drinking, and by going to AA meetings I am ACCEPTING my alcoholic problem.

9. WHAT CONVINCES YOU THAT YOU NO LONGER CAN USE ALCOHOL OR DRUGS SAFELY?

My own experiences, AA meetings, the presentations of the Staff, reading, the bull sessions and experiences of my peers in this program, and the deep gut feelings I have discussed with my God.

10. ARE YOU AN ALCOHOLIC?

Yes.

UNMANAGEABILITY

1. WHAT DOES "UNMANAGEABILITY" MEAN TO YOU?

To me "Unmanageability" means there are things in my life that I should be able to manage but cannot manage them.

2. WHAT COULD YOU IDENTIFY AS "SOCIAL UNMANAGEABILITY"?

A. I enjoy social interchange with others and yet I prefer to drink alone. I drink a lot and that cuts into my time with others.

B. I often feel that others are talking about me and I distrust them.

C. I am often jealous and envious of others and this makes me angry at them.

3. GIVE THREE (3) EXAMPLES OF SOBER PERSONALITY UNMANAGEABILITY.

A. After having had a drink, but when I am still sober others testify to dramatic mood swings in me.

B. I often get totally involved in TV, Movies, Books, Games, etc. and give rather heated advice, encouragement, corrections, etc., to the characters. This is especially true at basketball games. This causes me to get very excited. Sometimes I lose sleep over it.

C.

4. WHAT GOALS HAVE YOU SET IN YOUR LIFE?

A. To finish High School, I did, but in the United States Air Force.

B. To finish Medical Technology School, I did.

C. To become a priest, I did.

D. To become a pastor, I did.

E. To have all the people at my first pastorate to like me, I failed.

F. To get a new parish started and the first and second phase of construction finished, I did.

G. To get all the people of my second pastorate to like me, I failed.

73

H. To stop drinking, I failed.

I. To finish the book on which I have been working for many years, I failed.

J. To read a certain number of pages per week in the books that I have been given to read here, I have succeeded and failed.

K. To start again on the book I have been working, I succeeded.

L. To FULLY cooperate with this program. Damn, it is hard, but I am hanging in there. The most difficult part is being honest with myself and as a result being honest with others.

5. PRIOR TO TREATMENT, HOW DID YOU TRY TO ACHIEVE THESE GOALS?

Where I achieved I think it was due to my ability to work with and trust others, and to call the best out of them. I had good organizational skills and a willingness to study.

Where I failed I think it was due to my preoccupation with what I see as my addiction, my declining self image and my inability to get along with, or trust others.

6. GIVE THREE (3) EXAMPLES OF FEELINGS YOU HAVE TRIED TO ALTER WITH THE USE OF ALCOHOL AND/OR DRUGS.
1. A Feeling of Inadequacy.
2. A Feeling of loneliness.
3. A Feeling of Fear.

7. HOW HAVE YOU TRIED TO CHANGE YOUR IMAGE PRIOR TO TREATMENT?

There was a time when I listened to people without fear, went to annual retreats, and went on vacations that were fun.

In the last 10 years I have listened less to people, done more complaining, went less and less to retreats, took fewer vacations or days off. I have made a lot of vague promises and done a lot of pretending.

8. WHAT CRISES, OTHER THAN THE ONE THAT GOT YOU INTO TREATMENT, WOULD HAVE EVENTUALLY GOTTEN YOU INTO TREATMENT?

Prior to coming here I had thought more than once or twice that I might have some pre-planned accident that would end all my problems. These were just vague musings. Had I continued drinking I am certain that my ministry would have been a disaster and I would have died in some way related to alcohol.

9 HOW DO YOU DIFFER FROM OTHER PEOPLE?
1. I don't drink as other people do.

2. I think I have a rather poor self image.

3. I think I am overly sensitive to others, that is I let them walk all over me.

4. The way I look at my sexuality.

5. I am different from others in the sum of what makes me, me and most of this is not only good, but very good, some of it is not so good. In the last 15 years I have been looking only on the bad things and this causes me to be a person that I am not, and don't really want to be.

10. GIVE TEN (10) REASONS WHY YOU SHOULD CONTINUE ON WITH THE PROGRAM?

1. I want to live.

2. I have a lot to give.

3. I have talents I want to develop.

4. I have people who depend on me.

5. There is much beauty that I have missed.

6. I believe in the Good News and that the News is Good.

7. I have a Church to build.

8. I have a book to write.

9. Many people love me and I have a true love for others that I want to express.

10. My dog loves me.

Last night I used my computer to do my first creative writing - "The Scarf." I finished the 3rd draft. Very shortly after I arrived here I knew that I had not brought enough winter clothes. Ron, the young man in charge of House Keeping, gave, or loaned, me his scarf. I was really touched. He told me to give it back to him when I left because it was from the University of Michigan. "The Scarf" describes my feelings about the favor Ron did for me.

The scarf that Ron loaned me in cold spring weather is just one example of the unconditional love shown by all the members of the staff of Guest House.

75

Now I can begin to put my Guest House Journal on computer. I slip up, and I'm late for 3:00 p.m. appointment with Len. Len is good counselor, but he is not a "Father Figure," nor is he "My Confessor." I see him as one I can share my problems with, as one who can guide me, not guard me, he can help me be the real me, the guy I want to be. He points to a book, and says that I ought to read it. Good God!! I have so many books now, I am afraid I will let the sheer number seduce me into procrastination.

"Masada" is the video for tonight. I watch parts of it. It is not as good as the first time I saw it. It is about the Jews defending themselves against the Romans. Besides I've got books to read and letters to write.

APRIL 22, 1989
Saturday

An easy day. I do too little reading. Edit my sex history, and do the fourth draft of "The Scarf." I write a letter to Bob, my brother. I'm afraid I laid it on a bit thick, but I am unfamiliar with talking to others about my feelings, so I guess I'll just have to put up with over doing it, or under doing it for a while. It's like target shooting, you gotta' practice. I'm going to miss the target a lot, but if I hang in there I'll get better at it. I'm discovering that I'm still pretty much of a loner. This is surprising to me. I always thought of myself as an extrovert.

Mass was good, the Deacon preached: The Monk looking for an Ox. *(I wish I had written more about that Monk and the Ox, because now I have no idea what it was all about. I just remember that at the time I liked it.)*

APRIL 23, 1989
Sunday

Another easy day. Breakfast is late on Sunday. I take my walk and pray the Office before breakfast. My walk becomes a little longer as the weather warms up. I begin to realize that I have been here one month. One third of my time here is gone. So much to learn, so little time to learn it. I remember when I got here I was so anxious to get started. But now I feel that I will not have enough time to really get into "recovery" before I leave here.

I see Jim McD. at breakfast, he is going to the parish at which I had my "heart attack". He asks me if I have a message for the people. I say, "Tell them I'm coming back."

The weather is finally getting to be more the way I like it. I can spend more time outside. But I have work to do inside so I take the afternoon to complete my Sex History.

The AA meeting is In House at 6:00 p.m. There is mention of The Surrender Prayer on page 64 of the Big Book. I remember nothing of it. I am struck with the need to read, and reread, and reread the Big Book. Ted is the Table Leader. He is in relapse. He says, "I only complied, I never surrendered." I'm not at all sure what that means. Instead of asking I wait for an explanation that never comes. I am fearful for myself. I have no idea why I am so hesitant about asking questions.

After the AA Meeting we have a cookout. The cookout is in the side yard which is just off an immense porch. I call it a porch, but it is rather large and made of flag stone. I guess that's what they are called. I'm a country boy - I don't know these things. The cook out breaks the routine. I like it. Don C. and I are clean up detail. I even like that.

APRIL 24, 1989
Monday

The breakfasts here are great. I really enjoy them. It always seems so much more relaxed. There are no assigned seats, as at the other meals. But then assigned seats would be difficult since people are coming in at different times. I really enjoy my walk this morning. The weather is great and the Office of Readings is meaningful.

9:00 a.m. – 10:30 a.m. – Ken Adams is the sex man. He says that according to the Big Book it is not unusual for alcoholics to have some kind of problems with sex. When I review my sex history, especially my experiences while in the Air Force in Japan I realize that my conduct left a lot to be desired when it comes to respect for women. I begin to wonder how, or if this effects the way I look at celibacy.

11:00 a.m. – In group we talk about family histories. Dad may have had some problem with alcohol. I don't know. I don't recall seeing him drunk, more than once or twice. Maybe I just didn't know what to look for. A little high, yes, but not drunk. I do know that there is certainly a history of alcoholism in my family. I have no doubt that he had the difficulty of raising us (five brothers and four sisters) without a wife/mother. He did it the best he could. Many of my close relatives had drinking problems. The question for me is: What to do about it??

I am celebrant at 4:30 Mass. I forget, and am a little late. Will is impatient to get started. Just as I am ready to start, two more guys come in. I wait until they get settled. Will is signaling, "Get Started." I respond by saying out loud, "Hey, I'm presiding, not you." Will leaves. A month ago this would have upset me a great deal more than it did. *(I have absolutely no recall as to what the problem was between Will and me. It must have been a simple personality difference.)*

I walk with John K. and take some pictures after supper. His knee replacement is working out very well. John introduces me to some of the writings of Anthony DeMello, S.J. I look forward to getting to the Book Store at Manresa.

The AA Meeting is at Rochester at 8:00 p.m. Lloyd talks a lot. We are on Step 3, I acknowledge my drinking pattern was, "just drifting along and so was my relationship with God."

APRIL 25, 1989
Tuesday

My day begins, as usual with breakfast, then my walk while I pray the Office. It looked like rain before I started my walk, but it held off 'til I got through, thanks Lord.

9:00 a.m. – Earl talks on the Stigma of Alcoholism. I can relate to this 'Stigma' thing. I remember at the first few AA meetings all I could say was, "I have a problem with alcohol." I just couldn't bring myself to say, "I'm an alcoholic." I'm still not totally convinced.

10:00 a.m. – I take a brief and quick nap. I am very, very sleepy.

11:00 a.m. – In Group I discuss my relationship with Dad. I have always felt that Dad's discipline was directed more at me since I was the only boy left at home. The others were in the service. Bob was too young. Dad worked on the morning paper. He would go to work around 5:00 p.m., and come home about 1:00 a.m., or 2:00 a.m. If ever there was anything out of order in the kitchen he would get me out of bed to clean it up. Most of the time I was awake in bed when he came home, just waiting to make sure the kitchen was okay. My stomach would tighten up, and stay that way until he went to bed. Even the good adult relationship I had with him could never do away with my memory of my fear of him. I come away from Group feeling better about my feelings. I also am becoming more aware that all people make mistakes, including parents and their kids.

1:00 p.m. – Jack Gregory's group is about getting around the law. I begin to hope that Jack may help me understand, and cope with myself. I ask him for an appointment.

I find a letter from Larry, my Deacon in my mailbox. It's good to hear from him. In the afternoon I get calls from Father O., and Billy, our janitor. There is trouble brewing there, but there is nothing I can, or should do about it. *(When I returned to the parish I find that Billy would usually drink a beer at lunch time. He had a breathing problem and I have never seen, or known him to get drunk. At any rate Father Oglesby could not put up with it, and fired him.)*

The 4:30 p.m. Mass is Ted's last here. His stay here sparked a lot of conversation about relapse. This strikes a bit of fear in my heart. My thinking has been: I come here; I learn from Guest House; I work at putting into practice what I have learned; and I stay sober. Relapse scares me.

(I think it is about this time that we were given A Checklist Of Symptoms Leading to Relapse. I include it now.)

A CHECKLIST OF SYMPTOMS
LEADING TO RELAPSE

While the individual himself must maintain the disciplines that insure sobriety, there are ways in which others can help. Nearly every person close to the alcoholic is able to recognize behavior changes that indicate return to the old ways of thinking. Often these individuals and fellow AA members have tried to warn the subject, who by now may not be willing to be told. He may consider it nagging, or a violation of his privacy. There are many danger signs. Most alcoholics, if approached properly, would be willing to go over an inventory of symptoms periodically with a spouse, or other confidant. If the symptoms are caught early enough and recognized, the alcoholic will usually try to change his thinking, to get "back on the beam" again. A weekly inventory of symptoms might prevent some relapses. This added discipline is one which many alcoholics seem willing to try. The following is a list of common symptoms leading to "dry drunk," to possible relapse - - or to what AA commonly calls "stinking thinking."

Exhaustion:
Allowing yourself to become overly tired, or in poor health. Some alcoholics are also prone to work addiction - perhaps to make up for lost time. Good health and enough rest are important. Feel bad enough and you might begin thinking a drink couldn't make it any worse.

Dishonesty:
This begins with a pattern of unnecessary little lies and deceits with fellow workers, friends, and family. Then, come important lies to yourself. This is called rationalizing - making excuses for not doing what you know you should do, or for doing what you know you should not do.

Impatience:
Things are not happening fast enough. Or, others are not doing what they should or what you want them to.

Argumentativeness:
Arguing small and ridiculous points of view indicate a need to always be right. "Why don't you be reasonable and agree with me?" Looking for an excuse to drink?

Depression:
Unreasonable and unaccountable despair may occur in cycles and should be dealt with - talked about.

Frustration:
At people and also because things may not be going your way. Remember - everything is not going to be just the way you want it.

79

Self-pity:

"Why do these things happen to me?" "Why must I be an alcoholic?" "Why doesn't anyone appreciate all I am doing - (for them)?"

Cockiness:

Got it made - no longer fear alcoholism - going into drinking situations to prove to others you have no problem. Do this often enough and it will wear down your defenses.

Complacency:

"Drinking was the furthest thing from my mind." Not drinking was no longer a conscious thought either. It is dangerous to let up on disciplines because everything is going well. Always to have a little fear is a good thing. More relapses occur when things are going well than otherwise.

Expecting Too Much From Others:

"I've changed, why hasn't everyone else?" It's a plus if they do — but it is still your problem if they do not. They may not trust you yet, may still be looking for further proof. You cannot expect others to change their life because you have.

Giving Up On Disciplines:

Prayer, meditation, daily inventory, AA attendance are important, even necessary. Giving up on disciplines can grow out of either complacency or boredom. You cannot afford to be bored with your program. The cost of relapse is always too great.

Use of Mood Altering Chemicals:

You may feel the need to ease things with a pill, and your doctor may go along with you. You may never have a problem with chemicals other than alcohol, but you can easily lose sobriety starting this way. This is about the most subtle way to have a relapse. Remember, you will be cheating. The reverse of this is true for drug dependent persons who start to drink.

Wanting Too Much:

Do not set goals you cannot reach with normal effort. Do not expect too much. It's always a treat when good things you were not expecting happen. You will get what you are entitled to as long as you do your best, but maybe not as soon as you think you should. "Happiness is not having what you want, but wanting what you have."

Forgetting Gratitude:

You may be looking negatively on your life, concentrating on problems that still are not totally corrected. It is good, even necessary, to remember where you started from, - - and how much better life is now.

It Can't Happen To Me:

This is dangerous thinking. Almost anything can happen to you and is more likely to if you get careless. Remember you have a progressive disease, and you will be in worse shape if you relapse.

Omnipotence:

This is a feeling that results from a combination of many of the above. You now have all the answers for yourself and others. No one can tell you anything. You ignore suggestions or advice from others. Relapse is probably imminent unless drastic change takes place.

THE IMPORTANCE OF AA IN AVOIDING RELAPSE

Between 80 - 90% of repeaters or relapsers reported at least one of the following:

No attendance at AA meetings, no sponsorship, relatively few meetings. They also stopped reading AA/NA literature such as the Big Book, Twelve and Twelve, NA text, One Day At A Time, etc. One of the other major reasons for relapse was people associating with those that were still using.

After supper I take a walk and take pictures. It is staying light longer and even getting warmer. I encounter what I think of as my pet squirrel. He lets me get very close for a picture.

I also had a letter from Harry Sullivan. In the evening I have difficulty with the computer. The best thing for me to do is leave it alone, so I do. I go to the basement to play pool and relax. That was wrong!! I don't seem to be able to make many of my shots. I feel anger rising and recognize it as an inappropriate response. I'm glad that I recognize it. I don't deal with anger as well as I like, but at least I'm beginning to recognize it. In Group last week someone told me that I had a problem with anger and my quick response was denial and anger.

I have got to talk to Len, my counselor, and some of the guys about the idea that alcoholism is a progressive disease. Now this is where it gets scary. It seems

One of the friendly squirrels I encountered on my walks.

that even though I quit drinking now, if I started again in 4, 6, 8 years from now I would encounter the disease, not where I stopped drinking, but where it would have developed in those years. It's not fair, but as the saying goes, "Life is guaranteed to be real, not fair!"

THE LETTERS

April 19, 1989

Dear Friends at Nativity,

Many of you have heard that I was taken to the hospital. Here is how that came about.

I was helping out at a parish, some distance from here for the weekend. It was a real treat to be able to get out of Guest House for a while. Now don't get me wrong this is a wonderful place. No prison, no bars on the windows, or otherwise. But it is good to get out now and then. At any rate the schedule called for me to celebrate reconciliation at 11:00 a.m. on Saturday morning. Then the 5:00 p.m. Mass on Saturday, and the 8:00 a.m. Mass on Sunday. The Church seated a little over 800 people, and was almost full for the two Masses. I was a little overwhelmed at the size, and discovered that I was actually nervous. At one point during Mass my hand was actually shaking. After the 5:00 p.m. Mass the pastor took me out to dinner. Something I ate gave me a headache. I took it and a cup of hot chocolate to bed. In the morning most of the headache was gone, but I found I was still nervous at Mass. Crowds, or the size of them, have never bothered me before, and everyone said the sermon was very good. I thought so too. When I started to give communion I noticed some chest pain, and light headedness. I almost stopped two, or three times. After Communion, while sitting in the Presider's Chair I thought, "This is just not right, far from home, in a strange parish, and this happens." I did not want to think of what I thought it could be. I finished Mass, greeted the people. I thanked the Lay Ministers, and headed for the rectory. I could still feel the chest pain and was a bit light headed. The people who were to give me a ride back to Guest House stopped me. I told them I just did not feel well, and wanted to rest a bit. The pastor came by, and I told him what was happening. I told him I wanted to lay down. I was surprised that I had difficulty getting up. Needless to say I was quite shaken up at this time. I decided that I had better get it checked out, so I was taken to St. Joseph Hospital. The tests showed nothing wrong with the heart, but they decided to admit me anyway since I still felt some chest pain, especially when I took deep breaths. I stayed in the Hospital CCU without a phone 'til Tuesday morning. The doctor, who just happened to have been at the 8:00 a.m. Mass said that I had some neuromuscular spasms. The cause of which he could not determine.

When I returned to Guest House the medical staff had some better insight. It seems that there is a bit of stress involved in being part of the program here. My usual way of dealing with stress is just to deny that it exists. So what happened was that I had nervous muscular spasms brought on by a stress that I was unaware of, or

82

what some call an anxiety attack. Thank God, part of the program here is to learn how to cope with stress.

I am feeling fine now, and the weather is getting warm enough for comfortable walks. Would you believe we had snow flurries yesterday.

I missed being there for Confirmation and will miss the solemn celebration of First Communion. In the letters I get, people tell me that everything is in bloom. If anyone gets a picture, or two I would love to see them.

The food here is so much better than my cooking. It is not at all like institutional food. Funny thing is that they never serve wine with meals. Even the Altar wine is non-alcoholic.

I was out walking the other day and saw a rabbit under a bush. I see squirrels on a regular basis. I think I see the same one often. Some of the guys have even seen deer grazing, but I have not.

Even though I do miss all of you so very much I can tell you that I am enjoying life so much better without alcohol. Now don't worry, I know that not everyone who drinks is an alcoholic, nor do they become alcoholics. I also know that not everyone who becomes an alcoholic gets the opportunity I have. So I give thanks to God for this grace, and the graces that I receive through all of you. By the way did you know that non-drinking alcoholics often develop a "sweet tooth." I was just remembering some of the home made candy and cookies we used to have at those Nativity Bazaars.

God's Peace and my love,

Father Bill
Pastor

The Tabernacle
in the chapel at
Guest House.

83

Dear Father Bill,

(I have lost this next letter, but it had a very important effect on my recovery so I will try to relate what it was about. The letter was eight handwritten pages.)

The letter was from a man named Jim. He had heard my letter read at the Easter Sunday Mass. Jim was not a Catholic, but he came to Mass with his wife that day. He is a recovering alcoholic. The letter told me what I have come to know as "his story". I was totally knocked out by the letter. I don't think I could ever share with another human being the things he shared with me. He told me that one of the ways he manages to stay sober is to share "his story" with another alcoholic. He concluded by assuring me that he would like to meet me when I return to the parish and that he is willing to take me to meetings and help me in any way he can.

I shared this letter with Len, my counselor, and he told me that "Jim" might be a good person to have as a Sponsor when I get back to the parish. I will fill in more details about Jim and his letter later.

Dear Father Bill,

There is no reason for you to thank me. You are such a special friend who means the world to me. Friends reach out to each other because they care. I have to thank you for being a part of my life and my ministry. You do more for me than you will ever know.

Fr. Bill, I miss you but I know that when you return, there will be time for us to share our feelings. I want you to know that for me there is nothing for you to be embarrassed or ashamed about. As you stated in your letter to the parish and the Bishop also stated, problems with alcohol, is a disease which will respond to proper treatment, and is not a moral weakness. I know this and I feel that most of the parish knows and understands.

I read the enclosed letters from you and the Bishop this past weekend. This was very hard to do, but because I care so much for you, I could not let anyone else read it to the parish. Both letters will be published as an insert to the bulletin, as well as posted for all to read.

You are very much missed by all of the parish and we all look forward to your return.

If there is anything I can do for you please let me know.

Peace,
Larry.

P.S. I was really surprised, when after reading your letter, several members of the parish came to me and shared that they were recovering from a problem with alcohol. I asked that they write to you and share this with you. Also make a note that our address is 2876 not 3876. I'll get it corrected in the computer.

I got a card from the Bishop the other day. It had his motto on the front of the card: "I Seek Your Face, O Lord." On the inside he wrote:

Dear Bill,

It was good to learn the health scare turned out less serious than it seemed at first.

We prayed specially for you at Confirmation - You were missed - but clearly are loved and supported by the Nativity community. The ceremony was beautiful. Fr. Bruce and Leonard fixed a nice supper after.

All goes reasonably well here in W. TN. (West Tennessee) Please keep up your commitment to your program of recovery. We love you and need you.

Always with fond prayer
Bishop Daniel

Dear Bill,

I'm glad you are getting some help. I know the feeling. A few years ago I had a drug problem and had to get help. In the beginning I didn't think what the professionals were trying to help me to do was all that helpful. I was sure they had no idea what I going through.

It took a while before I could accept that I was responsible for what I was doing wrong.

I don't even like to take aspirin now. I still have friends who take drugs. Some use street drugs, some abuse prescription drugs. I don't like what they are doing to themselves but I tolerate them because they are my friends and I care about them.

I don't try to suggest to them that they need help because I know from experience that they will reject any suggestion that they need help until that time that they themselves decide for themselves that something is wrong.

Sometimes in being a friend you have to step back. You have to let them know that you care and that you are there. But until they decide that there is something wrong there is nothing you can do.

I knew you had a problem when you were here last time. You were overly sensitive about a lot of things.

They lied to us as we were growing up. They let us believe that things would get easier as we got older.

I'm still here and I still care.

So go on and get well and get back to work.

Love,
Bob

P.S. I haven't seen Magy in about eight months.

(I received this crazy letter from my friend Barbara. I guess that I had not written to her as I should have. I am following it with my answer.)

4/12/89

Dear Father,

Please mark the appropriate blank with an 'X' and return to sender. How are you? Great ___, fine____, so so ____, breathing ____. How is the weather? Cold____, raining____, sunny____, snowing____, all of the above____. Are you living in a palace ___, hotel ___, house ___, barn ___, a tent ____. Do you have? Room service ____, do it yourself ____, fast food ____, or a live in cook ____. Do you dress in? jeans ___, jogging suit ____, black tie, ____, white collar ____, swim trunks ____, or nothing ____. Do you bath in? A shower ___, Jacuzzi ____, tub ____, tin cup ____, or the lake ___. Do you get up? Early ____, late ____, noon ____, or never ____. Do you? work ____, study ____, play ____, chase the cook ____. When you go out do you go by? Car ____, horse ____, dog sled ____, or boat. Have you gone to? Town ____, the movies ____, the races ____, or the casino. Are you? Thinking on me ___, missing me ___, happy I am your friend ____, wish you had never met me ____. For fun do you? Read ____, watch T.V. ____, listen to music ____, or dance ____.

I am praying for you, thinking of you often, wishing you were here, wishing I was there, glad I met you, happy you are my friend, loving you very much, wishing you happiness, joy, and peace.

Sincerely, Barbara
P.S. Bart, Tamara, Jake and Helen send their love.

4/19/89

Dear Barbara,

How kind of you to think of me so often and so nicely. Be sure to read the letters that I have sent to the parish so I don't have to repeat myself.

Let's see now - How am I? Well I just got back from the hospital yesterday. I was taken there Sunday right after Mass with chest pains - but all of this is in the letter to the parish. Right now I am fine and enjoying life, except for a bit of gas.

I get up each morning between 6:30 and 7:00. Breakfast is any time between 7:00 and 8:30. They have just about anything you want. I had some grits special ordered from the parish. Not many people up here are familiar with grits.

At 9:00 a.m. we have a class that is an hour long on some aspect of alcoholism. From 10:00 to 11:00am is free, unless I have an appointment with my counselor. At 11:00 a.m. there is Group Therapy. This goes on til noon. At noon there is lunch. Afternoons are usually free. Except once a week there is a one hour session with the psychologist and a group of 6 to 10 people. On Wednesdays there is a trip to a mall. This is voluntary. On Friday a trip to K-Mart, which is close by. Individual meetings with my counselor could be scheduled from 1:00 p.m. to 2:00 p.m. Monday through Friday. Mass is at 4:30 p.m. daily, except Saturday. On Sunday Mass is at 10:30 a.m. Dinner is at 5:15 p.m. Free evenings are Tuesday - with a voluntary trip to a movie at a Mall with 12 screens. Fridays and Saturdays are free. All other evenings are open to trips to AA meetings. AA meetings take place all over the area and someone in the office makes up the schedule of who goes where, unless a person signs up for this or that meeting. We are picked up here at Guest House by volunteer drivers and taken to the meetings. Two, or three, or four guys are scheduled for each meeting. We go to at least 3 meetings per week. One of these is here in the House. The meetings are extremely interesting, but I always have to work myself up to going. Once I get there I always enjoy it.

On weekends we can volunteer to help out in a parish nearby. That is what I was doing when I was taken to the hospital.

From time to time side trips are planned. These take all of Saturday.

There is one hell of a lot of reading to do. I am reading five books right now. *(For most of my life I have preferred to read several books at the same time rather than finish one and start on another.)* There must be time for daily personal prayer and time for relaxing with others and by one's self. I am trying to keep a diary, or journal, of what I experience here. Right now all my writing is by hand, but soon my computer will be here.

Please share this letter with Helen. I have a few more letters to write and it is late.

Bye now - God's Peace, and my love,

Father Bill

A quiet moment of reflection in the courtyard at Guest House.

The Madonna and Child in the Chapel at Guest House.

Fr. Bruce
visited me
and enjoyed
the beautiful
mosaic of
Tobias.

CHAPTER SIX
WEEK SIX

APRIL 26, 1989
Wednesday

Breakfast is good. Most of the guys have no idea what they are missing when they refuse grits. After breakfast I take my regular walk, and pray the Office.

9:00 a.m. – Tom talks about Surrender. There is a difference between Surrender and Quitting, but right now I can't remember what it is. All I remember is that Surrender is better than quitting. I gave the Bishop control over my life, why not God? I discover six things I should be doing:

1. Don't Drink Today
2. Total Honesty
3. Openness to Guest House.
4. Openness to AA
5. Surrender (get rid of) False Pride
6. Surrender to Victory.

Today is the Departure Mass for Marsalis, Marcel, and Ed C. This Departure is more personal, I have begun to know these guys. The Departure Mass is a formality. Often the guys leave at separate times, and on different days.

After the Departure Lunch we have a trip to the Shopping Mall. I no longer even think about "One Flew Over the Cuckoo's Nest." I look for a poster for Ed. B but cannot find it, so Jim McD, gives me one that he has found. It is close to what I was looking for.

Back at Guest House I write letters to Larry Howell, and Ann Cissell. I run into some computer trouble and had to rewrite half of a letter. Anger is still a problem. I'm learning to cope with it, and to just accept it as one of the problems I'm working on.

APRIL 27, 1989
Thursday

Breakfast, Walk & Office. I'm out of grits and I don't think I'll worry about getting any more.

9:00 a.m. – The talk today is by Sister Jean. Health Enhancement Program. This could be very helpful. It is hopeful.

Dr. Lyons tells me to stop worrying - I'm in good shape. He says that he is sorry he didn't tell me a few days ago when the report came. He said he would have told me right away if there was anything to worry about. Do I feel relieved? You bet I do.

11:00 a.m. – Group is good. I am quiet. I guess I should have brought this up in Group, but I didn't. I have feelings of nonacceptance by two people that I very much want to be accepted by. I am tempted to "do anything" for acceptance. I know that would not be good. What to do about these feeling? I did the only thing I could do since I didn't want to talk about them, or give in to them. I just held on as tight as I could. It was not comfortable. Next time I'll talk to my counselor. *(As it turns out it is now just two months later and I have no idea who those two people were or what the problem was. I did not revert to my "people pleasing" ways. But neither did I do anything positive. I did learn that time is on my side even when I finally get around to doing something positive.)*

AA is at Manresa, Jesuit Retreat Center. It is a very good meeting. The topic is on 12 Step Out Reach. Every meeting is different. I have no idea how I would ever be helpful to a person still drinking. I think I would try to do too much, or too little. We also talk about anonymity. I don't see how I can ever be Anonymous, and that is of no concern to me.

I met a man named Bob at the meeting. He is dying of cancer, and he gives me a "Serenity Medal." When I carry it I will remember that as he faced death he was glad to die sober.

The Book Store is not supposed to be open, but somebody does me a favor and I do manage to get a little book, "The Song of the Bird." by Anthony DeMello, S.J. John K. recommended it.

Meanwhile, back at the ranch, I work on the chalice that Gordon made for me. Gordon comes to Guest House once a week and teaches us - that is, anyone interested - about ceramics. I have worked with him making a chalice and paten. I like this type of stuff, I guess because it is creative. If I let it, it can also teach me something about patience. There are certain steps in the process and you can't rush any of them.

APRIL 28, 1989
Friday

My day begins with the usual: Breakfast, Walk & Office.

9:00 a.m. – Jackie, the nurse, talks about Shame and Guilt. With my record I have a lot to be ashamed of, and an equal amount to be guilty of. According to her I am not going to be able to accomplish much that is good by letting Shame and Guilt weigh me down. But it don't go away by saying, "Out, out, damn spot!!"

11:00 a.m. – In Group someone speaks of a different sexual orientation. That took courage and honesty.

John K., and I walk to Villa. He is moving to the Villa, we view his room. He is not ready to go home yet. He needs the Villa because it is equipped with a handicapped bathroom. I am enjoying "The Song of the Bird" that he suggested. Later I write to Helen H. I let her know that I have not forgotten about May first. It was on May first that I received her into the Church and helped her and Don to make a sacrament of their marriage.

I have time to write my sermon for the weekend. I'm going to the parish that was the site of my "heart attack." I look forward to going and I am not nervous at all. All I have to do is relax.

Harvey Carter calls - Margie is dying. It could be any minute. I am still working on bad feelings about not being able to be there. I am also dealing with feelings of rejection. I don't really know if I am being rejected by anyone. I just feel it. I've always had feelings that had no rational basis. The way I dealt with them was either denial, or Jack Daniels. Now I have to learn to cope with them and recognize that feelings are neither good nor bad. They are just feelings.

I like the sermon so far, and finish it after dinner. I put final touches on my sexual history and work on my chalice. As I look at that last sentence it sure seems an odd combination, but after I finished with the sex thing, I did go to work on my chalice.

APRIL 29, 1989
Saturday

The pick up for the weekend Mass is right on time - 9:30 a.m. There are two ladies who pick me up, and I forget their names. There I am sitting in the back of the car, and what do I see? Beer cans on the floorboard. I start to laugh and they explain that they belong to a teenage son. They don't tell me which one of them is the mother of that teenage son, nor why a teenager is drinking.

I have time to edit my sermon, and then take a nap. I hear Confessions and find them spiritually helpful for me. Fr. Jim is out for funeral. The Mass and sermon go well. I do have slight chest pains, but I'm not worried since I know the source. After supper I take a walk, pray the Office of Evening Prayer and the Rosary.

APRIL30, 1989
Sunday

The Mass and sermon go well. Again I have slight chest pains but I apply relaxing techniques (deep breathing). The doctor who treated me at the hospital was there. He liked my sermon, and asked for a copy of it. It was mostly about Family. The music during the Mass was great. I feel good that I was able to go back to the place of my "heart attack" and know what is going on.

When I return Helen H. calls. She is all excited about the approach of May first. She also still does not accept the reality that I am an alcoholic. That's okay because sometimes I wonder about that myself. I like the AA Meetings once I get there. There is one thing that is beginning to grate on me. I keep hearing people say, "My name is John, or George, or Mary, and I haven't found it necessary to take a drink today." You know why that bugs me? I'll tell you. It bugs me because I never found it necessary to take a drink. I always wanted to take a drink.

MAY 1, 1989
Monday

9:00 a.m. – Dr. Ken Adams talks about Family Systems. It gives me some hope of understanding myself. I have completed my Sexual History and turned it in. (No I'm not going to tell you what's in it.)

I finish my reply to George's letter. (See pages 94-97.) There is something about his letter that sort of upsets me: I cannot compare to hardly anything that he experienced. My drinking pattern was so very different. Again I'm not supposed to compare. I'm supposed to relate. But still I wonder.

I recall what I wrote yesterday about whether it was necessary for me to drink, or did I drink because I wanted to. Now I keep seeing more and more things where my drinking pattern suffers by comparison. So the question keeps coming back am I an alcoholic or not? Am I powerless over alcohol, or do I just have a problem with alcohol? Can my life be all that unmanageable, if I can start a parish from nothing but a list of names and an empty lot? Everybody thinks that I'm making such good progress, so why do I keep slipping back to these questions. I'll have to ask Len about this.

I find time for a nap, and then it is time for Mass. I make a special prayer for Helen and Don H.

There is an AA meeting tonight. I should feel up for it, but I feel down. So many things I am discovering about myself. I feel like I am coming apart. I wonder if anything will be left of me. Perhaps this is good. Paul speaks of the "OLD MAN OF SIN" being replaced by "NEW MAN IN CHRIST." I hope this is what's happening. I just feel very tired, and depressed. Maybe this is one of the things I should bring up in Group, or with Len, my Counselor. I'm hoping for good night's sleep.

MAY 2, 1989
Tuesday

I had a good night's sleep. The weather is getting warmer, I'm beginning to see signs of Spring on my walk, and I'm almost on top of the world. As I look back on yesterday I wonder if my ups and downs will ever cease.

9:00 a.m. – Dr. Russell Smith talks today from 9:00 a.m. 'til 11:00 a.m. about the chemistry of alcohol. There's that "X" Factor again. I still don't know if I believe it. I want to, but that's not enough. I think it has to do with my need to hold on to some kind of guilt. But Jackie says that guilt and shame can kill me.

1:00 p.m. – Small Group Meeting with Jack Gregory. I always enjoy Jack's group. I need to talk to him one on one, so I ask for a one on one with him. Surprise, surprise!! He says, "Come on." So I followed him to his office up on the third floor. It is just a little cubby hole, but it is a place a man can be comfortable in. I'm comfortable there and I tell him of my feelings of depression, and how I feel like I'm falling apart sometimes. We had about an hour. He told me one thing that really helped me: "You set yourself up." And I did. I defined the results. It was like telling God how to answer my prayer. You'd think I'd know that, after all I'm a priest. Ha! There's still a lot I don't know.

Jack also tells me that I want results, and I want them right now. He tells me about His Majesty, the Baby who wants what he wants and he wants it now. Then I hear another one of those "sayings": "Plan your work, and work your plan, but don't plan the results." You know something? That makes no sense whatsoever. Maybe, in time, it will. *(It makes sense to me today.)*

In the afternoon I write cards and letters. Bruce called. He doesn't have much news, but I was happy that he thought enough to call. Just talking to someone at Nativity, even just in residence at Nativity, is helpful. And right now I know that I need some help.

THE LETTERS

April 27, 1989

Dear Family at Nativity,

First I must tell you how much your cards and letters mean to me. Without them I would be the loneliest person in the world. I am sorry that I am unable answer each of them individually. If I tried I would never be able to do all the things they tell me I should be doing here. I am not the world's fastest reader, and there are a lot of books to be read. One of them is simply entitled, "**The Big Book of Alcoholics Anonymous.**" but it is generally referred to simply as: The Big Book. It is 575 pages long. I am more than half way through it, and I made a disturbing discovery the other day. In an AA meeting someone brought up the Prayer of Surrender on page 64. I had to admit to myself that I had absolutely no recall of it. I was rather embarrassed until someone pointed out that The Big Book is not something that is read once, but something that is read again and again and again and is consulted frequently. Something like a research book, or even the Bible. *(I have been in recovery for a dozen years now and I still read The Big Book.)*

Well, Spring is about to arrive up here. The temperature has been in the upper 60's for two days in a row, and it was in the 70's one day in a row. Our trusty Parish Secretary has kept me informed about the temperature in Bartlett. You may think it is hot. I think you are lucky. You may, or may not, know that I enjoy walking, except when it is too cold, or too hot. At this time of the year in Bartlett I would walk early in the morning, up here I often have to wait til it warms up a bit. I do manage to walk at least an hour each day. I always take the Divine Office, (my prayer book) or my Rosary with me, and in some walks I take a taped lecture, or my camera. If I remember I will send you some pictures with this letter.

This morning at the 9:00 a.m. lecture we heard about physical fitness from a young lady, who is also a Sister from the Adrian Dominicans. She is associated with the Meadow Brook Health Enhancement Institute. What she had to say was very interesting, and will be part of the program I am enjoying here. NOW DON'T EVERYONE START WORRYING. When I get back requirements for member-ship in Nativity will not include meetings on Bethlehem Plaza before Mass on Sunday for exercise, and taking "The Pledge" not to drink for a period of time, or forever.

One of the important things they teach us is that unless drinking, or not drink-ing, is a personal decision it ain't no good. As for me, and my decision, I don't want to ever drink alcohol again, but I know that I have to take that one day at a time.

I am on the road to recovery. That road will not end when I leave here, it will go on for the rest of my life. It will be a long road, but not a lonely one. I have God, AA, my Family, my Family at Nativity, my friends, and many other supports. In the end I realize that I, and I alone, am responsible for my sobriety. When I return please don't think that if you invite me to dinner you have to hide the liquor. Many people in the real world drink, many people don't, I am one of those who don't, but I have to live in the real world and that is a mix of people who do, and people who don't.

The time that separates us grows shorter, and I've always liked short better. After all I've been short all my life. *(I am five feet five and a half inches)* My heart longs to be with each and every one of you, and I know that I soon will be. Let us pray for each other.

God's Peace, and my love,

Father Bill

(The writer of this letter is relative of mine, but I have changed
his name to protect his anonymity. I referred to him earlier as George.)

April 26, 1989

Dear Father Bill,

After learning of your illness I felt compelled to write. I was sorry to hear that you were stricken with the disease that has affected so many millions of us. It is a devastating disease that affects the body, soul, and mind and knows no socioeco-nomic demographics.

I am a recovering alcoholic with slightly less that a year's continuous sobriety. I thought you might be interested in hearing what it was like for me as a practicing alcoholic, what happened, and what it is like now. If you are not interested it is at least therapeutic for me.

I'll not bore you with a teenage, or early adult drunk-a-logue it will be enough to say that alcohol has been part of my life since the age of 15, or 16. The early drinking seemed to be more of peer motivation rather than an allergic reaction, or obsession. However in looking back I now realize that even then I didn't drink like everyone else. I always drank more and longer than most. There were times when alcohol related problems began to crop up during early adulthood and college years. Wrecks, fights, drunken weekends, etc. It was while I was in the Marine Corps that I began to experience blackouts and loss of memory, however I did not consider it to be unusual. I considered it to be the norm. During my time in Vietnam I did not drink at all since it was hardly available. On those rare occasions when we were pulled back to the rear for R & R and unlimited quantities of hot beer became available I drank until I could hold no more —forced myself to throw up and drank more. I repeated this until I finally passed out.

It made me feel good inside, it gave me courage. It made me forget where I was and how scared and lonely I was. It made me feel that everything was going to be O.K. Except for the few experiments with marijuana I was able resist the temptation to use other drugs which were readily available. At the ripe old age of 21 John Barleycorn became my drug of choice. As it has turned out, Vietnam and alcohol would play a very important role in my daily life for the next twenty years.

I was discharged in 1970, married and with no career opportunities I went back to school while working at night. In 1972 my first of three girls was born; 1973 I finished my formal education with degrees in Chemistry, History, and Political Science. During this period of time with school, work, and a young family, and no money my alcohol consumption was limited to weekends, but again, when I drank I drank past acceptable levels of intoxication.

At this time I took a position with xxxx Scientific Company as a Sales and Technical Representative traveling a two state area. I was quite successful in this position, and began enjoying the financial rewards of this job. A good salary plus commissions. Traveling quite a bit and on an expense account my drinking escalated enormously. I drank almost every night but not to excess during the week.

In 1974 my second daughter was born. My career took a gigantic leap with a Company out of Boston. I began as a sales a rep, was promoted to Sales Manager, then District Manager, then Regional Manager in charge of the east coast. By 1977 I had hit a phenomenal income level for that period. I was successful basically because I worked hard and had the uncanny ability to hire the right people who were able to keep sales at a high level with or without my direction. About this time (1976-78) alcohol began to dominate my life. I began to miss work. I was traveling a lot, some internationally. I drank in airport lounges prior to departure. I drank during the flight, and I drank upon arrival at the next airport. I rented a car to drive to my hotel and on the way I stopped off at several bars. Upon arrival at the hotel I would go directly to the bar. When I closed the bar I would go to my room where I had a bottle in my suitcase and I drank until I passed out. I would purposely not schedule anything until the following afternoon. Sometime around noon the next day I would get up with a hangover and go down to the hotel restaurant for lunch. This lunch usually included several drinks. I would make my appointments and be through in time for Happy Hour. This pattern was to continue for sometime to come. To make a long story short, in 1979 I resigned to keep from being fired or demoted. My stock settlement with the company left me with quite a large sum of money at my disposal. I was unable to find a job for a one year period. I drank as a full blown alcoholic during this year. Always promising my family that I would cut down just as soon as I found employment.

When I found a job I did cut back some at first, then after a short period of time I was back to the same old pattern. My mediocre performance soon began to deteriorate and that job was gone. I had become friends with some very influential people in the hazardous waste industry, and managed to land a very good job with a company based in England. The company had patented a new process for treating inorganic industrial waste. I became director of Marketing for the U.S. and Canada. I knew that alcohol was a problem for me, but I didn't think it was something I couldn't handle by myself.

With all the enthusiasm of the early pioneers I launched into this new venture. I seemed to gain some semblance of control over my drinking for a period of time. During which time I was successful in getting this new venture on a sound footing. Heavy drinking soon returned with the same results: No job. Still another good job came and went in the same manner.

This has taken a heavy toll on a wife I love very much and who loves me very much. Not to mention what it has done to three beautiful children. By this time all savings are gone. Our creditors call daily threatening legal action; I am very close to losing my house.

I promise my wife, and the kids, that I'll never drink again, only to drink the next day. I begin to promise myself, and a God I don't believe in, that I'll quit. But I can't stop. I am mentally, spiritually, physically, and morally bankrupt. Suicide is a very real alternative. Two feeble attempts fail miserably. It is a living hell for me and those around me. There were D. W. I.'s, jails, hangovers, bumps, bruises, etc. I became mean when drinking, abusing my family terribly, verbally and to a lesser extent physically. I sought help from Doctors and ministers, only to have the doctor prescribe tranquilizers, and the ministers a dose of the Bible. I continued to drink. In 1985 I was diagnosed as having moderately advanced cirrhosis of the liver. I was told that to drink would mean to die in a short period of time. I continued to drink knowing with some relief that I would soon die. I learned of a treatment center that had a 28 day program for alcoholism. My insurance will only cover a very small part of the $15,000.00 fee so I borrow enough money to stay 9 days. Needless to say this did little more than dry me out. One thing did happen that may very well have saved my life or at least create a life worth living. I was taken to two A.A. Meetings.

Upon returning home I found a way to keep me in good stead with my family was going to AA Meetings. I attended several AA Meetings a week and did just enough to stay dry. I put up a good facade. I could talk the talk. I tried to act "joyous, happy and free" and for a few weeks I was. After that I was as miserable as ever. Things got better at home. I got a job and after a while we could see the light at the end of the financial tunnel. I wasn't doing anything in AA that I was told I needed to do to stay sober. The first of the twelve steps in AA says, "We admitted we were powerless over alcohol - that our lives were unmanageable."

There was this lingering doubt in my mind: Was I truly an alcoholic?? I didn't wear three overcoats, sleep in the street, and eat out of garbage cans. My life had become manageable. Therefore I might not be an alcoholic. The end result was I tried some controlled drinking and stayed drunk for over a year, consuming between a quart and a half gallon of hard liquor everyday.

I was one of the lucky ones - I made it back to AA. This time I was willing to go to any length!! I made about 150 meetings in the first 90 days. I listened to the winners and did it one day at a time. I tried to enjoy each day.

The hopelessness is gone. There is meaning in my life. It's not always easy but today I'm able to deal with life on life's terms, not mine. It was very hard for me to understand that the only way I could win was to surrender completely. Today my wife loves me, my children aren't afraid of me, and love me as much as I love them. Without alcoholism I doubt I would ever have reached this level of happiness in my life. Emily is involved in ACOA and ALANON and the kids are in ALATEEN which has added meaning to their lives.

Father Joe Martin says that alcoholism is described as a Catholic disease. He says he can't figure out why he has to go to the basement of Protestant Churches to recover.

I truly wish you the best in your recovery and hope that you might find time to drop me a line or two.

I still struggle with the "God" side of my program of recovery. This being your forte I welcome any help. It took me years to tear it down so I don't expect too much too soon. But I wouldn't mind being "zapped" and having it done with.

With love and Hope,
George

This is the letter that gave me so much trouble. I kept trying to compare my drinking to his and when this did not occur I began to wonder: Am I an alcoholic? Of course I should have, and could have easily found traits that I could relate to.)

My friend Father John K. making a flower vase for me. It has been deliberately distorted.

Another of the friendly squirrels. This one I called 'Pete.' He lived in a manhole.

CHAPTER SEVEN
WEEK SEVEN

9:00 a.m. – Erik has his guys in Aftercare in for "Bridge." It is good. There was a guy there named Bill. I wanted to talk with him, but I let the chance slip away.

11:00 a.m. – I had a one on one with Len, my Counselor. I filled out more forms. He tells me that the Staff seems to think I am doing well and I agree with them - sometimes. One day I find myself fully confident, and the next day I'm wondering what's going on. I am in a hurry to get things done, but this is a slow process.

Len gave me a progress report today so I will share it with you;

TREATMENT PLAN REVIEW - APRIL 27, 1989
FATHER WILLIAM F. STELLING, S.J.

(The S.J. stands for Jesuit, but I'm not a Jesuit, but now and then mistakes are made.)

PHYSICAL - CLASS I -17

Problem:
1. Alcoholism
2. History of hypertension

Plan:
1. Guest House treatment.
2. 120/70 on Corgard, 40 mgm daily.
   To Discontinue Corgard.

PSYCHOLOGICAL - CLASS II -14

Progress:
Realizes need to live a drink and
   pill free life.
Problem:
Concerns about negative aspects
   of his early years.

Goal:
Use RET ideas to improve current
Attitude towards past.
Plan:
Group and individual therapy.

SOCIAL - CLASS II - 14

Progress:
Has begun taking the risk of self-
disclosure. Interacts more candidly

Goal:
Become socialized in area AA beyond
Guest House.

Problem:
Wants big improvements in self
too soon. Needs to trust more in
the process of slow change.

Plan:
Group counseling. Regular AA
attendance.

VOCATIONAL - CLASS II - 15

Progress:
Values priesthood. Has begun
pastoral work in area parishes
on weekends.

Goal:
Renewed ministry.

Problem:
Is dissatisfied with the quality of
his spiritual life. Recognizes
the need for more abandonment
to the will of God.

Plan:
Individual and group therapy.
House Confessor.

ALCOHOLISM - CLASS II - 15

Progress:
Has achieved a working understanding of the disease concept
of alcoholism. Verbalizes intention of remaining sober in AA

Goal:
Prepare for Fourth Step inventory

Problem:
Has difficulty letting go of old
ideas. Likes to be in control.

Plan:
Group counseling.

Shopping at Mall. I never thought I would really enjoy just walking through a Mall, but I do.

The AA driver is a no show. I read about 4th Step and have a BLOCK. The 4th Step is: "Made a searching and fearless moral inventory of ourselves." "Bill", the guy I heard in Bridge, just happens to walk by. I do not take opportunity to talk. I need to talk to someone about this 4th Step, and I think "Bill" would be the right person. I liked what he had to say in Bridge. I guess Len would tell me that I'm afraid to take a risk. He'd be right. I continue to read - frustrated by my BLOCK. I wonder if there is something I am afraid to look at in me. I decide to go to talk to Don K., and who do I run into? Bill, of course. We talk, I have a better understand-ing of FAILURE, it can also mean failure to have accomplished because I just didn't try to accomplish something. Why? Maybe I didn't attempt it due to lack of motivation, or fear of failure, etc. Well this is a beginning for the 4th Step.

MAY 04, 1989
Thursday

Today is Ascension Thursday.

9:00 a.m. – Jack Gregory talks about Honesty. It seems that any program of recovery is going to depend on Honesty. However, Jack counsels us not to go overboard. Total Honesty is required in dealing with yourself. But when it comes to others it must, **at times**, be tempered with prudence and charity. If a friend asks, "How do you like my shirt?" If it is absolutely terrible, be prudent, be charitable. I can remember Harry Sullivan's stock answer to that sort of thing, and now it makes sense. One time I ask him how he liked a new, and very colorful liturgical stole that I recently purchased. He said, "I'll bet you are really going to enjoy that." Or he might have said "I can see that's going to make you happy."

No Group today. There is an 11:00 a.m. Mass for Staff.

I was taking pictures today. I wanted to take a picture of Joe H., one of the Counselors. She didn't want me to take it. I took it anyway. Now that I'm being honest with myself I gotta' ask myself: What kind of selfishness was that? Is it just another form of control? It worries me. I know it's not rape, but it is an invasion of space, or the privacy of another person. I must apologize.

The trip to K-Mart brings a haircut, and a photo album. I get back in time for Mass at 4:30. Fr. Joe, the house confessor, is here tonight, and I plan to make use of the opportunity.

When I checked my mail I find that Len has put some 4th Step material in my mail box. There was also a letter from Jeff Marx. He tells me of Philip Offerle's accident. It involves a death. I will write him a letter.

MAY 5, 1989
Friday

I am still walking and praying. Everyone has been somewhat excited lately: The Canadian Geese are returning. I hope I can get some good pictures of them.

Schedule is off today. I write a letter to the Youth of Parish. I try to spend a lot of time on this letter, because I think it is important.

11:00 a.m. –Group is Good. We play the Card Game again. The card I draw is, "What do I do for protection?" What I used to do is HIDE. Now I am trying honesty. It may hurt for a little while, but then it will be over. Hiding hurts for a long time.

After lunch Harry calls, Marge died last night. I'll have to call Harvey, or at least write to him.

Dr. Russ Smith has us in conference from 2:00 - 4:00 p.m. –The "X" factor. I'm beginning to see that the "X" factor is not only possible, but probable. In a real way this does not relieve me of any responsibility. It points more clearly to a responsibility that I have, which is to do something about it. In other words I've got to play the hand I've been dealt. I can see, or I'm beginning to see, that it does help to get rid of "useless" guilt and shame. I wonder why it is so difficult to let go of that stuff.

I call the Office at Nativity and get more details on Philip's accident. I walk after supper with Matt S. I'm beginning to wonder what responsibility I have to Zeke, and how to fulfill it. If Group is working properly we should be able to help each other constructively to see our own faults.

After dinner I read more on 4th Step. This can be a fearsome thing. And yet the 4th Step says to make a "Fearless Moral Inventory". There are so many things that I have been hiding for so very long. Some things that, as the saying goes, "I want to take to my grave". I may share some of these with you, but I will save the rest for my confessor and my counselor. One thing I have noticed: My moods go up and down. I don't know if that should be part of my 4th Step or not.

I expect Joe and Jackie Lemanski on the 13th. I am really excited about this. I have known Jackie since she was a little girl. *(Jackie is the daughter of Harry and Mary Alice Sullivan and Joe is her husband.)* I officiated at their wedding. They live in this general area, and the fact that they want to come to see me tells me that I am not in disgrace.

MAY 6, 1989
Saturday

The usual, breakfast, walk, and Office. I see three mature Canadian Geese with 12 goslings. Then I rush back to get my camera for pictures. I almost lose them. I don't know where they go during the winter, but they come back here each year. They come back and have their babies. Each time they come back they make something new. When I go back to Nativity I will go back renewed and ready to make something new.

I never tired of watching this goose and her goslings.

102

There are no classes on Saturday. I seek out John K. for a walk and a talk. I want his advice, input, feedback about my problem with my responsibility for helping Zeke. John just listens and says little. I realize that I have great fear about saying anything to Zeke about what I think is his problem with authority. What will he think? What will others say? Will I have anyone left to relate to? I really am chicken. Len tells me that I'm afraid to take risks, and I know it's true. Down deep I am a "people pleaser". I don't like this, but I think I have taken the first step in dealing with the problem. I have recognized it, and I have called it my own. That's two steps, and I hope that is progress. But about Zeke, I keep asking myself: "Why is it my responsibility to say anything?" I don't really know the answer to that, except that it is on my mind, and will not leave me in peace.

I work on my sermon, write cards in the afternoon. Frank is due to return from his TL, (Therapeutic Leave) and I'm sure that this adds to my risk with "Zeke." DAMN.

I am celebrant at Mass with Barry as Deacon. At the "Momento for the Living" in the Mass I present my problem to the Lord.

I wonder about Raymond. Is he drinking? He complains so much. Now I have another problem. If he is drinking, and I know it, or think it, what is my responsibility? I recall how the guys who formed my Intervention Squad had a responsibility and how they fulfilled it. It would be so easy for me to just let nature take its course. Now if those guys who intervened me had done nothing, I think I would have been much worse off. *[As you will see in My Story (Chapter 16), I am convinced that I would have died an early death.]*

MAY 7, 1989
Sunday

I get to go out for Mass today at Holy Family Parish. The scripture tells about Stephen and how he was stoned. There is one part where it says that Stephen was talking, but the people covered their ears so they wouldn't have to listen. In the sermon I tell them that I'm reminded of some TV Talk Shows. Often on those shows everyone talks and it seems to me that no one wants to listen. It's as if they cover their ears to keep from hearing anyone but themselves. I also I include my ideas on John, chapter 17. This is one of the chapters in John's Gospel dealing with what Jesus had to say at the Last Supper. I think this makes an excellent prayer that parents might use for their kids as they leave the nest.

Roger Bendel calls and drops by. Good to see him, he brings his son. He and Pat, his wife, may come by some Sunday. Roger was a member of Nativity. In fact he was chairman of the Building Committee. He and his family moved to somewhere near Detroit. I am really excited, no I'm overjoyed. I don't know the right word, but like Joe and Jackie they really build my self confidence.

I had a strange, but comforting dream last night. It was all about sex. Now don't get any ideas. The dream was also about celibacy. As I understand sex it's an intimate and profound way of saying that I am special to this one person and that person is special to me. Well in the dream I am offering my sexuality to God and this frees me to be special to many, many people, and it allows those people to be special to me. It was a strange dream, but I really felt good about it. No, I guess a better word would be I felt at peace.

MAY 8, 1989
Monday

Ken Adams is good. He's talking about adult behaviors which Ken, et. al., say are adult defense mechanisms against shame, such as rage, blaming others, intolerance, isolating, addictions. I can spot those behaviors in myself. Now I just gotta' trace back to the cause, get hold of it, and then (most important) throw it away, or let go of it.

Len has given me a good book: "RISKING" by David Viscott. I took a RISK today: I talked to John K. about Zeke again, and my fears of approaching him. About my idea of what responsibility I have of telling him about what I perceive as his problem with authority. I think that I should do this in Group, but I am very much afraid of doing it. John K. encourages me to do it. I would like for him to do it, that is one of the reasons I mention it. John sees through this and does not take the bait. Frank O. returns from TL and that makes my task more difficult (Frank and Zeke are good friends, I would risk losing both of them and they would carry others with them.) My resolve waivers. Finally I regain it and decide to definitely bring this up in our next Group. I discover that Zeke will be on TL for the next Group. I decide to approach him privately. I spoke with him about what I perceive as his problem with authority. He disagreed but thanked me. I am learning much about my fear to risk the approval, acceptance of others. I feel good about it, and take a walk to rejoice. I see my Canadian Geese and their goslings on my walk.

There is a trip to Greenfield planned for Friday. This is the home of Henry Ford. It also has workshops use by Edison, and somebody else. I plan to go.

MAY 9, 1989
Tuesday

9:00 a.m. – Earl speaks on ATTITUDE. What is my attitude in reference to alcohol? How long have I been reinforcing it? Alcohol is only part of my alcoholism. The disease is in me not in the alcohol. Attitude is not based solely in fact, but also in feelings, feelings about facts. The important thing is that feelings can be changed. There are many things in the life of each alcoholic that act as triggers. Triggers can act to bring about a craving for a drink. I should become aware of what these are in my life so I can break the power the trigger has over me.

S A M = Sober And Miserable. There must be ten thousand of these cute little sayings. Earl talks about the difference between sober and sobriety. I got sober every day but I did not enjoy sobriety. I still had bad attitudes. To be happy try A B C = Attitude - Beliefs - Conduct must be in harmony.

104

11:00 a.m. – We have a new person in Group. His name is Paul. He is not a resident Guest. He seems to be a counselor in training. He does have good insights. He's quite a bit younger than Len. I was beginning to wonder if he was taking over the Group until Len introduced him. Len is still my counselor. I have no problem with this. I am certain that not too long ago I would have been very upset. It has taken me a while to be open with this group. Could it be that I am learning to be open? Learning to risk? Learning to trust? I think so. I hope so.

1:00 p.m. - Jack Gregory's Group is okay. I have another one on one with Jack. I feel great about me. I am really enjoying that book: RISKING. I think I am beginning to take risks. I am also getting ready for the 4th Step.

THE LETTERS

May 5, 1989

To All the Youth of Nativity,

For a long time now I have been wanting to write to you but I was wondering just what I would say.

First, thanks to all of you, especially those in the PRE classes for the cards and notes you have sent. They have really helped me to keep my spirits up.

Second, congratulations to all of you for completing another school year. I know that it is exciting to go from one grade to the next. Not only exciting, but a reward for your hard work. Many of you have made your First Confession, your First Communion, and accepted Confirmation. I am so glad that I was there for First Confession.

Confession is so very important, and I am glad that we can share it in such a friendly way at Nativity. No matter how young, or old a person is, Confession can be a very special way in which we can come to know God's friendship with us. Being up here, and so far away from all of you, it's important for me to be aware of God's friendship. I am able to talk to a priest who visits here often for Confession, and that has truly helped me to experience this special friendship.

I know that you had the Solemn Celebration of First Communion recently. This is a special occasion. I know you had a special Mass and music. I hope you wore special clothes and had a party. I sure missed being there with you, but Mrs. Brigance sends me the bulletin each week and I read the name of each person and I keep you in my prayers.

I wrote a special letter to those who were Confirmed. I don't know if those who were Confirmed at St. Ann's got the letter. If not I now ask Mrs. Miller to make sure that they get a copy of it. The Bishop wrote and told me how impressed he was with all the people of Nativity when he was there for Confirmation. Most, if not all, of those Confirmed will go on to High School now. That will be exciting, and it will also be a challenge to live as young Catholic Christians while in High School. Don't be afraid to call on, and use the Grace of Confirmation.

To those of you in High School, some will go on to the next grade, some to college. I have often said from the pulpit that Nativity has the greatest Youth Group in the Diocese. I say it again now. You don't have to be the best in anything, all you have to do is be real. I have seen how you work and play together, how you help each other, and help those who are not of our parish, but are in need. I have seen you get mad, get hurt, get depressed, and get over it. I have seen you build happy and joy filled memories and I'm so glad to have shared in some of that. You are real, at least you try to be, you are learning to be. For that you, and I, can thank your parents and the fantastic adult leadership we have at Nativity. I will see you again in June, until then, remember that you are mine and I am yours, let us treasure each other in thought and in prayers.

God's Peace and my love,

Father Bill

Thursday - the Ascension
May 4, 1989

Dear Bill,
(A letter from Leonard)

This letter/ report is long over due so I will try to catch you up on things at Nativity. The Parish Picnic/Outdoor Mass/Crowning of the Blessed Mother will be Sunday, May 21 at the 10:30 Mass. Barbara Bozzle is in charge, along with Mike Offerle. So I guess all will come off ok. You might want to drop Philip Offerle a note. He was driving his pickup truck last Saturday night in the vicinity of Bolton High School - had three teenagers in the back bed of the truck - lost control on a curve. The only one hurt was a girl in the back bed of the truck - pinned underneath the truck when it turned over - and was killed. Philip is a senior at Memphis Catholic.

When you come home for your visit, I will be glad to turn your room over to you and go to the Lake for a few days, or whatever you wish to do. Fishing is suffering this Spring. And it is all your fault (Ha Ha) but I will catch up this summer and I am enjoying the people and the work at Nativity. They are good people.

Billy Jolly's departure created no problems. It was really a blessing for the parish. He is getting retirement and $400.00 monthly now in Social Security since March. And he really was a liability rather than an asset.

Have had several lengthy talks with xxxxxxx trying to help him in her P.R. with people and improve his image. S/he knows that there is no way s/he can pull the Xxxxx Program back together here at Nativity. I am personally contacting some of the people and trying to schedule some of the talent here - plenty of it. I am trying to convince xxxxx *(I have not revealed the name or gender of this person on purpose.)* that you can't be so rigid and inflexible. People are more important than rules - regulations - guidelines Although you need those things. That has always been my principle, otherwise you needlessly alienate people. S/He seems to be listening.

The dinner Friday night with Ken & Shari Lee and Helen Harrington was a delightful evening. We talked a lot about you. I am sure you have heard, or will hear from Helen about it. The Lee's have some plans for a really luxurious home at Lakeland. Robbie *(their son)* drew the plans. Pat Patterson and Robert Edwards are still critically ill.

I took Gay, Eva, Mary, & Betty out to lunch on Tuesday for Secretary's Day. Went to Jim's East. They seemed to enjoy it. The Lee's, Helen, and you are invited to a filet crappie dinner at my place in Enid after you return and get settled in. I am still trying to do some cleaning up of grounds around the rectory. Also clean up the garage. Hope to get to that with Pat Trainor's help. He is really a good worker and fine young man. I had a talk with Lloyd Kneller about Jolly and Lloyd agreed it was for the best. John Tindle is working hard around the place. The Ground Crews for Saturday morning are back in operation.

John Tindle and Eva Holloway are the most under paid people I know of. I will talk to Eva and try to adjust her check some what. I am not sure I will say anything to John.

I am sure you know about the big celebration at the Coliseum for Mother Teresa - the Bishop's 25th anniversary, and the marking of the first Mass in Memphis 150 years ago.

I will do the Lisa McQuestion wedding here at Nativity, Saturday evening June 10th. She wants to have the Mass and reception here which is good. I have had Fred Wiseman come look at a few problems with John Tindle. Fred has offered to help John if needed. Fred still gives one day a week at St. Ann. I believe he gets paid for that. Charles Holloway is going to take care of a few problems up at the Church building. The new bulletin looks good - only problem is that it must go in early Wednesday A.M. So Gay has to get it finished by Tuesday afternoon. I am trying to reconcile the Mass Fund account with Mass Intentions receipts and special contributions you have placed in that account with the bank statement. Just about have it in order. It appears that you have not received the Mass Intentions stipend for Masses you offered in January, February, and March.

(The rest of the letter is lost.)

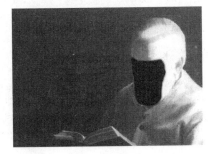

My friend and walking partner, Father John K., at prayer in the chapel. The picture has deliberately been distorted.

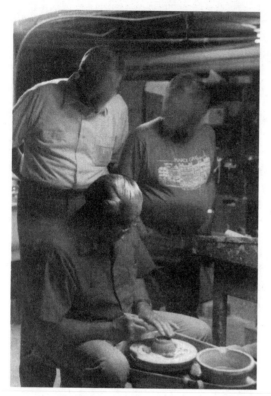

This is Gordon, the Pottery Instructor and two students. The faces of the "students" are deliberately distorted.

At the 'elevation' during Mass celebrated at Guest House

CHAPTER EIGHT
WEEK EIGHT

MAY 10, 1989
Wednesday

Breakfast is the usual good meal. No grits, but good. It is a good day for my walk and I feel like taking my time. I try to pray the Office but distracted by nature. I see more of my Canadian Geese and the little ones. The little ones are great. I've seen pictures but they just can't tell the whole story. I guess mine won't either. I also saw a groundhog today.

9:00 a.m. – Len has film on Fr. Joe Martin, it is good. Len concludes his talk by telling of a P.O.W. who was in solitary confinement for at least 18 months. During this time he begins a relationship with a rat. Shares food with it, watches it raise its children. They grow up and leave, finally the rat leaves, the P.O.W. cries, but rat gets pregnant and returns to have babies and raise them. *(I think the point was that when lonely and deprived of normal relationships we will establish a relationship wherever we can. Relationships are that important.)*

11:00 a.m. – Departure Mass for Jim McG. He asks me to take some pictures for him. I am becoming more, and more aware that this is a place of anonymity, and I wonder if I'm violating that for anyone. I take the pictures. At the luncheon Jim says something that catches my attention: "As I leave here, there is no one here who was here when I came." I notice that there are more people who arrived after I did, than there are of those who arrived before I came. This is both scary and encouraging.

1:00 p.m. – Shopping at the mall. I find a joke book on golf and buy it for Will. They had a novelty balloon packaging so I took that too. It really looked funny, the book was inside the balloon. The whole thing cost about $10.00. Why did I do that? I don't know. I don't get along well with him, so why? I think it's because I think he needs the attention, and I have received so much without being worthy of it. I recall how quickly people like Don K. and Ron, the Housekeeping Supervisor, came to my aid simply because I needed it. I am more aware of temptations to selfishness, and begin to realize how difficult it will be to overcome them. So things like the book in the balloon may be a help for me.

The AA meeting is at Beaumont, and it is a good meeting.

I write letter to Parish in reference to my awareness of what Father Oglesby is doing, and the fact that I agree with it. The problem that I want to head off deals with one particular ministry. Before I came here I was planning to move that ministry from one person to another. I had discussed this with him/her. I saw this as a solution to the problem of some people not getting along with xxxxx, and though I didn't think the solution was the best, I did see it as a way of solving a problem. I am coming to see that I should have done something about the problem long ago but I just let it be because of my "unwillingness to take a risk." This is not going to be fun working through. I don't want the people to think, "Well it took getting Father Bill out of the picture for a while, but the problem got solved." I talked to Len by phone about this, and I'm certain that he is following the plan that I had, whether or not he knew that, I don't know. But I let him know that I agreed with his appraisal. I introduce this subject in my letter talking about the 4th Step.

MAY 11, 1989
Thursday

Don K. goes on TL today. He's the guy who acted as my unofficial guide when I arrived. Thomas M. makes the team. In my mind this is one of the things that gives Guest House its credibility - some people are not accepted - only those who make the team.

9:00 a.m. – Lecture: Jack Gregory talks about sexuality: funny, interesting, very good. He is nothing like Ken Adams. He is serious, interesting, and amusing.

10:00 a.m. – I have a one on one with Len. He reports that Jack Gregory says I'm growing. I agree that I have decided to be set on a course that is growth. Len gives me my dates for 5th Step (May 23 at 1:00 p.m.), TL (May 27), Departure Mass (June 14) Departure (June 18. Father's Day). We talk about 4th Step, I look forward to it. Something like a General Confession but not dealing with sin.

11:00 a.m. – Group. John DeC. is having a tough time adjusting to being here. The Group comes through for him.

Thomas, the seminarian, tells me at lunch that he has made the team. He will return to his school for exams, then to Memphis and then return here on Tuesday. I make arrangements to meet him. Paul tells me that he and Len have assigned me a pigeon *(This means that I will act as a guide for a new person coming in.)* and that I am to meet him at the airport, same time as Thomas arrives. I am a little surprised that Paul seems to be taking some responsibility for me, and I somewhat resent it. However, I like Paul and I think he could be very helpful to me. I just am not ready to switch counselors. I must talk to Len about this.

3:00 p.m. – I move to the Villa. Ron helps me get everything, including my computer moved. It occurs to me that if someone had done this for me just two

110

months ago that I would certainly be obliged to offer him a drink. The room is nice. It is somewhat like a motel room, and I'm sure I will like it. I don't know how to describe this move. It is certainly a milestone in my treatment at Guest House.

MAY 12, 1989
Friday

I sleep late, walk in the rain to Breakfast. This is the only drawback about the Villa. It is quite a distance from the main residence and when it rains you just walk in the rain. However they do provide umbrellas for each room at the Villa. Today is the day for the Greenfield Trip.

9:00 a.m. – Tom talks about 5th step, I find it helpful, he also gives a check list as a hand out. The list is very thorough and it is divided into logical divisions. But he also tells us that the way 5th Steps are made varies with each individual.

10:00 a.m. – Mail brings medical bills from my hospital visit and volume III of the Breviary. Jackie calls, confirms that she and Joe will be here tomorrow. I tell her a joke about alcohol. She interprets it as a longing for it. Got to straighten that out tomorrow. As I look back over my notes and review my past thoughts and desires, I can't believe that at times I thought, or hoped, that this treatment would prepare me to be able to drink responsibly. I can see that I have always said that I was giving up drinking for good, but there was always that thought about being able to drink responsibly. Well that is no longer a part of my thinking, or desire.

11:00 a.m. – In Group we play the card response game. My card reads: "I only get angry when..." I add whenever someone disagrees with me. This is not as true as it used to be.

We are about 15 minutes late leaving for Greenfield. It is cold and rainy but I, along with Frank , Jerry, & Barry tour the village instead of the museum. We see the house in which Henry Ford was born, a Plantation House - it was much smaller than the movies make you believe. We see how wool goes from the sheep to thread. There is also a border collie in training. This reminds me of Jock. There are a couple of workshops: the Wright Brothers, and Edison's. Noah Webster's home is here. We have dinner at an Italian restaurant and it is good. I realize that it is not half as expensive as when I was drinking. I did not miss having before dinner drinks, a during dinner wine, and after dinner drinks. I was able to talk to, and listen to, people. We returned late and I catch up my Journal on computer.

Jackie & Joe are due today.

I slept late, til almost 8 a.m. The walk from the Villa to breakfast is long and cold, but no rain. I ask if they have any more grits, but they have lost my grits in the kitchen. Well I'll let them stay lost, perhaps they will lend a blessing to the kitchen.

I take time to write to the Bishop giving him the dates I have, and requesting an appointment during my TL. I also ask him to have all the members of the intervention team there. I want to thank them again after I meet with the Bishop. I start a letter to Victor.

Jackie and Joe arrive around 11a.m. I show them around, and we have lunch in the dining room. Everyone is very nice to them. Jim McD. gives Jackie, the teacher, an apple. After lunch we walk and talk. I tell them about the program and me. Jackie tells me about her family. I invite them to be in Nashville on the weekend of June 3-4. I will be on TL then, and I plan to visit her family, and my other friends in Nashville.

Later in the afternoon we go shopping at the Mall. I am looking for a small hot water heater, the kind you stick into a cup and heat the water. We get back to Guest House for the 4:30 Mass, and then Joe, Jackie, and I go to Lake Orion for dinner. I am told that Jimmy Hoffa, the Teamsters Union boss, enjoyed his last meal at a restaurant around here. We have a great time. Jackie remembered that I enjoy gardening and she brought me a bulb to plant when I get back home. Then it is time for them to leave.

I finish my letter to Victor in which I give him the dates for my TL and ask him to meet me at the airport. John K. and I enjoy a short walk and brief talk. I try to call Victor - no answer.

I have set my clock for 6:00 a.m. I will be going out to a parish to celebrate Mass. It's good to have a coffee maker in my room. At the Villa it is a good idea to have coffee before that walk to the main building. I am scheduled to be picked up at 7:00 a.m. by people from St. Hugo's Parish.

St. Hugo's church is beautiful, but not $6,500,000.00 beautiful. The people are very friendly and participate well. I tell them that May 17th is my 25th anniversary of ordination, but that in 1964 that was Pentecost Sunday, so I always celebrate both dates.

I get back to Guest House in time for breakfast at 10:00 a.m. The cook has found my grits, so I have a special treat. I spent the rest of the morning writing notes and letters. At 2:00 p.m. we have spare ribs. They are not very good, full of grease. They are definitely not up to the standards of Corky's in Memphis. I make time to write a letter to Steve and Mary Miller and then nap. I call Victor and ask him to meet me at the airport on the 27th. I am a bit concerned about my own emotions and returning home. Victor is reassuring. He will have my office call me Monday afternoon.

A gas attack starts about 5:00 p.m. just as we are having a House Meeting. I am elected Sec/Treasure. I'm not at all sure what my duties are. I know there is no money involved. From what I have heard the three officers serve as a go-between with the Guest House Administration and the Guests. (Us). In other words if there are any suggestions, or complaints we take them to the powers that be.

The gas is too much for me to stay for the AA meeting. It is very painful. I try the Health Institute's method to no avail, it only spreads the pain. The back of my mouth fills with warm liquid now and then. I return to the Villa to lay down with music. Frank O. stops by around 10:00 p.m. just to see if I am allright. I am touched. I join him in the Villa recreation room and we watch the conclusion of War and Remembrance.

MAY 15, 1989
Monday

The gas is still a bother, so I am unable to eat much breakfast.

9:00 a.m. – Ken Adams is good. There is no group today.

I am still not up to eating much lunch. After lunch I check with the office about the medical bills I have received as result of my trip to hospital, they say that I should send them to my parish secretary for insurance claims.

I take a nap in the afternoon trying to get rid of gas. If I can just lay down and get perfectly flat and relaxed the gas will usually pass.

I get card for Francis R.'s 25th anniversary. His anniversary and mine are on the same day. The gas is mostly gone by time for supper.

I go to airport with Bob (the driver) to pick up Jim B. He is to be my pigeon, that is, the guy that I'm supposed to help get acquainted with Guest House. This takes three hours. I recall the time when I arrived. Jim is scared. He has also had a few drinks on the plane. I try to help, hope that I did. I show him around the building and introduce him to Jackie, the nurse. Later I introduce him to a few people, and generally get him settled. I have a bad headache, but I have to write the parish a letter. I go to bed with the Rosary. The gas lets up.

MAY 16, 1989
Tuesday

Nobody knows when Tom M. (the seminarian) is arriving, so I call Bruce and get his flight information, and give it to the office. Today is a strange day, the schedule is all mixed up. Dr. Russ Smith is talking this afternoon but about 7 people will be out.

9:00 a.m. – At Group Frank ventilates his feelings about what he considers Len's neglect. I think that this is just a cover for his insecurity about having nothing to do for the next five weeks. When he returns home he knows that he will have no assignment for five weeks. The Group offers several suggestions. I think he feels better about this five week period.

A group of us go to the Health Institute this afternoon for an evaluation of the physical they gave us a week, or so ago. This is a Health Maintenance Program, and I think it has great value. I have little, or no, control over my diet at this stage but when I get home I will try the suggestions they made the last time we were there. They told me that I should lose 10 pounds, avoid red meat, pork and fried foods. I should try being a vegetarian two days a week. We also discussed my age old problem of GAS. Several options were discussed. Today they told me that abdominal pain could be resulting from diet, or gallbladder disease. The report suggests that I could use something called Thorazine for abdominal pain since it is an alternative to narcotic type medications. I will have to read over their report. The Health Institute went so long that I was unable to meet Tom M. at the airport.

I got back just in time for Mass at 4:30 then supper. After supper I take a walk with John K. Then we watch the news together. This is the first time in many a day that I have paid any attention to the news. Does this mean I'm getting back into my old routine? I used to think, or act as if, the world could not function unless I watched the news. I give Helen H. a call and arrange for picnic on Sunday, May 28th with her and several others. Then I call Harvey Carter to arrange for a Mass for Marge on the First Friday in June. I also call Jim H. and arrange a time when we can meet. He says he will meet me after the Sunday Mass on May 28th. This is the guy who could be my sponsor.

I walk with Tom M. and remember that I am supposed to order pizza for an in house party. I also order soft drinks thru Ron, get plates and napkins, etc for the party before each departure. I discover that this is one of the duties of the Secretary/Treasurer.

THE LETTERS

Dear Family at Nativity,

The 4th Step in the 12 Step AA Program is: "Made a searching and fearless moral inventory of ourselves." The 5th step is to present that to another human being, that will be my counselor here. Now that is a pretty tall order. I must take a serious look at both the good and the bad. It's fairly easy for me to recall the things I'm proud of, they stand out in my mind. Sometimes they're colored a bit more than they should be. It's more difficult to recall the things I'm not proud of. But once I have made the decision to be honest, and I have made that decision, then things begin to become clearer, not necessarily easier.

There are many good reasons for making this inventory and the counselors supply us with plenty of help. Everyone has character defects of one sort, or another. I'd like to think I have only a few, and not very important ones at that, but I know better. My concern is my defects and virtues. How to get rid of the former and to strengthen the latter.

Let me quote from "Twelve Steps and Twelve Traditions." "By now the newcomer has probably arrived at the following conclusions: that his character defects, representing instincts gone astray, have been the primary cause of his drinking and his failure at life: That unless he is now willing to work hard at elimination of the worst of these defects, both sobriety and peace of mind will still elude him; that all the faulty foundation of his life will have to be torn out and built anew on bedrock."

I got to tell you that word, "failure" has been very hard for me to take. I've done a lot of good things in my life. Of course I have, and the Fourth Step doesn't deny that. Everyone has failures in life. I've learned, and grown from some of them. Ah, but it's those that I cover over, or deny, that I stubbornly cling to, that I must deal with and learn from.

I realize that some, perhaps most of you, reading this will think I'm really feeling down. The very opposite is true. My character defects have caused me, and others enough trouble. I am anxious to be rid of them. At least to start the process of working on them. I heard something the other day at an AA meeting, "I'm not afraid of the future. I don't know what the future holds, but I do know Who holds the future." God's in charge of the future. I've turned my life over to Him, of course I realize that's not a one time decision. I've got to work at it every day.

Why mention all this? From the beginning Father Oglesby has sent me progress reports on the parish. We have discussed the problems at the parish. I seek his advice and point out directions that I want to follow. I can see the wisdom of his suggestions and with the program up here I am able to see problems that I didn't see, or was too stubborn to see before. I am so glad that Father Oglesby is there. We work together well. I'm filled with hope for my recovery, and for our recovery as a parish. The proof is in the pudding so I invite you all to stay around for dessert. As a result of my experience and yours we all have an opportunity to grow. We will never be the same again. We will be better.

God's Peace and my love,
Father Bill

May 11, 1989

Dear Bill,
(This is from my sister Micki and her friend, Nancy)

We both enjoyed your letter of the 26th. Your program seems to have given you some insight into yourself and that is good. I am so glad that you are doing this. You are in my prayers every night. Keep up the good work. Also keep in touch. I will try to answer soon. My biggest problem with the computer is that I am not a typist. I use a sort of hunt and peck system with all ten fingers. However, I look at the keyboard. But it gets the job done. Now, Nancy is a typist, and it takes her about half the time to write a letter as it takes me. But I love it anyway.

Your parish house *(the rectory)* sounds like you really have an ideal one. Remember our house on Canby? It was 2100 square feet so I have some idea about the size of your place. The planning of it seems to be well thought out, too. You were smart to get good furniture. One of these days we will come and see for ourselves. But that won't be for a while yet. Just think about it and we will too.

We finally got our spa opened for the Summer. It needed to have the skirt restained and the tub polished, then filled, and heated. Yesterday was our first dip, and we were in it again today. We both get a lot of therapeutic value from it. No, we didn't get to take it off the income tax.

I had hoped to have a letter from Bob, but I haven't heard from him since February. We were supposed to make a trip to Las Vegas this June, but when we bought the computer we used the money that we had set aside for that trip. I don't know if he was upset because we weren't coming or if he just hasn't found the time, *(Bob, our brother lived in Vegas.)* But no matter, I'll get a letter from him one of these days. He told me that Rosemary and Cook *(our sister and brother-in-law)* had given him an airline ticket to Winston Salem and that he was going in August for her birthday. I think that is really great.

Bill, this letter may take more time that I have right now so I will just store this and come back to it later. [Two Days Later]

I just read this over and there really isn't much more news for now. I will close for this time. Write again when you have the time. I'll try to get back to you soon.

Love from both of us,
Micki & Nanc

CHAPTER NINE
WEEK NINE

MAY 17, 1989
Wednesday
My 25th Anniversary

9:00 a.m. – Russ Smith is the speaker today. I think he is very good, and I decide to buy his tapes.

11:00 a.m. – The Departure Mass for Frank O. and Jim McD. and the luncheon go well. Francis R. and I are remembered in the Prayer of Faithful for our 25th anniversaries. (surprise) It is Frank who had lung cancer discovered in a routine physical when he came to Guest House. He sees the Hand of God operating there. It is this Hand that gives him a joy that is so evident.

Today is also shopping day at the Mall. I get some cards for future Departure Masses, and find a poster for Jackie, she likes cats. Mary Miller calls to congratulate me on my 25th. Four people from the parish send flowers for my 25th. At supper the cook has provided two cakes for our anniversaries. One for Francis and one for me. The guys sing "Happy Anniversary." Man oh man!! This treatment center is nothing at all like what I expected.

Today I order my ring. Guest House has a ring that those who have finished the course are entitled to wear. It comes in silver or gold. I order the silver. The face of the ring carries a two fold message, or graphic. At first glance it seems to be two hands holding a chalice. Closer examination brings out the image of a face held by two hands. It is the face of despair. The message is: From the despair of alcoholism to the joy of sobriety.

After supper I look at a video that came from the parish today. Somebody took a video of the people in the parish and various activities. It brought tears. I truly enjoyed it.

The AA meeting is at Beaumont. This is a meeting that I enjoy except for one thing. Every meeting is closed by the same guy. I guess that whoever is chairing knows to call on him as the time runs out. One of the things that I really like about AA meetings is that they start on time and they end on time. Another thing is that no one is giving advice. Everyone who speaks is simply sharing his, or her, personal experience. This means that there is nothing to argue about. It's not a case of somebody being right, and somebody being wrong. If I can apply what someone says to my life, that's good. If not, that's okay too.

I find out tonight that June 14th is not only my Departure Mass but it is also the Departure Mass for Will C. and John K. I have to fight my temptations about judging Will. I don't get along with him, but that's okay. Perhaps he has a difficult time getting along with me. I never thought about it that way.

MAY 18, 1989
Thursday

9:00 a.m. – Jackie speaks on "The Courage to Change." Jackie is so sincerely serious. She has a real wisdom. After the lecture I ask her about the place of the "X" factor and "Instincts that run wild". Which is responsible for destructive drinking? She helps me see that the "X" factor provides the predisposition for destructive drinking, while the instincts running wild take advantage of the opportunities. In the final analysis I am responsible.

11:00 a.m. – Group is wild. I say that I am uncomfortable with what is happening. It seems that Len is going after Zeke. Does Zeke need to be "gone after"? Is group the place to do it? The purpose of Group is for us to help each other. SO??? I don't understand. It's not really a case of choosing sides. There is no question in my mind that Len is not only the counselor, but he is MY counselor. It is certainly a time for me to learn patience.

After lunch I get to play with the baby squirrels. A few days ago someone discovered some baby squirrels in the end of a fallen tree trunk. The mother squirrel had been killed by a car. One of the secretaries made the discovery and she started bringing them food. Soon some of us joined in. The babies seem to have no fear of us. One climbs all the way up my arm. I try to get several pictures.

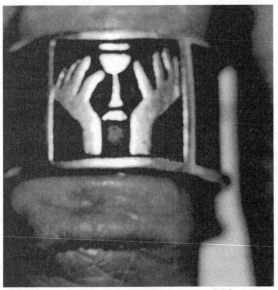

This is my Guest House Ring. The image is a double image. At first glance the hands of the priest can easily be seen offering the chalice. A second more intense look can discern the hands of the priest holding or covering his face in despair. The top of the chalice with the line across it is the forehead of the priest. The eyes are covered. The stem at the bottom is the nose of the priest. So the message of the logo is that of a priest returning from despair to happiness.

I get a good nap at least an hour. I have come, not only to accept, but to appreciate, Paul (the counselor in training) and since I have consulted with Len, I think I'll ask him to sit in on my 5th Step, I trust him, and I want to offer him a learning experience.

I am celebrant at Mass today and I make the intention one of Thanksgiving for our 25 years of priesthood not only for me but for Francis also. I use the scripture from Ezekiel about the Dry Bones, and Gospel from vigil of Pentecost. The way I see it, my spiritual life had become like the dry bones during my drinking. My time here is a time when the "dry bones" of my spirituality begin to come to life again.

The AA driver is a no show. I begin work on the 4th Step. Walk up to Administration Building and back with John K. I have a little problem with Gas. Perhaps it is due to that nice piece of red meat I had for supper. After supper I call the Trainors, and arrange for supper with them on Saturday, May 27th.

MAY 19, 1989
Friday

9:00 a.m. – Tom speaks about High Quality Sobriety (HQS), and Sober And Miserable. (SAM). HQS must be voluntary and sought after. I must accept my alcoholism and acknowledge my need for help. I must want to be sober FOR MYSELF, but not BY MYSELF. I must accept responsibility for my own Sobriety. It is necessary for me to actively strive for Spiritual, Physical, and Emotional goals as best I can. This takes planning, and AA meetings. Tom says that sobriety will not be done to me. I'll have to work for it. I must forgive resentments, but to forgive resentments does not mean to change the truth, a crook is still a crook, forgiven or not.

SAM (Sober And Miserable) involves "Stinking Thinking." 1) I'm not really an alcoholic; 2) I don't need any help to stay sober; 3) I don't need a Higher Power; 4) All I have to do is quit drinking; 5) If only they would leave me alone, get off my case, etc., I'd be allright. Self pity leads to a drink: "Poor me, poor me, pour me a drink." Resentments are the killers of the soul. Yes, I got a lot out of Tom's presentation.

11:00 a.m. – Group is good. Len talks about some of his story. I am still surprised when people share the story of their drinking with, not only me, but with the group. I'm still surprised but not as much as I used to be. I wonder: "Could I ever do that?" I get the impression that, in light of yesterday and the ongoing situation with Zeke, Len is trying to show us how seriously we should take this sobriety business. He does say something about that at the beginning of Group.

After Group, Len tells me that he has not scheduled me for 5th Step since Paul will be doing it. I tell him that there has been a miscommunication, I wanted the three of us, but he says a 5th Step is only for 2 people. I assure him that I did not mean to exclude him, or to insult him. He tells me he has not taken it that way. Nevertheless I do feel bad about how it turned out. Now this is something new. If something like this happened a few months ago I would have lost a whole lot of sleep. I would have fallen apart. I would have talked it over with my friend Jack Daniels. This is progress, I hope.

K-Mart trip is uneventful. I forget to get peanuts for the squirrels, but I do pick up movies for the Villa.

I work on my 4th Step most of the evening. Later I go down to the basement and get some pictures of John K. working at Gordon's Potter's Wheel.

MAY 20, 1989
Saturday

A lazy day. I sleep late 'til almost 8:00 a.m. The walk is good. I enjoy my squirrels, the geese, and I pray the Office. I take time to write my sermon for Trinity Sunday, and a few letters. After a good long nap I finish the sermon. The Bishop encouraged me to get plenty of rest, and I am doing just that. The Mass is at 4:30 p.m., and my sermon goes well. After supper I watch a video movie on TV with John K. and Frank S., and then catch up my computer journal. At 10:30 p.m. it is to bed with the Rosary.

MAY 21, 1989
Sunday

I sleep late again 'til almost 8:00 a.m. The Mass is at 10:00 a.m. After Mass I arrange the photos I have been taking in an album. I am going to put them on display so the guys can order any pictures they want. John and I take a walk, and talk about Anthony DeMello.

Lunch is late, but the usual time for Sunday lunch is 2:00 p.m. After lunch Don C. and I take a walk. He tells me that I have grown. That I am not as suspicious as I used to be. We talk about the points Ken Adams made about Abandonment. I can see how the orphanage experience, and the early death of my mother may have had an effect on me that I never realized. We also talk about my difficulty as a people pleaser and the difficulty I have in receiving and giving love. I surprise myself with ease with which I discuss these things. I don't ever remember talking to anyone about these things before I came to Guest House. The way I see it, talking about these things is a way of dealing with them. At least it's a beginning. It's not finding something on which I can blame my attitudes and actions. It's a way for me to understand myself, and go on from there. Jackie says that the most dangerous secrets are the ones you don't talk about. I think she's right.

The AA meeting is in the House and it is good. Later I am able to sit through an entire movie on video at the Villa with friends without having to make an early exit.

MAY 22, 1989
Monday

Breakfast - Walk & Office.

9:00 a.m. –It comes as a revelation to me that most families are not "normal families." When I begin to discover that most families have difficulties within them, I feel more at ease and less guilty. I guess I just assumed that the "average family," the "normal family" was what I saw in the movies, or on television. It becomes more and more clear to me that it's okay that there were problems in my family. There is no doubt left in my mind. Now begins the recovery.

The Steering Committee (I am Sec/Treasurer) meet with Ed Higgins. We discuss unmet needs in the House. I mention that there must be some follow up lest the Steering Committee appears to be a joke. The only unmet need as far as I'm concerned is that the pool table needs to be refurbished.

Len advises me of my travel arrangements for my departure. I will leave here on Father's Day, Sunday, June 18th at 3:40 p.m. for a flight at 5:40 p.m. and arrive in Memphis at 6:30 p.m. Memphis is an hour behind us, so the flight is not really that short.

Everyone knows that I have been taking pictures all around Guest House, and I have had many requests for pictures. I arrange with Matt S. to set up a display of the pictures so the guys can order any pictures they may want.

I work in earnest on the 4th step. I feel good about what I have done and finish up work on 4th Step at 10:45 p.m.

MAY 23, 1989
Tuesday

The headaches are coming back. They do not interfere with my morning walks. They start in back of the neck on the right side, pulsing, reaching up into the head on the right side to the forehead. These may last anywhere from a few minutes to 20 to 30 minutes. They reoccur several times during the day. I have been troubled by these for 3 days now. Have I seen the doctor about them? Of course not. A headache is a headache, and besides that by the time I get to the doctor the headache is gone. It reminds me of taking a car into the shop. You tell the guy what's wrong, but can you get the dumb car to perform? Not a chance.

9:00 a.m. – Jackie talks about Grief. The 5 stages of Grief: 1) Denial, I am denying if I say "but" instead of "and." For example: My dad was a strict disciplinarian but.... or My dad was a strict disciplinarian and..... (I still love him) I did not know this yesterday but... or I did not know this yesterday and that's allright. 2) Anger (Why me?) 3) Bargaining: Yes But -. Yes I did this but I will never do it again, *(never say never)* 4)Depression: God has forgotten me, I am unworthy, 5)

Acceptance: I am as sick as my secrets. I must learn to accept me, and forgive me, or others, for what I, or they have done to me.

10:00 a.m. – I check with Dr. Lyons about headache. He recommends a hot pad for my neck and aspirin. Now this is something new. Me going to a doctor. Yes the aspirin and hot pad help. He tells me that a cold pad can also help. Sometimes the simplest things are the most difficult to accept.

11:00 a.m. – Group is about unreasonable FEAR. There is a lot of discussion. Fear is part of living. Most of the things that I fear never come to pass. And I have survived all of the things that I have feared. (I'm here and alive - right?) I can't get rid of fear, but I can learn to cope with it.

1:00 p.m. – I do my 5th Step with Paul.
(I did not write my 5th Step into my Journal, but I did keep a copy of what I wrote as my 4th Step on my computer. I have since destroyed it. What follows is taken from that and current memories.)
The 5th Step: "Admitted to God, to ourselves, and to another human being the exact nature of our wrongs." In other words, as I understand it, it is a spoken 4th Step. I have been told that there is no exact right way to do this, but there is a wrong way. The wrong way is to be dishonest in what I include and in what I exclude. Len told me that the 5th Step, should be done between two people, therefore I will not share my complete 5th Step with you. I will touch on some things that may be helpful to others.

THE FOURTH STEP
MADE A SEARCHING AND FEARLESS
MORAL INVENTORY OF OURSELVES.

Using "Twelve Steps and Twelve Traditions" preparing for my 5th Step I made several puzzling discoveries. I list two:

1) "Alcoholics especially should be able to see that instincts run wild in themselves is the underlying cause of their destructive drinking." (Twelve Steps and Twelve Traditions page 44.)

2) "By now the newcomer has probably arrived at the following conclusions: that his character defects, representing instincts gone astray, have been the primary cause of his drinking and his failure at life...." (Twelve Steps and Twelve Traditions page 50.)

My response was, "Where does this leave the "X" factor?" I thought it was responsible for "my destructive drinking." And, if so, why the 4th and 5th Steps? After much reflection, peer discussions, and listening to professionals I have come

122

to a different understanding that not only justifies these two steps but makes them necessary.

My understanding is: there is indeed an "X" factor. It provides a predisposition for destructive drinking, but of itself is not responsible for it. Being born into the human race gives me a predisposition for pain and suffering as well as joy and happiness, but being born into the human race is not the cause of either.

My instincts run wild, my character defects have been the primary cause of my drinking and failure at life. For me to accept this, without being driven to drink, is nothing short of a miracle, and I would not have been able to do it without the Guest House treatment.

The lectures have given me an understanding of some of the root causes of my character defects. The reading list gives me hope by showing me there is a way out. Both have shown me that there is, in this world, a life available to me without unmanageable shame, guilt, and fear. The program at Guest House and the AA program provide me with tools for a task to be accomplished.

When I made my surrender to God in the 3rd Step, in regard to my alcoholism, I was sure that I knew just what that meant, and how the AA program works. Now I realize the meaning of my surrender is a matter of continuous discovery, and I am sure that I have no idea how, or why the AA program works. So I make a new surrender in these terms: I have ample proof that my way does not work, AA has more than ample proof that their way does work, so with more faith than knowledge, I surrender my alcoholism and other problems to God, in my Church and following the AA program.

All of the above enables me to make a fearless moral inventory.

I am aware that I should set boundaries to help me overcome the character defects that I list. I list first a rather general category of my instincts run wild, or character defects:

1. TO BE LOVED, OR LIKED, AND TO LOVE, OR TO LIKE.
To be loved is certainly an instinct of human beings. In me this instinct has run wild and produced some serious character defects, such as being a "People Pleaser." I then spoke of several examples of this behavior:
Compromising values.
Remaining silent.
Not leading; not holding people responsible.
Not expressing personal likes, or dislikes.
Difficulty in saying "no" and an ease of being intimidated.

2. RESENTMENTS:
With me Resentments are connected with Envy, or Jealousy . Then I spoke of people of whom I was envious, or jealous, and people who had positions or talents that I did not have.

3. SEX:

Here I spoke of times that I had used the sexual instinct selfishly, and without respect for others. This was particularly true for the time I was in the Air Force, and stationed in Japan during the Korean War.

4. PRIDE:

For me unwarranted pride expresses itself in the way I accept correction from others. If I can find the fault I have no difficulty correcting it. When someone else points it out I become defensive and find clever ways of denying the truth. Then I spoke of the examples I knew of.

5. ANGER:

Anger has been a life long companion for me, it is almost like it was in the genes. I grew up with anger, often being expressed in the form of strict discipline. One of my idols is Hodding Carter, Press Secretary to former President Carter. He always seemed to be in perfect control of his emotions. For many years I felt that it was normal to get angry and get over it. I realize now that anger in me is a character defect. I spoke of the times I would kick, hit, throw things, or bang the table with my fist when alone. I spoke of the times I would make others uncomfortable by sulking, isolating, being unkind, or inconsiderate of the feelings of others.

6. IMPATIENCE:

My impatience is solidly rooted in selfishness. I often act like His Majesty The Baby, I want what I want, when I want it. It may deal with traffic, coffee, the phone, getting the mail in or out. I then spoke of the events that I could recall.

7. PREJUDICE:

I've often said, "There's nothing wrong with being prejudiced, but there is a whole lot wrong with being satisfied with being prejudiced." By this I mean that I think it is almost impossible for a person to grow up in just about any society without some kind of prejudice, but it is not a situation that I have to be content with. Nevertheless I am often surprised by discoveries of my own prejudices. I see them as a pathetic attempts to establish self worth at the expense of another. I then spoke of the prejudices I had discovered in myself.

8. FEAR:

I spoke to Paul of the ways that I permit fear to, at times, rule my life. I gave many, many examples of this. I also talked about the book *Risking*, and the help it has been to me.

Then, since I understood it to be a complete moral inventory, I listed the virtues I had discovered.

I am basically a good person because God made me that way. While many of my instincts have run wild resulting in character defects, I also have instincts that I have developed well, and result in honorable characteristics.

FAITH: I have faith in God and try to live that faith. I have faith in people and try to accept them as they are: people with strengths and weaknesses. In my position as pastor I try to accept people where they are, and to call them to where they can be.

HOPE: I am basically an optimist. I expect good things to happen. When bad things happen I can, and do, look to the future. I expect people to be good. When they are not I call them to where I think they can be. When bad things happen to good people, or good things happen to bad people, I trust in the mystery of God's love. I have difficulty in applying this to myself, but I am working on that.

LOVE & COMPASSION: In spite of the temptations I have to selfish love, I believe that I am truly a loving person. That is, I work and pray for the good of others. I comfort the sorrowing, rejoice with those who are happy, bring good news, not good advice, to those who are in doubt, and are searching, I offer forgiveness to the sinner, and to those who injure me, and correction to the erring. I offer company to the lonely, and I urge others to be aware of the needs and feelings of others.

WILLINGNESS TO LEARN: After some initial hesitation I can and do admit my mistakes and make adjustments. Although I am plagued with procrastination, I enjoy study because it benefits me, and the people I lead, by freeing us from error, or outmoded ways.

WILLINGNESS TO WORK: Again, although plagued with procrastination, I do enjoy the spiritual, administrative, and physical work that I do as a priest. I look forward to reviving my work on hobbies that can be of benefit to me and to others.

SENSE OF HUMOR: I think I have a good sense of humor. I can and do laugh at myself. I use my sense of humor to help others: lifting them out of the dumps, helping them to have a more positive attitude, just letting them know that I care.

PRAYER AND SPIRITUAL LIFE: My life is enriched, and made meaningful by my concept of God. My relationship with God is an ever growing thing, and usually an exciting adventure. I share my Spiritual Life with others through the way I live, the way I care for others, letters, private conversations, my writings, preaching, and public prayer.

That was the outline of my 5th Step. Afterwards I thanked Paul for listening to me. I am more and more impressed with him. I'm glad we talked about fear this morning. It helped me deal with my fear of the 5th Step. One of the fears that I had was that in doing the 5th step I would invite sympathy, I feared that I would do this on purpose, but I really think that Paul could see through any "B.S." I even mentioned this to him, and he said, "It's not important."

After my 5th Step I spend some time in the Chapel. I was filled with a spirit of Gratitude. I remember saying to myself, and to God, "Now, let me get on with the rest of this program." It was a good experience.

Mail brings a problem: GMAC says I have no insurance, I know that I have. I also receive a notice from Insurance company in which I note that they are covering my old car. I called Gay, my secretary at Nativity, about this. She said she would check with Nashville. She did and called back to say that they are covering my new car also. It is the "also" that concerns me. I asked her to tell them that I no longer have that car. I am amazed that I did not resort to anger to handle that situation. I call Fr. Oglesby and make some plans for a few social events while I am home on TL. He accepts my invitation to take the weekend off.

This closes week nine, and I have one of those pulsing headaches.

THE LETTERS

May 19, 1989

Dear Family at Nativity,

I didn't realize that I would be home on Therapeutic Leave when I started this letter, but I have decided to write it anyway. I will be on Therapeutic Leave from May 27th 'til June 5th. The leave is supposed to be THERAPEUTIC, not TRAUMATIC so I will not be involved in the parish activities except for the Masses on the weekend of the 27th - 28th, and the Masses on Monday and Tuesday. After that I will visit friends in Jackson and Nashville. This will give Father Oglesby some time to do a little fishing on the weekend. I will be coming home for good on June 18th, Father's Day. I do not know the arrival time but I will let you know.

I went out to St. Hugo's parish to celebrate Mass on Pentecost Sunday. St. Hugo's is a suburban parish, and has been there for some time, but they have just recently built a new Church with offices and everything else. It only cost $6,500,000.00. It is nice, but a bit out of our price range.

I have recently moved from the building in which I was living. I think I sent some pictures of it. I am now living in what we call, "The Villa". Those who still live in the main house call it the "Sharecropper's Shacks". It is somewhat like a motel. It is a nice walk in the morning to the main building, of course on cold and rainy mornings it's a cold and rainy walk.

I see some real nice things on my walks. I'll send you some pictures. We have Canadian Geese up here. They make a honking noise that can be heard from a long distance. I think they are very beautiful. They nest here on the property and raise their young, called goslings. The goslings are cute. We also have mallards here, they are much smaller than the Canadian Geese. I have one picture of a pair of Mallards with a Canadian Goose, so don't mistake them for goslings. On my way to the Villa I pass a squirrel who lives in a manhole. He is becoming friendly, since everyone feeds him, or her, as the case may be.

The apple trees are beginning to bud and other trees are opening up. Spring is finally arriving in Michigan. Those yellow flowers that grow on a bush are blooming. I never could spell the name of the flower.

Today one of the priests is celebrating his 25th anniversary. He was the celebrant for our 4:30 p.m. Mass. Wednesday I, and another priest here, will celebrate our 25th anniversary. For a while I felt very sorry for myself. Today I know that I have an appreciation of the priesthood that is unmatched by any that I have ever had. Had all this not happened I would have gone on drinking and fulfilling my ministry somewhat routinely, but who knows for how long. Gradually everything would have slipped away and who knows how many people would have been hurt. As it is, all this has happened, and I celebrate my 25th anniversary in circumstances far different than I would have imagined. I also celebrate with a far better understanding of God's love for me and what it means to be a priest and a pastor. Learning this lesson has been painful and that is my fault. It has also been a joy for me and that is your credit. Thank you and I look forward to being home again.

God's Peace, and my love,
Father Bill

Dear Father Bill,
(This letter is from Mary C., a friend. I have no date for it.)

How happy I was to hear from you yesterday. You have been on my mind and I had planned to call and tell you that I have your cane. I will give it to you in June.

I am glad to know that you have gone for treatment. It's a blessing that you are able to do something about this problem. One of the other pall bearers at Bud's funeral was Joe R. *(Bud was Mary's husband. Neither of them were Catholic but at his funeral I was honored to serve as a pall bearer.)* Joe was an alcoholic, and went for treatment eleven years ago. Joe gives New Year's Eve parties and drinks tomato juice. He is so very proud of his new life - his non-drinking life. He also attends AA meetings regularly. We were with them last year at their home. He was able to offer us drinks, but he had none. He said this made him stronger.

My dear Bud, I miss him terribly. It seems he had given up in so many ways, as he just wouldn't take care of himself. The last five weeks of his life were the happiest - he was working in Batesville, Mississippi for Joe, as a consultant. He actually ran Joe's office for him. He overdid it, I know, as he drove there each day and back and worked at home at night. He was there when he had the heart attack. I had worried about Bud's drinking for several years. He really depended on it to unwind and relax. I am thankful that you made the decision to do this for your health, for your friends, and for your parish.

These days since February 18th have been very depressing, and lonely for me. Things have been in a mess with lots to do. Hopefully, I'll get on with my life. This June 7th would have been 36 years since we walked down the aisle together in the First Methodist Church in Greenville, Mississippi. Did I ever tell you that we met in Church? When I was in college at Mississippi State College for Women in Columbus, Mississippi. I went to the Cumberland Presbyterian Church with a girl-friend, and she introduced me to Bud. He was a Deacon in his church and sang in the choir. This makes me sad, but I wanted to tell you.

Please know that you are in my prayers daily. Write again and let me know how things are going for you.

May God Bless you,
Mary

These are pictures from a Field Trip to Greenfield Village and the Ford Museum.

CHAPTER TEN
WEEK TEN

MAY 24, 1989
Wednesday

The headaches continue, but they do not interfere with my walk and prayer. I talk briefly with Jackie, the nurse and try aspirin and cold pack. I do get some relief.

9:00 a.m. – Bridge is interesting. I really enjoy this part of the program. I am surprised that this part of the Aftercare Program dates back only a few years.

11:00 a.m. – Group is exciting: I receive feedback on ANGER. I don't know how to be angry appropriately. Len directs me to a book on ANGER in the front office. He writes to my Bishop and shares the letter with me. It looks OK to me.

I am intense about TL, and perhaps, about my Picture Project maybe this is the cause of my headaches???

1:00 p.m. – Shopping at the Mall.

The AA meeting at Beaumont is good. There is a newcomer. His name is Bill. He is a young guy and is there on the orders of a Court. The meeting focuses on Bill. He is welcomed by all. Many people at the meeting tell their story, that is, how they got into recovery. I find that this called a "Newcomer's Meeting." The meeting is good, it is better than good to see how Bill is welcomed.

MAY 25, 1989
Thursday

My walks are getting better and I'm sure it is because of the weather, the flowers, the squirrels, and I guess this program of recovery. Of course praying the Office adds to it also.

9:00 a.m. – Earl tells us about the History of AA, and its Spirituality. The Spirituality of AA consists of many things: Experience of the Members; Language of Recovery. Spirituality of AA includes: Thinking; Speaking; Living. There is nothing new in the Big Book, so what does it have to offer? The Big Book separates the Fly Poop from the Pepper. ("The Fly Poop & the Pepper" comes from a saying of one of my professors in the college seminary.) In temptations a good question to ask myself is, "Not what do I see at the moment? But what do I see at the end of the day?" Some time ago Karl Marx said: "Religion is the opiate of the people." TODAY I think he might say: "Opiates have become the religion of the people." It seems that Spirituality is not a part of AA, it is the very essence of it. *(In the course of my recovery a few people have wondered why the Spirituality of my Church, my Faith was not enough. I guess my answer would be that I was not using it properly. My Church, my Faith calls on me to discover the Spirit of God, Spirituality, in all things. I see no contradiction with the spirituality of my Church, my Faith, and the Spirituality of AA.)*

Earl tells us that when Ed Higgins interviews those who have lapsed he asks two questions: 1) When did you stop going to meetings? 2) What are you hiding?

No Group Today. Headache is back I lay down and it goes away.

After Lunch I speak with Len. I thank him for his help and friendship. John K. has made a vase with the help of Gordon, and he gives it to me. He left it unfinished so I could paint it the way I want it. I hope I didn't mess it up. I painted it in many different colors. It reminds me of the multicolored coat of Joseph, and the many ways in which the Spirit of God is to be found in the World. *(I still have that vase.)* The headache got real bad during the painting. This could be from the fumes. I lay down it goes away. Mo volunteers to fire the vase for me.

The AA meeting is at Manresa, it is good. I have four more AA meetings to go to up here outside the house. I look forward with eagerness, and some fear to going to meetings at Home.

MAY 26, 1989
Friday

9:00 a.m. – Earl continues the Spirituality of AA.

The Spirituality of AA flows from 1) The Experience of the members: The Grapevine (a publication of Alcoholics Anonymous) is a good source; It must be Mystery not Magic; Open Ended, i.e. not having all the answers. The minute you think you got it - you don't have it any more. It's like being awarded a big beautiful medal for humility for being the most humble person in the world, as soon as I put it on I don't deserve it. Spirituality is not part of the AA program it is all pervasive.

Other notes: Fr. Dowling: "The thirst you have had was not for alcohol but for God." "If you can name the thirst it is Not God." "Prayer is not telling God how to run the Universe." "Life is not a problem to be solved, but a mystery to be lived." The Language of Recovery:

RELEASING: differs from "freedom;" letting go is a preparation for release;

EXHIBITIONISM: is showing yourself off without giving yourself away.

HONESTY: knowing and accepting yourself as you are.

The vase made for me by Fr. John K. and the flowers the chef placed on all the tables in the dining room one day.

GRATITUDE: response of one emerging from the Kingdom of Darkness. A responsibility we have to share.

TOLERANCE: is not putting up with what is different, but appreciating what is different in God's plan.

Other notes on Spirituality: We are "both" "and" not "either" "or." We are less than God - more than animals, i.e., both and. We are united by our flaws, and weaknesses, not by our strengths. Bodies are united by pleasure, souls by pain. Christianity will be revived when people go to Church the same way they go to AA meetings: hoping to learn and to share.

Len gives me another one of those progress reports. Perhaps you might be interested in it.

GUEST HOUSE

Treatment Plan Review - May 25, 1989 Father William F. Stelling

PHYSICAL - CLASS 1 - 17

Problem:	Plan:
1. Alcoholism	1. Guest House treatment
2. History of hypertension	
2. Blood pressure normal - no medication	

PSYCHOLOGICAL - ON VACATION

SOCIAL - CLASS II - 15

Progress:	Goal:
Is developing a more stable pace in confronting his issues.	Master basic assertiveness techniques.
Problem:	Plan:
Tends toward "people pleasing"	Read assertiveness primer provided.
Needs to learn when to assertively say "no."	Role play "no" exercises in group. Process feelings.

VOCATIONAL - CLASS II - 15

Progress:	Goal:
Has experienced more spiritual abandonment to will of God by working 2nd & 3rd Steps of AA	Renewed ministry.

131

Problem:	Plan:
Needs to confer with Bishop while on TL	Experience a successful TL to begin 5-27-89

ALCOHOLISM - CLASS II - 15

Progress:	Goal:
Reads voraciously. Has opened himself to the simplified principles of AA.	Continued responsible use of the of 12 Steps & AA groups.
Problem:	Plan:
Needs sponsor. Also needs to become socialized in home AA.	Therapeutic Leave.

MAY 27, 1989
Saturday

I go on TL today.

John K. and I have a good walk. It is the usual easy day and I take the opportunity to work with Matt to set up the display of the pictures I have taken.

(Until I returned to Guest House all of the following notes for my Journal were made on yellow legal pads.)

Jim, the Guest House Driver, comes to the Villa to pick me up. The ride to the airport is an opportunity to build tension, and I make the most of it. I experience vague fears, uneasy stomach. Conversation is forced but not difficult. Headache is ever present. The trip takes about an hour and I have an hour before takeoff. Jim helps me check the baggage outside and then he tells me to go right to gate 17. I get nervous doing this alone - you'd think I was a kid. I go through security and head for the gate, then I think I should have checked in at the ticket counter. I go all the way back only to find out what I already knew: I had checked in outside. I go back through security, they are a bit amused. I find gate 17, and take a seat. I can feel nervousness in my mouth, tingling in my hands and feet. I take deep and slow breaths - a drink sounds good but would be a disaster. I can see my group's disappointment, and Len's, and the people of the parish, the Bishop, the priests etc., But most of all I can see my disappointment in me. All of this time, all of this work, wasted.

I talk this over with myself. I have never been so aware of my feelings of vulnerability. Pains in my neck are very strong, I try some relaxing techniques. Thirty minutes 'til flight time, perhaps a club soda would help, but I would have to go into the bar to get it. I have the book, "RISKING," but I am too nervous to read it. Saved by the bell!! Boarding is called with 27 minutes to go. The flight goes well, I get the club soda on the plane, head and neck aches continue.

Victor meets me at the airport. Rick is outside with my dog Jock. Before I meet Victor I encounter Peter, a parishioner, who is going to catch a plane. I have vague fears about meeting the people. Jock is overjoyed to see me, it takes about 20 seconds for him to change loyalties from Victor to me. The ride home is restful. Jock is all over me and that is good.

Several notes await me at the rectory. From Len Oglesby there is a reference to a staff member and job he/she wants to take at the beginning of the new fiscal year. The headache is ever present.

I get ready for the first Mass back in the parish. *(Saturday evening.)* I am really nervous. I do not go out in the Narthex to greet the people as they come in. Larry, our Deacon, sits with me in my office/sacristy before Mass. I am so glad he is present, he is keeping others out. That's good, I am just not ready to greet them yet. Finally it is time to start Mass. As I enter our temporary sanctuary I am over-whelmed - WOW - applause before I even start. There are many tears during Mass. I use Deacon Barry's sermon. *(The one about the Monk and the Ox, and I still cannot remember what it was about.)* I stand at the door greeting the people after Mass. The greetings are gracious, sincere, and filled with joy. I am overcome.

I have supper with the Trainors, as planned. It's good to be with a family and friends. The talk is easy and natural. After supper Bob, Kathy, and I walk in the neighborhood. I get a gift of roses from one of Bob's neighbors. *(I don't know why I was given the roses. But it was perfect. I have always planted roses in every parish in which I have been assigned.)*

I return to an empty house, and triggers go off: this is my usual time to have a drink, and one more, and one more. Tension, awareness of headache, nervousness, I must learn that Christian Yoga. The Lisa McQuestion wedding reception is going on in the Fellowship Hall. I am concerned about who is going to clean up. I check it out, and remember that it was planned before I left. The Youth Group will clean up. It gives me something to do, instead of thinking about my usual drinking time.

Bruce and Greg return. Our conversations eases the triggers. I take a cup of hot coco to my suite, watch a little television and get ready for bed. I think to myself, "I'm home." But in a real sense I know that Guest House is still home to me. It's where I feel safe.

MAY 28, 1989
Sunday

I am up early and fix breakfast and play with Jock.

I have those pre Mass jitters again. Larry shows up early for the 8:00 a.m. Mass. How thoughtful of him. He is a big help. Everything goes well. The people are wonderful and I stand by the door and greet each one as they leave. Larry goes home, but agrees to return for the 10:30 Mass. I return to the rectory.

I lose track of time between Masses, and am not able to get to my office before people show up. Gay, my secretary, calls from the office, wondering where I am. I tell her I will come up just before Mass, I do not want to greet the people before Mass. I am nervous and scared during Mass. I forget to tell the people when my return date is. After Mass I greet the people as I did at the other two Masses. I have been wondering if Jim H. would show up, and wondering how I would recognize him. All of the sudden he is there. He is the last person in line. I have no trouble recognizing although I don't recall ever having met him. I think of this as God's coincidence. We arrange for him to stop by, and take me to an AA meeting at 7:00 p.m.

After Mass I nap. Helen H., Barbara B., and Ollie T. come for a picnic in my back yard. At her insistence I mix drinks for Helen (3). Lots of friendly talk. Helen says she wants to go to an Open AA meeting. She also wants me to drop by for a talk. I tell her that I will not be able to until I get back permanently.

Jim comes by at 7:00 p.m. and we go to an AA meeting at White Station Towers. I feel very good, relaxed. I am not nervous, or uptight. It is really a very good feeling. There is a man in his 80's there. I recall Marsalis at Guest House. There is also a teenager at the meeting. He seems to be in late teens. After the meeting he surprises me by stopping to quietly speak to me. "Aren't you Father Bill? I used to serve Mass for you at St. Ann's." I simply smile and say, "Yes, but my name is Bill and I am an alcoholic." He smiled, slapped me on the back, and said, "Well I'm glad you're here. Keep coming back." Jim was standing by and guided me out of the meeting. As we got in his car he told me that I was going to have to get used to that. He also says that I handled it well.

We stop by his house after the meeting and I meet his wife Denna. She offers a glass of tea, I feel right at home. We sit at the kitchen table and talk. We talk with an easy familiarity that I have come to know as natural to alcoholics. This is a new and very welcome feeling for me. Jim gives me a set of tapes: A Big Book Study - as a loan. We make arrangements for a noon AA meeting tomorrow.

MAY 29, 1989
Monday

For the Mass at 8:00 a.m. there are about a dozen people. Afterward I take a walk and pray the Office. John Tindle comes to work. It is so good to see him, he has done such a good job on the flowers around the rectory. Billy, the man Father Oglesby fired, comes by with his sister. Billy will always be a friend, but I don't know about a job, and he does not ask about one. I don't know what I am going to do in that regard. I take a drive through the neighborhood, and the old Johnny Maher property. Construction on houses for a new neighborhood is going along very fast.

Jim H. came by with Larry W., his sponsor, and we go to a noon meeting in Bartlett. At Jim's urging I picked up a white chip. I didn't really need one. A white chip is a symbol for coming into the program for the first time, or coming back into it after a relapse. My last drink was March 22nd.

I ask Jim and Larry if they have any information about meetings in Nashville. They give me a good noon location. I enjoyed meeting Larry. I am considering asking Jim to be my temporary sponsor. The drawbacks are that I am his pastor, and he is considering becoming a Catholic through the RCIA program. Well, I'll talk that over with Len at Guest House.

Back at the house I take a brief nap and then visit with the Malls. I have dinner at the Brigance's with Eva & Charles, Mike & Betty, Steve & Mary. Greg comes along, too. Some of them are concerned about drinking in my presence. I assure them that should be my problem, not their's, and that I'm doing okay. Dinner and conversation is very good. I eat some cake for desert and it gives me gas all night. I ask Bruce to arrange with his Dad for me to go to a meeting with his Dad on Tuesday. I make arrangements with Greg to walk to Charlie's in the morning for coffee and a visit.

MAY 30, 1989
Tuesday

I am up early after a very bad night with gas. Greg has been up, and has coffee made. We walk to Charlie's with Jock. It is an absolutely delightful time. The air is warm but not yet hot. *(Charlie is the man who built the rectory. Many months ago I encountered him on one of my morning walks. He was building his house. I just got in the habit of making his house the turn around place on my morning walks. We became good friends and I hired him to build the rectory.)*

The Office of Readings has some good points about Step 3 . This is Tuesday, the 8th Week in Ordinary Time and the reading is from "The Confessions of St. Augustine:" *"O Lord, the depths of a man's conscience lie exposed before Your eyes. Could anything remain hidden in me, even though I did not want to confess it to You? In that case I would only be hiding You from myself, not myself from You. But now my sighs are sufficient evidence that I am displeased with myself; that You are my light and the source of my joy; that You are loved and desired. I am thoroughly ashamed of myself; I have renounced myself and chosen You, recognizing that I can please neither You nor myself unless you enable me to do so."*

After Mass I write my letter for the bulletin. I have lunch, then a nap. There is no trigger for a drink that I am aware of, but the desire is there. Yesterday I discovered that we have had yet another burglary. This time it was the trailer. Father Oglesby has been turning the lights off at night to save money. I suggested that he leave them on. Today Wally and I go to Sears to replace the trailer.

Then it is Happy Hour time and I recognize the reason for more triggers. The triggers are there but I deal with them. Bruce, his dad, Greg, and I celebrate Vespers and then we have a cook out. After the cook out Bob C. goes with me to an AA meeting. There is a Newcomer there. Every one is very supportive. Many people tell their stories. This still amazes me. Some meetings are better than others but all are growing experiences for me. Two people pick up White Chips. I have been to two Newcomer meetings. One guy was ordered by the court, the other guy decided on his own. I'm like the first guy. I had to be pushed. It wasn't the court. It was the Bishop, and in my life the force is about the same.

Bob and I return to rectory and we talk with Bruce for a while. Bruce tells me that he, and my other interveners, will be at the meeting with the Bishop with me tomorrow. I am happy to hear this. I had mentioned to the Bishop that I thought it would be a great idea, but I didn't know that he had followed up on it.

THE LETTERS

LAKE ORION TREATMENT CENTER
1840 West Scripps Road
Lake Orion, Michigan 48305

Most Reverend Daniel M. Buechlein, O.S.B., D.D.
Bishop Of Memphis
1325 Jefferson Avenue
P.O. Box 41679
Memphis, TN 38174-1679

CONFIDENTIAL
Re: Father William F. Stelling

Your Excellency;

Father William Stelling will commence a ten (10) day Therapeutic Leave from Guest House, Lake Orion, on Saturday, May 27, 1989. For your general information, he is scheduled to arrive that day in Memphis at 12:51 p.m. on Northwest Flight 293. After he completes this brief stay at home, Father will have approximately two (2) MORE WEEKS LEFT AT Guest House before he is finally discharged.

I have watched Father Stelling grow and change for the past couple of months. From initial wariness and distrust, he has learned to interact freely with staff members and conferees. He risks disclosure and then talks about the benefits of having done so. He now has a working knowledge of what it means to remain continuously sober with the help of the fellowship of Alcoholics Anonymous. He lends proper cognitive weight to the concept of alcoholism as a disease. This idea was not an easy one for him to assimilate, but he can now see that the first drink is representative of a meaningless life and possibly an early death. Father Stelling is one of the lucky ones who has already realized many benefits from his efforts at continuous sobriety. He is a gifted and sensitive man who sees beauty in the simplest things. He now reports a clearer vision and his memory is beginning to improve. "There is no way," he says "that I could ever find happiness in a lifestyle which included drinking." He is now working at quality sobriety.

The purpose of Therapeutic Leave is for the man to locate and attend Alcoholic Anonymous meetings in his home area. He can also, at this time visit with family, friends and conferees and take a needed rest. Assignment problems, if any, can be discussed with you or your designated representative. It is a time when the man can see how he feels sober in an environment where before he more or less had recourse to alcohol on a regular basis. After this time away, he can come back and process, with the help of staff and friends, any possible troublesome feelings which he might have encountered.

If you should have questions or concerns, please contact me.

Sincerely yours,
Lynwood E. Buysse, Counselor

136

CHAPTER ELEVEN
WEEK ELEVEN

MAY 31, 1989
Wednesday

I sleep late but I take a walk to Charlie's house, and find that he is home. We have coffee and conversation. I pray the Rosary on the walk back. Bruce has the Mass and I attend, but I do not share the Cup. After Mass I have breakfast with Bruce then go to pick up that condiment server I had re-silvered for Rosa.

On the way to the Bishop's House I begin to listen to The Big Book Study tape that Jim loaned me. I remember my last visit to the Bishop's House. It was on March 22nd, the first day of Spring. I was nervous then, and for some reason I am very nervous today. Last time, he asked me to come to his house. This time, I asked him if I could come to his house, but I am still nervous. I wait in the car 'til the last minute. A maid answers the door and I wait in the entryway of the Bishop's house for a few minutes. It seems like hours. He is very gracious, I am very nervous. He asks why I am so nervous. I mention that I have entertained the thought that I could have lost my parish.

He says, "I told you that you were still the pastor."

I reply, "Well you could have changed your mind."

The Bishop laughs, that deep and gracious laugh of his, "No, I haven't changed my mind."

He is gracious, very gracious. I don't deserve it. All of those thoughts mix up together in my mind. I am so nervous that I cry. I didn't expect to cry. In fact I had rejected the thought trying to show the Bishop just how sincere I am by crying. Boy I really do have vain and selfish thoughts. I share with him that I have come to appreciate the importance of AA meetings, and tell him of my personal experiences, especially my meeting with Jim H. I also tell him that I am having a difficult time knowing how to make amends to him, and to the people for all that I did not do because of my drinking. He says, "Just be the best priest you can."

The Intervention Team comes in, and I express my gratitude to all. There are no words like, "You were wrong." "We were right." It is not even the welcome back of a sheep, or pastor, that had strayed. We just embraced, and the conversation focused on the future. The Bishop did mention the big celebration of the 150th anniversary of the first Mass in Memphis, his 25th, and the presence of Mother Teresa. I told him I didn't think that I was ready for a celebration of that size. He understood. The whole meeting took about a half hour. On the way home I marveled at the fact that I had actually told the Bishop that I would not be able to attend that big celebration.

I had lunch with Victor. It's good to be with a trusted friend. I return to the rectory and talk with John Tindle. I agree to raise his salary from $4.00 per hour to $5.25 (especially when I find that Pat Trainor (a teen in the parish) is making the same hourly wage. I also urge Len to give him a $100.00 bonus.

Then I'm off to Jackson where I have supper with Sid and Rosa McDonald, and Father Al Kirk. They have many questions about Guest House. We talk 'til very late. I sleep on couch because that room is air conditioned.

JUNE 1, 1989
Thursday

I slept 'til 7:45 a.m. Rosa and Sid, and I enjoy a nice relaxing time at breakfast. Many is the time, when I visited, that I started the day with two, or three glasses of white wine. Today it's orange juice and coffee. I take time for the Office of Readings and Morning Prayer. Then I leave for Nashville.

I arrive at about half past noon, much earlier than I thought I would. This means that I have time on my hands. I am uncomfortable with that so I use it to visit with Harvey Carter at Waller Buick, where he works. Dawn, Harvey's daughter, drops by and we agree to meet at the house for a late lunch. On the drive to Harvey's house I pass several triggers, billboards inviting me to have a cool one. Dawn, and her boy friend, arrive at the house about the same time I do. We have lunch and talk. After that I get a good nap in.

I search the phone book for an AA number, Dawn asks what I am looking for. I am a bit embarrassed, but I tell her. This embarrassment is a new feeling for me. I finally find the number Larry gave me, and I call it. It is the 202 Club, they have an 11:30 a.m. meeting every day. I plan to go on Friday. Harvey comes in about 4:30 p.m. we have a good talk. He tells me about Marge's death then we go for a relaxing ride in the country. We have steaks cooked on the grill. Harvey, and I do nothing except "be together." He mentions the possibility of priesthood. I think that might be a real possibility, but it is a bit early to be making plans. He has been a Permanent Deacon for some time now. I don't think he would even consider priesthood until after Dawn finishes school.

During the evening there are several triggers for a drink. I mean that's what I always did in the evening.

JUNE 2, 1989
Friday

I have a good night's sleep. Dawn helps me with the coffee. I take a walk down a country road with Jock. (Harvey lives in the country.) After breakfast I pray the Office of Readings and Morning Prayer. Harry Sullivan calls and wants to know what time to expect me. I tell him between 2:00 p.m. and 3:00 p.m.

The AA meeting is at 11:30. I misjudge the time and arrive late. I remember what Jim said about getting there early, it makes sense. There were no seats available. The return trip to Harvey's is through slow traffic, so I stop to pick up lunch on the way. Jock and I enjoy a quiet lunch in the country. I say good bye to Harvey's house and drive to Harry Sullivan's. The traffic is bad, and I get there about 3:30 p.m. Harry and I greet like long lost friends, which we are. When Mary Alice arrives we all head for St. Ignatius of Antioch for the Memorial Mass for Marge. The traffic is still bad, but we make it by 6:00 p.m. Harvey's parents, Marge's brother, Jim, and his family are there. They have no non-alcoholic wine so I use alcoholic wine. I see that I am going to have to carry my non-alcoholic wine with me in the future. I just let it touch my tongue. I am surprised by the somewhat burning sensation. The thought occurs, "This doesn't hurt me." In this I recognize what I think could be called, "Stinking Thinking." "This little bit didn't hurt could easily, and quickly grow to be much more." The Memorial Mass is something I really wanted to do for Harvey, and there are tears all around.

We all go to the Knights of Columbus Club for dinner. They all have something alcoholic to drink, I have club soda, but I do not feel at all out of place. I meet Don and Jean Wells again. They are volunteers at the K of C Club. I gave them instructions years ago. He returned the favor by giving me instructions to be a pilot. I advanced enough to solo a couple of times, but when I moved to Memphis I had to stop flying. It was then that I discovered that Don and another friend had been paying my dues and flying time. I could not afford to continue. Don and Jean's daughter, Donna, drops by with her husband. She was just a baby when I baptized the whole family. When the dinner is over, everyone begins to leave. Harvey remains. He has an after dinner drink. I want to stay with him, but I don't want to stay in that environment. I feel a bit selfish leaving him. Harry, Mary Alice and I go for Frozen Yogurt, then home and to bed.

JUNE 3, 1989
Saturday

Another good night's sleep. Jock and I walk in the park as I pray the Office. Back at the Sullivan's I read 'til 10:45 a.m., then I'm off to the AA meeting at 11:30. I get there on time this time, and I get a seat. I enjoy the meeting, and feel right at home. I meet Harry and Mary Alice for lunch then enjoy a lazy afternoon. That evening we have a cookout at Pat and Rick's. (The daughter and son-in-law of Harry and Mary Alice.) At the cookout we are joined by more of the extended Sullivan Family. There is quite a crowd. They all have drinks during the evening. They drink normally. I have club soda and do not miss drinking. One of the visiting children calls Mary Alice "Grandmother" and me "Grandfather." Harry gets a kick out of that, I enjoy it. It is a very good evening with the kids playing.

Later that evening, back at the Sullivan's house I find that Mary Alice remembers more about my drinking than I do. I don't really believe her. I wonder if this is some kind of "denial"? I don't know. She has the advantage since I do not remember a lot of things. It is not a case of a blackout, although I have experienced a few of those. Mary Alice, and I disagree from time to time and it bothers me. Perhaps I just don't know how to disagree. I think it's going to take a while for me to learn something about disagreeing. I think that it just might be part of my recovery. At any rate I don't lose sleep over it like I used to. I used to lose sleep, and worry, but do nothing constructive. Now I am at least thinking about what to do, and not losing any sleep.

JUNE 4, 1989
Sunday

Another good night's sleep. I am up early. Jock and I walk in the park as I pray the Office. I celebrate Mass at 9:00 a.m. at Holy Rosary. The pastor there has my kind of wine and I am very comfortable. I use Barry's sermon. *(I still cannot remember what was so special about that sermon.)* I feel good about it. Harry says he enjoyed, and says that Mary Alice enjoyed it too.

The drive from Nashville to Memphis is uneventful. At home I write a brief letter for bulletin, but I must rewrite it. I call Jim H. but there is no answer, so I go to the AA meeting at the Tower alone. It deals with Honesty - people pleasing is a form of dishonesty for me.

After the meeting I go to St. Ann's to be with the priests and spend the night there. They have just come back from the big Diocesan celebration, and are all excited about it. As I listen I am glad that I did not go. I'm just not ready for that sort of thing yet. Victor remembers that he will be at "Study Days" this week so I must make arrangements for Jock. I check with Bruce about Greg, but Greg will not be available. Jock will simply stay at home, my rectory. Bruce says he will check with Len, I tell Bruce, I am not asking permission. I realize that I have been assertive without getting angry, and I like that.

JUNE 5, 1989
Monday

I am up at 7:00 a.m., and have coffee and conversation with Vic. Charlie, another priest, gets up and we have a little time together. I take Jock and go to Nativity. I talk with Len about the parish, and tell him what I have decided about a problem we have discussed. He agrees. Then I go up to office to write a personal note to solve the problem. I rewrite my letter for the bulletin, and take care of some banking. I return to the rectory, say good bye to Greg, and to Jock. Then I return to St. Ann leaving Jock at my rectory. Vic and I pray together and then we go to the airport. I feel much better about the airport than I did when I left Detroit.

The flight to Detroit was uneventful. Funny, I think of Guest House as "Home", and it is good to be home. Bob is late picking me up, and I am about ready to call and then have supper when they show up. "They" is a young priest here for aftercare. He is what I, in my superior judgement, call a typical "young" priest. I recall thinking that I hope he can solve all the problems while he still knows everything. While I was at Nativity I received a letter from Guest House inviting me to be in a video about Guest House that they will be filming June 26 - 30. I agree. I have one of those headaches, and I'm hungry so I don't go to any meetings. It is nice to have a free night.

JUNE 6, 1989
Tuesday

I sleep til 7:00 a.m. It is good to enjoy breakfast with the guys I have spent so much close time with. After breakfast I take my walk and pray the Office.

9:00 a.m. – The lecture is about Re-entry. Since John K. is still on TL only Will, and I are there for the Re-entry talk and a video entitled, "RELAPSE."

10:00 a.m. – I meet with Len and Paul. I recount experiences while on TL. Len is happy about the number of AA meetings I went to. He is a little upset that I served drinks to a guest, and he would have me get rid of the stock in the wet bar in the rectory. He also thinks it is a bit too early for me to associate with those who drink. I don't think this is possible, or necessary for me. Paul seems to understand. But I take seriously what Len says. He was right about MEETINGS!!

11:00 a.m. - Group is good. I recount my TL, it is here that Len expresses his concerns about me serving drinks, etc. Many in group sort of share his ideas. The Group expresses a concern about the departure of Dr. Ken Adams. They think it leaves a vacuum.

1:00 p.m. – Jack Gregory's group. He is startled when I tell the group that when hearing the confessions of those making their first confession I let them sit on my lap if they wanted to. I look at it as a way of helping them feel unafraid, he sees the possibility of sexual scandal. That really never occurred to me. Only a very few take the opportunity and it is only for First Confession. Also I always discussed the offer in the meeting with the parents. I tell them that I tell the children that when they come to confession they can sit down, kneel down, or sit on my lap if they want to. I have always heard those horror stories about fearful kids making their first confession and wetting their pants, and I wanted to put them at ease. I never considered that there was anything sexual about it. Nevertheless I accept his caution.

After Jack's Group I started to get ready for an exercise program, but when I saw Jim getting the van ready to go to the airport to pick up John K. I decide to get permission to go with him to greet John, besides I want to get out of the exercises. We return at 6:30 p.m.

After supper John K. and I talk with Will about making arrangements for our departure Mass, we agree to meet on Thursday. John and I walk and talk about our TL. We mention the real possibility that Will may think we are taking over since we are such good friends.

I get Raymond B. to help me sort out the pictures I have taken. I am missing one negative. I guess I'll have to take some more pictures to get the one that I want.

I call Nativity and talk with a staff member to check on my letter for the bulletin and to see how she/he reacted to my note which confirms that he/she will not be paid staff as the fiscal year begins and that Gay, Eva, and Father Oglesby know this. She/He is okay with that. I just wanted to make sure that the news is not out 'til this staff member knew about it.

Spring really did come to Guest House.

At the beginning of this book I showed you this picture, but there was snow everywhere.

THE LETTERS

(This letter was written while I was at Nativity on TL.)

Dear Family at Nativity,

It was good, very good to be home last week. I hope the emotions of the minute were easier to bear for you than they were for me. Tears are something that come easily to me, but are most difficult to share in public. Tears are not something of which I am ashamed, just something difficult to share.

I have enjoyed walking in the neighborhood. I drove through the old Johnny Maher property. They had already started some of the houses before I left but I was surprised to see how many had been completed. I sure hope that some new Catholic families move in and join our Nativity Family. I plan to drive through some other developing neighborhoods. The area is changing rapidly. I have made some major changes in my life and I think we have an opportunity, as never before, to reach out to new people. But as Jesus said on more than one occasion in one way or another, our first job is to those of our own house who have sought greener pastures. After I return in June I will be working with our Pastoral Council and others who are interested in a search for workable ways of reaching out to old and new alike. If you have some ideas please talk them over with any member of our Pastoral Council.

Tomorrow I will meet with Bishop Daniel to let him know what has been going on in my life in the last two months and to thank him for the opportunities he has offered me.

I will be going to Jackson to visit Father Kirk and other friends. Then I will go to Nashville to visit friends. While I was at Guest House the wife of Harvey Carter, one of my good friends, in Nashville died of Lou Gehrig's disease. She was only 40 years old. I married Harvey and Margie, baptized their daughter, Dawn, and have enjoyed Thanksgiving with them for 20 out of the last 23 years. Harvey is a Permanent Deacon and served with our Deacon, Larry Howell at the dedication of our first building. I will also be visiting with Harry and Mary Alice Sullivan. I have known them as long as I have the Carters and have celebrated all but one of the weddings in the Sullivan family.

I will come back from Nashville Sunday evening and then return to Guest House on Monday. On Father's Day, June 18th, at around 6:30 p.m. I will return to the parish for good, that is, for better or worse.

This whole thing has been a learning experience for me and will continue to be for the rest of my life. Alcohol has been part of my life for at least the last 40 years and the changes in my way of life will include more than just not drinking. I will be learning new ways of dealing with stress, emotions, friendships, and many other things that will affect the way I live. I think it is very important for you to realize that I know that I, and I alone, am responsible for my sobriety. When I come to your home, please don't hide the liquor. If you drink, that is your right. I know that just because I quit drinking does not mean that the whole world has to quit. Why, I have even heard of some alcoholics who took offense because their friends did not trust them enough to enjoy their favorite beverage when they were around. My favorite beverage, by the way, is Club Soda, with a twist of lemon, or lime.

Bye now, see you in June, God's Peace and my love.

Father Bill

======================================

GUEST HOUSE
June 6, 1989

Father Stelling,

Congratulations on your successful completion of treatment here at Guest House. We hope your stay here has been profitable, and will represent the beginning of an alcohol/drug free lifestyle that will add new meaning to your personal and ministerial life.

Your counselor has indicated that you will be taking part in the departure Mass/ Luncheon on Wednesday, June 14, 1989 with Fathers Will C. and John K.

We would like to offer the following procedures for your consideration when preparing your departure ceremony program. These procedures will serve to assure that this most significant event will be given the recognition it deserves.

1. When possible, a meeting should be held the Friday before departure for graduates to determine participation in the Mass, as well as the Luncheon ceremony.

2. Departees would meet with Mr. Higgins and/or myself on the following Monday for a quick review of the program.

3. The program could then be submitted to the front office by Tuesday afternoon for typing.

4. During the luncheon, we would request that the first speaker not be introduced until everyone has finished their ice cream and cake, thereby affording all staff, residents and guests an opportunity to attend to the speakers without distraction.

Thank you for your cooperation. Prayers for lasting sobriety.

Earl E. Kilbourn
Clinical Services Supervisor

CHAPTER TWELVE
WEEK TWELVE

JUNE 7, 1989
Wednesday

I enjoy my regular routine of breakfast, a walk & praying the Office.
I ask Ron to let me have his scarf again for a while, but I don't tell him why.

9:00 a.m. – We have a special lecture by a person named Marietta. I cannot recall her last name. The lecture is on Forgiveness. She tells us how she dealt with the experience of having her young daughter kidnaped, abused, and murdered. She recounts the spiritual experience she went through in being able to forgive the one who did this.

11:00 a.m. – In Group John K. asks this question of one who is trying to discern Unmanageability: "Was there anything about your life that you were unhappy with, and did it have anything to do with alcohol?" I find the question very helpful, and would have found it very helpful six weeks ago. I had a difficult time recognizing Unmanageability and I think this question would have helped.

Jim B. seems to be having a difficult time just being here. I think Len is trying to get the Group to help, but I also think the Group is too big for this. There are too many hiding places in a large Group. I think a one on one would be more helpful to him. It would have helped me a great deal to be able to help, but I'm just not there yet. Then I realize that this is what my peers, my fellow Guests, are here for. There have been many times when John and I, and others have walked and talked, and it was very helpful to me.

Shopping at the Mall in the afternoon. I get a heating and vibrating pad for my neck and back.

4:30 p.m. – The Mass is very good. I recall the first time I shared in the Mass here at Guest House. There are no tears this time. Just a great feeling of peace and serenity.

John K. and I talk and walk, he is having some anxiety problems the closer his Departure date is. This is very helpful to me. For some reason it always comes as a surprise to me when I find that other people are experiencing the same things that I am experiencing.

7:00 p.m. – The AA meeting is at Beaumont. It is a good meeting. It focuses on the First Step. I note that each time we say anything at the meetings we identify ourselves with: "My name is Bill and I'm an alcoholic." This, for me is an ever present reminder of the First Step. I think our driver is a bit preachy, but I take it as coming from a heart filled with love.

JUNE 8, 1989
Thursday

9:00 a.m. – Re-entry Group meets with Erik. We have a good discussion on Recovery, and what to expect and how long it will take. I am surprised that recovery takes as long as three years. I just note things like this silently. I mull them over in my mind, but seldom ask anyone anything about whatever I'm thinking about.

Paul is with us again at Group. Group is smaller and better. I try to remain silent and listen.

I get the address, and stats on Paul and Len. Paul is only 26, WOW!! If I had as much on the ball as he does when I was 26 I'd be Pope by now. I get my Flight information from the office: Sunday, June 18th, NorthWest Flight 884 departs Detroit 5:40 p.m., arrive Memphis 6:32 p.m.

Will, John, and I meet to plan our Departure ceremony, John will be celebrant at Mass, Will will preach, and I will give the talk at Lunch. We try to pick a variety of people from the staff to participate.

Len has given me information on Aftercare and has told me to work out an Aftercare Program. It looks pretty simple, but I must take it seriously.

I talk with Joe H. about using Jim H. as my sponsor when I get back to Memphis. She says, "It sounds like a good idea." I'll call Jim after the AA meeting. I take time to write to the Bishop and write my letter for the parish bulletin.

4:30 p.m. –Mass and then supper. A man named Michael talks. I am impressed with him. He works with AIDS victims, and is a man of great love.

The AA meeting is at Manresa tonight. I have one more meeting there. It is a good meeting. After the meeting I call Jim H., in Memphis, about being my sponsor. He agrees. We talk for about 10 minutes. I never talk that long on the phone. I think Jim will be good for me. So far he helps me bring out what is good in me.

JUNE 9, 1989
Friday

9:00 a.m. – The lecture is with Erik and it is on Re-entry. It is good, interesting. He goes over the time limit, but these sessions are building confidence in me about getting back into the parish.

11:00 a.m. – Group is about Response. I pay Jim B. a compliment. I tell him that he really listens well and gives his answers much thought. When it comes Jim's turn to talk, he tells us the story of the situation in which he was living. It was ghastly. The group begins to wonder how and why he put up with it. I mention that I would have put up with it because I don't like to make waves, I'm a people pleaser. I keep things bottled up inside and then explode in a disaster.

After Group Len mentions the particulars about coming back to Guest House for the video. He gives me a list of questions that could be used on the video. I then meet with the office staff and make flight arrangements to come back on Monday, June 26 and return to Memphis on June 27.

I make a quick trip to K-Mart and Video Store. I use the rest of the afternoon to finish my Aftercare Plan. Will, John, and I wrap up plans for our Departure Mass.

We had a good thunder storm this afternoon. I enjoy thunder and lighting. This thunder storm knocks out the power. It returns, but only dimly at the Villa, so I go down to the office to finish reading the book "The Negotiator." It's a good thriller.

Here is my Aftercare plan.

GUEST HOUSE
INDIVIDUAL AFTERCARE PLAN
PREPARED BY: REV. WILLIAM F. STELLING

Before changing anything on the Aftercare Plan, I agree to talk it over with my Counselor or my AA Sponsor.

I. THESE NEED MY ATTENTION FOR AFTERCARE:
  A. Alcoholism/Chemical Dependency
  B. Health
  C. Emotional/Psychological
        Personality Characteristics (good & bad)
        Sexuality
  D. Spiritual
  E. Social:
        Assignment
        Recreational
        Friendships

II. RECOVERY GOALS:

  A. Quality Sobriety
  B. Continued Growth in Good Health.
  C. Personality Characteristics: Peace through continued growth
     Sexuality Concerns: Peace through continued growth.
  D. To have a regular Confessor / Spiritual Director and
     Shared Prayer Experience.
  E. Assignment: Discern Spiritual & Physical Status of Parish
     Recreational: Daily Fun Time, Regular Day Off & Annual Vacation.
     Friendships: Strengthen old and establish new friendships.

147

III. MY PLAN:

A. At least 4 meetings per week for the first month and then a minimum of 3 until I return for Phase I Aftercare which will be December 11th through 15th, 1989. Continued reading and study of "The Big Book," "The Twelve and Twelve," etc. I have secured a Temporary AA Sponsor, Mr. Jim H. and agreed to his guidance.

B. Within two months find a doctor who will be "My Doctor" and establish annual physical date. Use the exercises given me by Meadowbrook at least three times a week plus daily walk of at least one mile. Use the diet recommended by Meadowbrook.

C. Personality Characteristics: Reading of related material at least once a week, e.g. Risking; Anger; etc.

D. Reestablish contact with Fr. David Knight as Confessor/Spiritual Director and initiate Shared Prayer with Father Victor Ciaramitaro (we have already agreed to this) for Wednesdays at noon.

E. Assignment: My Pastoral Council and I, with appropriate committee assistance, will try to ascertain, within the next 6 months, the Spiritual status of the Parish with steps for improvement. My Finance Council and I, with appropriate committee assistance, will try to ascertain, within the next six months, the Physical status of the Parish with steps for improvement.

Recreational: Begin to REALLY take one day off each week. If I do not physically go some place I will instruct the secretary not to contact me at home by phone or any other means except in emergency. I will make definite plans to take a vacation this Fall in Daytona Beach with family and make annual vacations a priority item. Schedule at least one hour of "fun" time each day. Establish, at least once a month, quality time to work on my book.

Friendships: By phone, personal visit, or letter to carry on some meaningful conversation with at least one friend each week. Lunch with Father Victor Ciaramitaro on Wednesdays. Look to the establishment of new relationships with people in the program with the help of my sponsor and priests of the diocese in the program.

IV. AA CONTACT: Jim H.

V. CONTINGENCY PLAN:

I have available to me my AA Sponsor; two priests of the diocese in the AA program and my Guest House Counselor, and others at Guest House that I feel free to call on in the event that I, or others, notice that I am: isolating; having mood swings; experiencing continued nagging headaches; am uptight, nervous, or irritable for noticeable periods of time; not trying to live out my After Care Program or am not working the AA Program.

VI. Aftercare contact person at Guest House is my counselor, Len B.

(Signed)

William F. Stelling

(Signed)
Guest House Counselor—Lynwood Buysse
(Signed)   *(Signed)*
Edward Higgins   Earl E. Kilbourn
Director   Clinical Supervisor.

JUNE 10, 1989
Saturday

WOW is it cold. I choose between a sweater and a suit coat for my walk from the Villa to breakfast. I should have used both. John K. and I walk after breakfast, but we both get added weather protection. I finish up most of my Aftercare Plan. At Lunch Dick K. joins Francis R. and me at the table. We have a very enjoyable talk.

After lunch Barbara B. calls: She says that Helen is depressed because I have not called her, and did not call before returning to Guest House. Barbara understands that Helen is VERY possessive when it comes to me. I am very uncomfortable about this. I do not think it is healthy for Helen, but I do not know what to do about it.

Tomorrow I will have Mass at Immaculate Conception and I am looking forward to it. In the scripture for Sunday there are two stories about restoring to life. The first is about Elijah and the widow's son. The second is about Jesus and the son of the widow of Naim. I choose to say that while these are important, the more important restoration to life is in the second reading: Paul says that we must invite Jesus to live in us, and that is a restoring to a greater life.

JUNE 11, 1989
Sunday

The Mass and sermon at Immaculate Conception go well. I return to Guest House about 2:30 p.m. and enjoy a nap from 3:00 p.m. to 4:00 p.m. Roger Bendle called a few days ago and said he and Pat would be here Sunday afternoon. The Office called me at the Villa to say that the Bendles will be here close to 5:00 p.m. I use the time to update my computer journal. Tomorrow I will order copies of the pictures I have been taking for those who signed up for them. Helen H. calls, and tells me that Dorothy T. will have surgery tomorrow.

Roger and his wife, Pat arrive right on time. I show them around the building, and then we go to Haymaker's Restaurant for dinner. It's great. No drinks. We have a great time talking about "old times" at Nativity. The times, they are a changing and thank God. I'm still amazed that I can have such a good time without alcohol. We return to Guest House, and walk and talk. They brought the "Clue Game" so we play a few games, talk some more and they leave a little after 10:00 p.m.

JUNE 12, 1989
Monday

9:00 a.m. – Connie's first lecture. It is very good. All about relationships. What makes them, and what breaks them. She recommends, "The Struggle for Intimacy". John K. and I meet with Ed Higgins and Earl Kilbourn about the Departure Mass and Lunch. Ed will not be able to be M.C. due to death of close friend. Will is playing in the Guest House Open Golf Tournament and unavailable for suggestions. We wait.

1:00 p.m. – Group is very good. Matt tells his story. What a man, what a very mature person. He is something I would like to be. It rains all afternoon which is not good for the Guest House Open Golf Tournament. It is good for nap, but I work on updating my Computer Journal instead.

Gay calls about my return and to ask if I want to order cokes from coke company, I say NO. I tell her it would be fun to have a cookout on the Plaza like we had for Evening Prayer. Even as I write this I wonder about my need for an AA meeting that Sunday night. I hope that Jim will be there.

JUNE 13, 1989
Tuesday

This day has been all mixed up. The 9:00 a.m. lecture for the Re-entry Group is postponed 'til 1:00 p.m. Len canceled group so I have nothing to do all morning. I spend my time making sure the pictures are in the process, checking with Earl about who is to be Master of Ceremonies, and then checking with Will and John about seating at head table.

1:00 p.m. – Joe H. has the Re-entry Group it's about sponsors and home groups. She gives me some things to think about: A sponsor is someone I need, not someone who needs me. Call your sponsor daily and let him know what is going on in your life. A good sponsor does not give advice, he waits 'til it is asked for. A sponsor tells me when I am letting my ego get in the way, and when I am being too sensitive. A sponsor protects me from becoming a priest at meetings. The job of making AA rewarding is mine, not AA's.

I nap from 2:00 p.m. 'til 3:00 p.m. I have a meeting with Jack Gregory from 3:00 p.m. 'til 3:45 p.m. I tell him how much he has meant to my life in the past three months. I recall how much I have changed and how much I enjoy the change. I don't tell him that it has been difficult getting to know him. I do tell him that knowing him has brought about good changes in me.

4:00 p.m. – I go to airport to meet Bruce. We get back to Guest House a little after 7:00 p.m. Which gives us plenty of time to talk. I share with him how I expected him to call me instead of Thomas with information about his arrival time. This does not call for an apology, just venting feelings, I think Bruce understands this. Bruce and I have supper. John K., Bruce and I walk and talk, after supper. The

150

mosquitoes are out in force and they bother Bruce a lot more than they do me. The mosquitoes in Michigan seem to bigger than those in Tennessee.

I continue to work on my talk for tomorrow. I have talked to Will and John about a significant change in their life as a result of being here. At 10:00 p.m. I take a break for pizza and conversation with Bruce, Thomas, and Greg. Then continue work on tomorrow's talk.

THE LETTERS

Dear Nativity Family,

This is my last letter from Guest House but it will not be my last letter for the bulletin. While I was home I had so many positive comments about these letters that I plan to continue them on a weekly basis. I started these as a way of letting you know what was going on in my life while I was away at Guest House.

There are several reason to continue them:

1) *As a way of sharing with you my concerns about what is going on in the parish.*

2) *As a way of responding to your concerns about what is going on in the parish.*

3) *As a way of sharing some spiritual insights that I may have from spiritual books or other sources.*

4) *As a way of sharing my ideas about what is going on in the Church.*

I know that this will be work to do this on time week after week, but I think it will be worth it. I will need your help. I would like to hear from you about problems in the parish. You can do this by seeing me, or calling me. Of course you can also drop an anonymous note in the collection. I am very much aware of how important it is to be anonymous.

I would also like to hear from you about other things: What are your spiritual insights: Have you had a meaningful spiritual experience lately? A Retreat? A Cursillo? A Marriage Encounter? A Search? Have you had an experience lately that you might not call spiritual, but you really think was a good wholesome Christian, or Godly experience? Have you read any good books, or seen a good movie lately? Again they don't have to be strictly spiritual, just a good wholesome, uplifting book, or movie.

Perhaps the Youth Group has done something they really enjoyed, or something they did that you really admired. Maybe you have found a new and exciting way to get rid of pornography, or drugs, or you know a good program on alcohol, not just for youth, or just for adults, but for us, for all of us who are really trying to know and love God and each other. Perhaps you have found a program that shows how to be better parents, or better students, or just better people.

I love you people, and I have found out just how much you love me. I know that you love each other. Well, I want to use my letters to talk about that. I want to use my letters to help us do that. God has called us to be something very beautiful. To be the living Body of His Son. No one can do that alone. No one can do that only with people they like. No one can do that only with people who like them. We can do it together and I want my letters to be one way to help us do that.

I need to hear from you. I already know that you love me. I know that you really do love and want to love each other. Help me to let each one of you know that each one of you wants to love and be loved by the others.

God's Peace and my love.
Father Bill

GUEST HOUSE

June 12, 1989

Most Reverend Daniel M. Buechlein, O.S.B., D.D.
Bishop of Memphis
1325 Jefferson Avenue
P.O. Box 41679
Memphis, TN 38174-1679

CONFIDENTIAL
Re: Father William F. Stelling

Your Excellency;

A departure Mass and dinner celebration will mark the graduation of Father William Stelling from Guest House. He will be fully discharged from the Lake Orion facility on June 18th, 1989. Father is scheduled to arrive in Memphis that evening at 6:32 p.m. on Northwest Flight 884.

Father Stelling made such excellent progress in our course of treatment that we have asked him to return, as a special favor, on June 26th and 27th, 1989, to take part in a public relations campaign we are conducting. There will be two high quality videos filmed that day in which Father Stelling will appear. Those alumni members whom we believe would be most representative of Guest House have been asked to take part in these presentations. Father Stelling exemplifies clinical success in the broadest sense. He has come to grips with the fact of his alcoholism, and has put into place the components of significant behavior change. He did a lot of hard work and is now ready to enjoy the rewards of his effort.

Soon Father and I will sit down and go over the details of his Aftercare Plan. When we have a finalized copy, I will be sending you one under separate cover. If you should have any questions or concerns, please do not hesitate to contact me.

Respectfully,
(Signed)
Lynwood E. Buysse
Counselor
LEB:njj c: Father William F. Stelling

152

CHAPTER THIRTEEN
WEEK THIRTEEN

JUNE 14, 1989
Wednesday

Today is the day of the Departure Mass and Lunch.

I slept late, that is until 7:00 a.m. I have no classes today. Last minute touches on my luncheon talk. Brother Mo calls just before Mass to offer his congratulations. John does a very good job at Mass, and Will is his true self. His sermon is simple and colorful. About Miracles in our life from Guest House. I was afraid that he might have "stolen" my talk. I am close to tears during Mass. I want so much to work the AA program with my God, and to be the person God calls me to be. The song "Gentle Woman" was very meaningful to me. Guest House takes pictures after Mass of the three of us together.

At lunch Paul and Bruce are seated next to me. Paul tells me he is pursuing a Ph.D. in Counseling. His speciality will be working with Alcoholics. He has the head, he has the compassion, he has the will, and I think he will make a good doctor. My talk goes well and Ron is there. At the end of my talk I give Ron his scarf. In presenting him the scarf I use that thing I had written entitled, "The Scarf." (Unfortunately "The Scarf" is lost.)

GUEST HOUSE FAREWELL
by Father Bill Stelling

I was looking through "The Big Book" the other day for some funny stories that I could tell you today. I'm not talking about "The Big Book of Alcoholics Anonymous." I'm talking about "The Big Book of Jewish Humor." I saw this book in the store and thought it was just the thing for an ex-drunk and a recovering alcoholic. There are some very simple jokes in here: Sam and Josh were together. Josh says, "Sam, please close that window, it's cold outside." Sam replies, "And if I close the window it's going to be warm outside?"

When I arrived here at 10:30 p.m. on the night of March 22nd, Jackie greeted me with warmth, kindness, understanding, and compassion. She told me to expect a miracle. There is a joke in this book about miracles. In one of his routines Bill Cosby tells of a conversation between God and Noah:

"Noah!"

"What? Whadya want?"

"You gotta take one of those hippos out and bring in another one."

"What for?"

"Cause you got two males down there and you need to bring in a female."

"I'm not bringing nothing in! You change one of them."

"Come on Noah, you know I don't work like that."

"Well, I'm sick and tired; I've had enough of this stuff. I've been working all day, working for days, I'm sick and tired of this..."

"Noah?"

"Yeah?"

"How long can you tread water?"

I don't know why but when Jackie said, "Expect a miracle." I really didn't. I didn't expect God to work that way. The fact is I was not real sure how God worked at all, I'm still not sure.

However I knew then, and I know now that Jackie was certain that I would find a miracle. I began to look for the miracle of which she spoke.

It seems like a miracle that I read even half of the books that were rather seriously recommended to me. But that was not the miracle of which she spoke.

Surely it is a miracle I didn't gain more weight than I did considering the tasty food and the cheerful way in which it was served. But that wasn't the miracle either.

Perhaps the miracle was that my counselors never lost faith in me. Close, but no cigar, 'cause counselors are supposed to be good at that.

I thought that I had finally discovered that miracle when after attending certain AA meetings I still believed that "Going is more important than content." But no, that was not the miracle.

Perhaps the miracle was that the Housekeeping Crew and the maintenance people could put up with us with such good grace and cheerfulness. That comes close but it just wasn't the miracle I was looking for.

Many will agree that the graciousness and efficiency with which the Office Staff met our every wish and whim is certainly a miracle, but it was not the miracle for which I was looking.

You want a miracle? Consider the safe and courteous way we are so often transported from place to place in the midst of Detroit traffic. Good, in fact great, but not the miracle I was looking for.

In various ways and at different times I asked Dr. Lyons, Jackie, Nova, Diane, and even Ed Higgins about the miracle - they just smiled and said, "Hang in there." I listened with care to Joe, Earl, Erik and his Bridge Group, too. I heard a lot of good things but I still didn't find my miracle. Then the Guest House Open came and Dick and I both hoped for a miracle. Many good things happened despite the rain, but that was not my miracle.

Finally I came to Will, John, and myself. The question was, "Has anything special happened to you." I'll give you the answers but I'll not tell you who said what, after all anonymity is highly prized here.

One answer was, "Of all the things I've discovered about myself, there is nothing that God, the Program, and I can't handle." Another answer was, "Although I've spent a lot of time drinking, I've discovered I've got a lot more to do, and I can start over again and live sober." Finally, "I've discovered some wonderful friendships and a better meaning of community, that's special."

In those three answers is Will's miracle, John's miracle, and mine. It may not seem like much of a miracle to you, but it's a miracle to Will, to John, and to me.

I have the opportunity to say, "Thanks" to all of you, from each of us. I have chosen to say it in something I wrote to celebrate a favor done for me when there was still snow on the ground. The simple act of lending me a scarf. It speaks of an act of sharing by one person but it is directed to all of you. It speaks of an act of gratitude of one person, but it comes from each of us.

(At this point I read what I had written entitled, "The Scarf." Unfortunately I have lost what I wrote. But I know that it ended with the words), ".... and so Ron I now give back to you the scarf you loaned to me. Your act of generosity was an act of love. It spoke, and speaks, well of the love that all at Guest House have showered on us. So, "Thank you, Ron, and thank you, Guest House, for your gift. My gift to you, our gift to you, Ron, and Guest House, is my intention, our intention to live sober."

Will and John left Guest House before I did. My actual departure would be Sunday afternoon. Today I was going shopping. But the shopping trip was delayed. Davie had to take John K. to the airport, so I opted to go with John to the airport and pass up shopping. John has been a very close friend, one I will miss, but one I want to write to. On the trip back and to the Oakland Mall Davie and I have some good close conversation. I have met so many people up here that I can say that I truly love and feel good about that.

Bruce, Tom, Greg and I have supper together (an all Memphis table). After supper Bruce and I walk and then he helps me by making backups for my computer.

AA meeting at Beaumont is good. I share the fact that I have finished the course and will return to Memphis on Sunday and that this causes fear. I think it is a healthy fear, but it is nonetheless fear and I am somewhat uncomfortable with it.

JUNE 15, 1989
Thursday

All schedules are mixed up. I begin packing. After sharing my feelings with Bruce about his calling Thomas and not me I feel I may have hurt him. After all he did come all the way up here to be with me for my graduation. I am amazed at how selfish I am. I tell Bruce I am glad he is here, but because of my new way of relating to feelings I some times express them poorly. We walk and talk but mosquitoes cut our walk short. They are very bad and very big.

I get a nap in the afternoon. Brian Timby, a priest of the Diocese of Memphis calls at 2:45 p.m. I am overwhelmed. Gay calls at 3:15 p.m. seeking more information about my return to the parish. I take time to write letters of appreciation to Len

155

and Paul (my Counselors). I also write note for Guest House for their donation letters. I fail to find time for the Recovery and Nutrition Video.

Due to the meeting of special people the 4:30 Mass is at 5:00 p.m. Bruce and I walk again, mosquitoes are still bad and big. It occurs to me that my time at Guest House began with snowflakes and ends with mosquitoes. The Manresa Driver is a no show and I did want to pick up some books at Manresa. I write my sermon for last Sunday at Guest House and then pack the computer.

(I was given some sample questions to be answered after I returned from my parish for the video to be filmed.)

Q. What part of treatment did you feel was the most beneficial?
A. That is very difficult to say. Personal counseling and rapport with Counselors. The respect and love accorded all the guests by every member of the staff. The experience of AA meetings and the value given them by Guest House. The Peer Group. Individual lectures. As I said it is difficult to single out any one thing.

Q. Did you feel that being among fellow clergy and religious who were also recovering was helpful to you?
A. Most certainly.

Q. What aspect of treatment did you find the most difficult?
A. Looking deep into myself. Coming to accept some of my warts.

Q. What kind of reception did you get upon return to your assignment?
A. Loving, kind, supportive, compassionate, embarrassing. My Bishop was, and is very understanding and supportive. My people knew from the very beginning where I was and why. I wrote to them the day I left and continued to write to them on a weekly basis to let them know what was going on. The Bishop also wrote to them. My first letter and the Bishop's were both read from the pulpit the Sunday after I left. (Easter) My other letters were published each week in the Sunday bulletin.

Q. Were there particular aspects of "Re-entry" that you found especially hard or rewarding?
A. Since I have only recently left Guest House I do not have a whole lot of experience on which to base an answer. I will say this: While on TL I met someone from the parish who is in the program seven years. He had written to me very soon after I entered treatment and shared the fact that he, too, is a recovering alcoholic. He invited me to get acquainted when I returned. I wrote to him just before TL and we were able to go to two AA meetings together. When I returned to Guest House I consulted with my Counselor and Confessor and then called him to ask him to be my temporary Sponsor. He agreed. I am a very nervous type of person and was very up tight the night before I left Guest House. My new sponsor called, just to

say, "Hi, how ya' doing? It's okay to be nervous, but try to relax and know that I'll be here to help you when you get home." For me that was very special and rewarding.

Q. Was it hard for you to accept your alcoholism?

A. Yes, and No. I was intervened by my Bishop, two priests, and my Permanent Deacon. They all were and are good friends. I could not argue with what they said. I had been trying to quit, or cut back on my drinking without success. The Bishop told me that he was taking control of my life since I had lost control. It would not have occurred to me to argue with the Bishop. So my first step in accepting my alcoholism was accepting my Bishop. When I arrived at Guest House I knew I had a problem but it did not sound like any of the horror stories I heard, so I thought perhaps all I had was a bad and strong habit. I was very suspicious of everything and just could not go any further. I accepted the program as a means of overcoming a bad habit. This was the second step in accepting my alcoholism. The program seemed to make sense to everyone but me. I could not understand why others were so easily taken in. Then I had to admit that didn't make sense. I began to accept the program and from that I came to accept the fact that I am an alcoholic.

Q. How did your entry into treatment come about?

A. I was intervened by the Bishop, two Priests, and the Permanent Deacon in my parish. This was with the cooperation of my office staff. I left for Guest House on the day of the intervention, which was Wednesday of Holy Week.

Q. How did you happen to come to Guest House? Were other Treatment Centers considered, recommended?

A. The Bishop was in charge, he decided on Guest House. Two other priests of the diocese had been to Guest House. It would not have occurred to me to argue with the Bishop.

Q. Do you think the intervention leading to your entering treatment could have been done better, and if so, how?

A. For me it was the best and only way.

Q. Did you admit or comply with being an alcoholic before you actually surrendered? What were the circumstances of your surrender?

A. For several years I suspected that I was an alcoholic. However my drinking pattern did not match my brother's, who was an alcoholic. For this reason I found denial easy. I knew that I had a problem but did not know how to solve it. I tried to quit, or cut back without a great deal of success. I had been able to quit smoking and I could not understand why I was having such a difficult time with my drinking. It did not occur to me to ask for help. This would have been too embarrassing. I was able to accept the fact that others, whom I respected, thought I was an alcoholic. This way I could use the treatment, with a clear conscience, and be able to

157

break a bad and worrisome habit. Through working with the program, listening to my peers, my counselors, and God I was led to the inescapable conclusion that I am an alcoholic. There was not a blinding light or anything like that.

Q. How important is spirituality to your recovery?
A. Well it may sound strange, but I think there is no recovery without spirituality and, there is no spirituality without recovery.

Q. What parts of your life as a priest, or brother made treatment and recovery either easier or more difficult?
A. Treatment was made easier because of my vow of respect and obedience to my Bishop. Recovery is effected by my openness to the varied ways in which I expect God to act in my life and I consider this to be an essential part of my priesthood.

Q. Do you believe in "Don't analyze, utilize." That you can "Act your way into a new way of thinking and living"?
A. I didn't used to, but I do now. I used to have to understand EVERYTHING about something before it could be of any value to me. I know AA works, but I don't know how. I'm also told that a Bumble Bee is not supposed to be able to fly, but it does.

Q. Did you have problems or behaviors that seemed separate from your alcoholism that cleared up once you received treatment and became sober?
A. My blood pressure is now normal. I have been on two kinds of blood pressure medicine for about eight years, now I take no medicine.

Q. What are the most common misunderstandings about alcoholism that you have encountered?
A. This question could concern the ordinary NON-alcoholic person, but I prefer to take it as concerning MY most common misunderstanding. For me the most common misunderstanding and most difficult to come to grips with was this: UNLESS MY DRINKING STORY MATCHES THE HORROR STORIES, OR AT LEAST COMES CLOSE, THEN I AM NOT AN ALCOHOLIC. You have no idea how long I struggled with that nonsense.

Q. What do you believe are the biggest obstacles to getting alcoholic clergy and religious into treatment?
A. I will name two: 1) Overcoming the shame and guilt that almost overpowers the alcoholic clergy or religious. It is with difficulty that the alcoholic accepts help when it is offered, even when offered with benevolent coercion. It is rare that the alcoholic voluntarily seeks the help he needs. 2) Overcoming the lack of information available to Bishops and religious superiors and to lay people in the parish on alcoholism as a disease. This lack of information is a large contributing factor to the guilt and shame experienced by the alcoholic priest, deacon, brother, or seminarian.

Q. Did the disease concept of alcoholism help your understanding of your condition in any way?
A. When I heard during treatment, for the first time, that the AMA had unanimously declared that alcoholism is a disease I was surprised. It was confusing to me. I wanted to believe it and I wanted to reject it. Finally it helped me to come to grips with my guilt and shame. It helped me to identify my responsibilities for my sobriety.

Q. Has AA played an important role in your recovery?
A. Yes. It has played an essential part and will for the rest of my life.

Q. Compare your current vocational effectiveness to what it was like prior to entering treatment.
A. It is too early for me to tell.

Q. Where would you be now and what kind of shape would you be in had you not entered treatment?
A. I would still be hooked and on the downward slide. My pastoral effectiveness would be declining along with my health. My interest in life and my vocation would minimal. My bar bill would up and I would still be wondering how I would ever quit drinking. *(Nine years after I quit drinking and entered this program of recovery I had quintuple bypass surgery. I am convinced that if I had not quit drinking I would not have survived my heart problems.)*

Q. Do you think that Guest House brings anything special to treating clergy and religious for the disease of alcoholism?
A. I have nothing to compare it with. I will say that I was treated with dignity, respect and love by all the staff. It provides a peer environment that made for easy and healthy sharing. This exchange contributed greatly to my recovery process.

Q. Describe your physical, mental, and spiritual condition upon arrival at Guest House. What kind of progress had you made by the end of inpatient treatment?
A. When I arrived at Guest House I had a long standing problem with blood pressure and I was very tired, not from the trip, just run down. Mentally I was very suspicious of everything anybody told me and evasive and reserved in most answers I gave. I had a short attention span and my concentration was not good. Spiritually I thought I was doing very good, above average.

When I left Guest House I no longer had a blood pressure problem. I had lots of energy and although I was very nervous I was also filled with hope and the will to go slow but steady. Mentally I had lost a great deal of the paranoia I had. I was working on my own honesty and openness. My reading and comprehension skills were slowly returning along with my attention span and ability to concentrate. I am more patient with the slow pace of recovery. Spiritually I thought that I had been doing well, in reality I had only been holding on. I can concede that my acknowledgment and acceptance of my alcoholism, the treatment program at Guest House, and the AA recovery program is the finest thing that has happened to me spiritually and other wise since my ordination.

JUNE 16, 1989
Friday

7:00 a.m. –I have coffee in my room. This is a luxury that doesn't take much getting used to. On my walk I'm beginning to say good-bye to the squirrels and the Canadian Geese. It'll not be hard leaving the mosquitoes behind. They grow them big up here. I finish the Office of Readings and Morning Prayer and then go for breakfast. I must remember to say good-bye to the cook. He has been very nice. A week or so ago, he had artificial flowers on each table. He told us that we could keep them if we wanted to. I was the only one who wanted them at my table. *(I still have them. They are in the little vase that John made for me. I keep them on the shelf in my study.)*

This is the day that I pack up the computer and start keeping my Journal on yellow legal pads. Actually I packed everything that was going to be shipped ahead.

10:00 a.m. – I meet with Len for the last time. I ask for his prayers. I never mentioned it before but he feeds birds, chipmunks, and squirrels right outside his office window. We have a good talk. This is the man who has helped me change my life, and I guess he has also affected the lives of each person I will touch.

When I think of the way Len brought about this change in me I am astonished. He never tried to control me. I am usually trying very hard to control others, especially the young adults in the parish. This will cause me nothing but grief. I can quickly tell them just how they should change their lives. Len told me that practice is known as taking someone's inventory. The only inventory I can really take is my own. The only person I can really change is me. The most, the best, I can do for others is share with them my experience, hope, and strength. That's right from the AA program, but it's true, and it makes sense. I wonder how long it's going to take me to live that way. All of this led me to apologize to Tom for taking his inventory.

In the evening I play a little pool and then switch to scrabble with Greg F. and John D. Oh, I forgot to tell you Greg is another priest from my Diocese. He has been here for a few weeks. John D. is not all that new. He and I have become friends because of our mutual interest in writing. We play scrabble 'til about midnight. That is late for me. I guess I'm a bit excited about going home.

7:00 a.m. – I am up early despite my late night. During my walk and Office I am distracted by thoughts of my problem of managing - controlling others and situations. Sometimes the awareness, the realization, is overwhelming and a bit depressing. Such a thing to discover this late in treatment. I wish I could talk to Len about this but he is not here today, and I leave tomorrow. John K. tried to tell me. I accepted it, but could not see how serious it is. Now what to do? Turn it over. How? In prayer, and once again submitting myself to the direction of others. I guess a sponsor will be helpful.

The last few days have really stretched out. I am feeling lonely. I recall what that guy said at his Departure Lunch. - What was his name? I can't remember, but he said, "As I look around I realize that as I leave here there is no one here who was here when I arrived." This loneliness brings up my problem with self esteem. Is too much of my self esteem derived from what others think of me? Wow!! Why are these problems coming up just as I'm about to leave. Perhaps I should stay another three months.

I tried a game of pool to lift my spirits and I'm interrupted by a call from Larry W. He is my sponsor's sponsor. Larry tells me that Jim will call me tonight. This really does lift my spirits. Larry tells me that Jim has not received the letter I wrote to him about my departure time. Jim does call a few minutes later. He encourages me to call him every day when I get home. I agree right away. My eyes are a little wet and I'm way above cloud nine. I play another game of scrabble with John D. and Mike T. I win. To bed at a reasonable time tonight.

THE LETTERS

Dear Len,

There is in the scripture a parable that our Lord uses to warn us not to sell ourselves for the material things of this earth. I will use the same words of that parable but give them new meaning to describe just how I feel about you. The parable asks, "What shall a man offer in exchange for his very self?"

What can I say to you Len? What can I offer you? I was in the process of losing my very self and you have changed all that. Oh, I know that it is the Guest House Program. The AA Program. And I know that some, perhaps, could have done a better job than you. I know all that and it is not important, for it is you who have given me back my very self.

What can I offer you in exchange? What a preposterous question! If I could offer you the world, it would not be enough. If I gave you myself, it would defeat your purpose.

I have been reading parts of my journal, parts from the early days. I am surprised and amused by how suspicious, how impatient I was. I am now surprised and amazed at how patient and understanding you were and are.

You have helped me begin to take risks despite my fears. You have helped me to accept compliments without suspicions. You have helped me begin to give honest compliments, not just "people pleasing" platitudes. You have helped me begin to replace cowardice with courage. You have helped me begin to understand that I can be a person that I, and others, can and will like and respect.

What can a man offer in exchange for his very self? I don't know what other men can, or would, offer, but as for this man: I offer you my love and respect; I offer to others, in honor of you, the same help you so generously offered me; and I offer to my God and yours my continuing prayers for your continuing sobriety.

Thanks, Len, for being there when I needed you and thanks for being you.

God's Peace, and my love

(Signed) *Bill Stelling*

P.S. Please feel free to use this letter in any way you think it may be helpful to anyone.

Dear Paul,

From the very first day that I met you I felt, rather than saw, something in you that helped me open up. I felt that you are a person with a willingness to listen, a person who wants to understand and help others. I felt that there is something driving you to be of service. Perhaps "driving" is too strong a word. Maybe it is closer to the truth that you are a person responding to what you believe your Higher Power is calling you to. Yes, I think that's it.

I thank you, Paul, for being there for me. Perhaps you don't know what you have done for me. Let me tell you:

First: You are young enough to be my son, but I don't see you that way. I see you as a brother, not a younger brother, just a brother.

Second: Most of my life I have done my best to be nice to others, to be understanding for others, to be willing to listen to them in a non-judgmental way but I have had a difficult time letting others be nice to me, be understanding, be willing to listen to me in a non-judgmental way. Then I would turn around and get upset because others were not nice to me, were not understanding, were not willing to listen to me in a non-judgmental way.

Len and I were breaking this down. Len was helping me to learn to take risks. Perhaps I was thinking, "Well Len has to be nice, understanding, etc., to me." My peers were all understanding, nice, etc., to me, but then we were all in the same boat and they did not really know much of my dark side. Then you came along. There was something about you, I don't know what, that said I could trust you, that said, "I care."

Well I took the risk and I'm glad I did. You did not disappoint me. You have a lot on the ball, you are going to be a great counselor. I'm sure many people will be glad they met you. But know this, I'm glad I met you and you will always have a special place in my prayers and heart. Thanks for helping me to be me.

God's Peace and my love,
(Signed) *Bill Stelling*

(A letter written to encourage donations to Guest House)

Dear Friend of Guest House,
When my Bishop sent me to Guest House I was filled with guilt and shame. Since alcohol had been part of my life for 40 years I was overwhelmed at the prospect of never drinking again. All of my vision was clouded with fear. I knew I was at the end of my effective priesthood. When I left Guest House I was filled with hope and courage. I was eager to enjoy sobriety, one day at a time. With confidence in the Guest House and AA programs my fear was a reminder, not a conqueror. This is the Guest House Miracle. Thank you for being part of it.
God's Peace, and my love,

Father Bill Stelling

June 18, 1989
Sunday

I'm up early today, my last day here. I take my walk and pray the Office of Readings and Morning Prayer. I finish all of my packing. Enjoy a good breakfast and just sit around and wait.

I have the Mass today. It is special and I have a special person assigned to do the readings. At the last minute he changes his mind. I am hurt, and get ready to overreact - the Serenity Prayer saves me.

The tough part about today is waiting for time to pass. Finally the driver comes to the Villa to pick me up at 3:00 p.m. On the trip to the airport memories race through my mind. I wonder how is it possible that I have experienced so much in such a short time. I will miss Guest House, but I will be back for the video and for Aftercare.

The plane trip is uneventful. Victor, and a small but enthusiastic crowd meet me. The reception was moved inside because of the weather. I called Jim and he meets me in the rectory. We talk from about 9:00 p.m. 'til 11:00 p.m. I feel good, and very comfortable with Jim. I hope that I do not become dependent on him in a way that would not be growth. *(I didn't)* I was also greeted by a card from Bishop Daniel.

From the Desk of:
Bishop Daniel M. Buechlein, O.S.B.
Bill, Peace!
And <u>welcome home!</u>

Thank you for your very touching letter from Guest House.
Know you have my love and respect also!
Congratulations on being included in the
Guest House video.
You're a gem.

Bishop Daniel

The chalice and paten that Gordon helped me make. I still use it at Mass now and then.

CHAPTER FOURTEEN
MY STORY

During my stay at Guest House I was often surprised. No, a better word would be stunned, by the ease with which people shared their experiences. I have come to know this practice as 'Telling My Story.' I didn't think I could ever do that. I have come to know that I can, and should tell My Story. "The Big Book" even gives guidelines for this. I should tell: "What It Was Like," "What Happened," and "What It Is Like Now." Every story differs, and my experiences may pale in comparison to others. However, I have learned that one should never compare, one should always find a way to relate. I have come to understand that there is something in every story to which all alcoholics can relate.

WHAT IT WAS LIKE

I grew up in a family of six boys and four girls. I had four older brothers and three older sisters. In our family adults drank and children did not. At least that was the rule. I looked at drinking alcohol, and smoking as badges of adulthood. I'm not sure when I started smoking, but it was before I went to high school. I was in Catholic Grade School when I decided that I wanted to be a priest. I told my mother and she said to tell my dad, but I just didn't feel like talking to him about that. Anyway, when I went to High School I discovered that God made girls as well as boys, and I thought He did a better job on the girls, so I forgot about wanting to be a priest.

I remember when I started drinking. That was when I was in high school. The thrill of doing something only adults did, and the relaxed, warm, light headed feeling was something that kept me coming back for more. We lived in a dry county, in fact, the whole state was dry, but there were certain cab companies that would deliver to your door step as long as you had the money. They were not too particular about legal ages since the whole thing was illegal from the get-go. My sister and I would call a cab on the weekends. I don't remember ever passing out, and we only ordered a half of a pint. I do recall getting high with a classmate who had a half of a pint of Old Crow in his locker.

I dropped out of High School in my senior year to join the Air Force just as the Korean War started. I did get my high school diploma by taking and passing the G.E.D. test. I learned a lot about drinking while in the Air Force, especially while I was in Japan. It was my considered, and expert opinion, that the major reason for drinking was to get drunk, and I did - often, but I did my work. I was stationed at a rear echelon maintenance base for jet fighters in Korea. I worked in a communication detachment known as AACS (Airways & Air Communications Service). We lived in large eight man tents, but we never had more than six men to a tent. The little town nearby had three main businesses related to servicemen: Bars, Pawn Shops, and Bar Girls. I took full advantage of all three. In those days I rarely practiced my religion, but one Sunday I did decide to go to Mass. I noticed three young ladies in the front row. They worked on the base, but they also worked in town. I felt it my duty to tell the priest after the Mass what was going on. I said, "Father you probably didn't know it, but those girls in the front row were prostitutes." You know what he said? He said, "Yes, I know, but how did you know?"

I never got in any trouble, except for the one time that a buddy and I got disorderly and spent the night in the lock up, and there was the time a month or two before I was to ship back to the States. A buddy and I were drinking late one night in the recreation tent. Apparently we were making a little too much noise for one guy next door. He came over and said, "Shut up!!" We thought he said, "Stand up!!" That was when the fight began. He had three stripes. We had two stripes apiece. After the fight and administrative action he kept his stripes; we lost ours.

When I got back to the States my enlistment was almost up. I was stationed at a separation center in California for a while. They had reenlistment posters and invitations all over the place, but they also had KP lists on the bulletin boards too. Although I had a glorious time in the Air Force I could not be enticed to reenlist.

At home in Johnson City, Tennessee I started college on the G.I. Bill at East Tennessee State College. After one year I became more interested in what my sister and brother-in-law were doing for a living. They were Medical Technicians and that sounded interesting, so I changed my G.I. Bill objective and went to Philadelphia to study. My drinking was what people call normal at that time. I got my certification as a Medical Technician and got a job in Clifton Springs, New York. The hospital was the principal industry there. They also had some natural springs. They smelled awful, but they attracted people.

While working there I drank heavily only on the weekends. I recall that we were located just on the boarder of the Eastern and Central time zones. I had become a practicing Catholic again, so if I was going to go to Communion on Sunday I had to quit drinking at midnight. Well, at midnight a gang of us would jump in our cars and head for the boarder.

I had a date for a St. Patrick's Day Dance with a nurse that I thought I wanted to marry. I had a few drinks before I picked her up and when I got there a half-hour late this upset her. (You never know what's going to upset some people.) I told her that she had every right to be upset since I was a half-hour late. So, to make things right I suggested that she go back upstairs and keep me waiting for a half-hour. (She lived in the Nurse's Dorm.) Well, she did, but when she returned she had on an orange outfit. I had never been aware of the significance of orange at a St. Patrick's Day Dance so it didn't bother me at all. This seemed to upset her a little more. When we got to the dance I was immediately made aware of the significance of orange on St. Patrick's Day by several of my friends, and enemies. Naturally my reaction was to get very drunk.

One very good thing did happen while I worked in Clifton Springs. The hospital administrator was a Catholic, in fact most of the people in Clifton Springs were Catholic. Every year, on the Monday after Easter he would throw a champagne breakfast for everyone who went to Mass every day during Lent. I couldn't pass up the challenge, so I went to Mass and enjoyed the champagne. But I also got something else. Going to what we used to call a High Mass all those days at 6:30 in the morning I rediscovered the calling to the Priesthood that I first knew in grade school.

I applied to the Bishop of Nashville in Tennessee, my home state, and he accepted me, and sent me to the college seminary at St. Mary Kentucky. After that I went to St. Mary's University in Baltimore, Maryland for four years. Of course I didn't drink at all during the school years, but I made up for that during the Summer. I saw nothing unusual about my drinking. I was still in control: I could drink, and I could not drink.

I was ordained a priest on May 17th, 1964. My first permanent assignment was in Knoxville, Tennessee. I served as an associate to a Pastor in a parish and I taught at the Catholic High School. There I continued to drink according to what I defined as normal. I did get acquainted with a drug called Darvon for my headaches. It was delightful and I had a lot of headaches. At the end of the school year it was discovered that the college from which I graduated was not accredited, so I could no longer teach there. I was transferred to Nashville.

In Nashville I served as an associate to a Pastor in a parish, but did not teach. I enjoyed my work there. But in May of 1969 drinking got me in serious trouble with the Pastor. This was the first time that I know of that I went into a blackout. While in that blackout I assaulted the pastor. The Pastor, himself, had some difficult dealings with the Bishop, and so the result of that affair was that I was transferred to another parish. During my time in Nashville I was also assigned as Spiritual Moderator of the Citywide Young Adults. We got along famously. They were all old enough to drink and they did, and I did. At the of the Summer of 1969 I was routinely transferred to Memphis.

I enjoyed serving five years as an associate to Fr. Leonard Oglesby at St. Ann in Bartlett. My drinking was fairly normal. Almost every evening he and I would have one drink together. He would always measure his, which I thought was rather funny. Later in the evening I enjoyed a few more drinks. I enjoyed the hospitality of many of the families in the parish. They drank normally and I thought I did also. Sometimes I would discover that the bottle from which they offered me a drink had been on the shelf for months. I thought this was a bit odd.

In June of 1974 I was assigned as a Pastor for the first time to St. Mary Parish in Jackson, Tennessee. At this point my drinking started to get out of control. I used the excuse that if I did not have a "nice" meal every evening I would soon be eating beans out of a can over the kitchen sink. I told myself that was a real possibility since this was the first time that I would be living alone in a rectory. Of course a nice meal included wine and before and after dinner drinks. I naturally assumed that this was normal drinking. There were times when I would be invited to dinner at the home of one parishioner or another and, just to make sure, I would always volunteer to bring a bottle of wine. If the family didn't drink I would think that was odd, and be sure to have a few drinks before I went to dinner. Of course I would use a mouth wash before I would go to dinner. This too I thought was normal, after all it was odd that they did not drink.

It was while I was in Jackson that I got into the habit of going to bed with Jack Daniels and Johnny Carson. It was during this time that I should have gotten a DUI, but because of the generosity of the Trooper I was sent on my way. I had been returning from a Wedding Reception in Memphis at which I had enjoyed too much champagne. It was also during this time that my headaches returned and Tylenol with codeine was prescribed. The headaches were real, but so was the abuse of codeine. In Jackson I managed to quit smoking. This gave me the impression that I was really in control of things.

In June of 1979 I was invited to establish a new parish in Bartlett, Tennessee. I would be neighbor to my old friend, Fr. Oglesby at St. Ann in Bartlett. This was a real challenge. I started with a vacant lot and a list of names. I had no place to live, so another priest friend, Victor Ciamaritaro, and I went looking for a place. We found a townhouse that suited my purpose. Across the parking lot from me lived a man who enjoyed drinking even more than I did. He worked for someone in my new parish and was also a gourmet cook. We soon became fast friends and established a regular happy hour.

It was at this time that my day off would begin with breakfast and white wine. It was my day off. If I wanted to get a little high in the morning who was that going to hurt. Besides it was none of anybody's business.

I was making some progress in getting the parish of Nativity started. I had built the first building. It was an all purpose building. It had a combination Fellowship Hall/Sanctuary, a Narthex, offices, a plaza, and my living quarters. I was not bashful about inviting people into my living quarters. However, if I happened to be having a drink during the day and someone came to my door, I would hide my drink. This was another signal I missed. Frequently I would have drinks on the Bethlehem Plaza in the evening, even when the Youth Group was meeting. I told myself that I was teaching them that drinking was an adult thing. I was an adult, they weren't. But again I was lying to myself. It seemed to me that I always had a drink in my hand, it was almost as if that glass was growing out of my hand, was part of my hand.

My friend, from across the parking lot, would frequently come to my new living space and prepare a gourmet meal. Of course we would have drinks before, during, and after. We loved to watch the thunderstorms, just the three of us: me, my friend, and Jack Daniels.

Next I built the rectory. It is important that you realize that I keep saying, "I did this" and "I did that." You see as long as I could say that, I did not have to even consider that I was out of control. I mean could I do all of that and have no control? Of course not!!

When I built a very good rectory, I made sure it had a wet bar. Victor and I worked hard on its design. It would be completely separate from the church offices. Victor didn't know it but it would also be a very private place for me to enjoy a drink or two. It was during these years that I began to notice, every now and then that almost 90% of my social drinking was done alone. My friend from across the parking lot had lost his job and moved out of town.

Something very good happened after I built that rectory. Father Bruce Cinquegrani moved in. He had lived with me for a while in Jackson. He was in the seminary and he stayed with me during the summers. The good thing was that he observed my drinking habits and how they had changed since Jackson. I thought I was being very careful. As I said I would always go to bed watching Johnny Carson and drinking Jack Daniels. Every time, just before my glass would be nearly empty, I would always replenish it. That way I could say that I had only one drink. I would go into the kitchen, which was just across the hall from my suite, to refresh my drink. I would slide the ice cube down the side of the glass, so Bruce would not hear the noise, then quietly add the Jack and water.

In 1987 I decided to give up drinking for Lent. I began to think I had to demonstrate that I was still in control. For the first two weeks I did good. Then, for some reason, I took another look at my decision and concluded that I had decided just to give up Jack Daniels for Lent, and it was okay to have wine with my meals. I coined the saying, "It's savage to dine without wine!!" That lasted for a week, and then I made the decision that I had been foolish to decide to give up drinking for Lent in the first place. I had fought the desire to have a drink all day long. It had been a good fight and I thought that I surely deserved a drink for putting up a good fight.

I remember the days when the liquor stores were closed on Sundays. It was an absolute terror to discover on Sunday that there was nothing in the house to drink. I would make up stories that a surprise guest, or group had come to visit, and try to borrow some whiskey from friends or parishioners.

All during the rest of 1987 and into 1988 I made valiant attempts to quit drinking just for the day. The results were always the same. I fought the good fight all day long and now at night, or evening, or noon, I deserved a drink, and I was damn well going to have one. But it never stopped at one.

I remember one night after having gone to bed in my usual manner I was awakened by an emergency phone call at 2:00 a.m. A man was dying. Could I come to the house? I was out of bed in a flash, I got the Holy Oils and rushed to the house. The man was lying on the floor, fully clothed. When I arrived he had just died. I anointed him on the condition that the soul had not yet departed. I stayed with the family until after the police arrived. On the way home I gave thanks to God that I had been able to get out of bed and help the family. I made a firm resolution to do something about my drinking. I mean this was serious. This was what a priest was about. No sooner had I gotten home than the resolution evaporated. I mixed a strong drink to quiet my nerves before going back to bed.

My friend, and drinking buddy, from across the parking lot died. I knew he had a problem with alcohol, and so did he. He had been in treatment for a while, and it worked for a while. Then he decided that he wasn't an alcoholic. Shortly after that he had lost his job and moved out of town. We would call each other frequently. There came a time when he stopped calling. He would not answer his phone when I called. I was shocked to discover the reason for all this. The police discovered his body in his apartment about a week after his death. His former employer had his ashes shipped back to Memphis and he, and I, a few friends buried them. We all knew his death was caused by alcohol. After the brief funeral service I hurried back to my rectory to have, you guessed it, a drink, or two.

Another time I was asked to visit a young patient at Lakeside, a rehabilitation center for many different types of patients. I called and made arrangements. They told me that since I was a minister that I could come just about anytime during the day. I said that I would be there tomorrow at 2:00 p.m. On that day I had my usual drink before lunch, wine with lunch, and an after lunch drink. I rested a while and then went to Lakeside. Of course they smelled liquor on my breath and were unwilling to admit me. I made a scene and they finally let me see the young person. We met in the library, but the staff kept coming in to check on us. I jammed a chair under the door nob to prevent interruptions. When I left I lodged a complaint with a supervisor. (They reported this to the Bishop and it turned up at my intervention.)

I knew I had a problem. I knew I had a serious problem. My brother had the same problem and I had seen the sorrow that it had caused. He had been in and out of AA. But my brother was not a priest. I needed help. But who does a priest go to for help? I mean I was the one people came to for help. Who was I supposed to go to? I truly did not know. Besides, the shame, the disgrace was more than I was ready to face. I decided that I might as well face it from the other direction: I was going to die drinking and there wasn't a damn thing I could do about. I might as well relax.

Christmas of 1988 arrived, and my closet and wet bar was stocked to overflowing with Christmas gifts of Jack Daniels. I was shocked when I had to go to a liquor store in February. For many months before Christmas I had been going to three, or four different liquor stores. I didn't want the sales clerk to know how much I was drinking. But help was on the way. I just didn't know it. I had a regular group of men coming to the rectory for a little poker on Friday nights. The most a guy could lose was ten or twenty dollars. We had good food and good fellowship. We would play from 8:00 p.m. until midnight. We all agreed that an evening that enjoyable would normally cost more than twenty dollars. One night I mentioned to the players, "You know, it used to take 5 or 6 drinks before I would even begin to feel good. Now with just one or two I get a buzz on. Well at least it'll save me some money." Bruce's father was one of the players and he was knowledgeable where alcohol was concerned. He reported my remark to Bruce. (When I revealed this to Doctor Lyons at Guest House, he told me that my liver was telling me that it was not going to process that stuff any more, and was dumping it directly into the blood stream.)

Lent of 1989 came and I made another decision to quit drinking for Lent. I did very well throughout the day of Ash Wednesday, and was beginning to think that I had this thing under control. I did very well until after the 7:00 p.m. Mass on Ash

Wednesday, and then I really did deserve a drink. After all I had gone all day without one. As soon as I tasted that first drink, it was like a snake bite, I knew it was all over. I knew it, and there wasn't a damn thing I could do. I had tried, I had really tried.

My drinking and my despair continued unabated at its usual pace throughout Lent. I was convinced of two things: I had a problem and because I was a priest there was nothing I could do about it. I could not face the disgrace from my parish, my brother priests, and my Bishop. I was tired of fighting and failing. There is a saying that I have learned in AA and it is most appropriate here: "I was sick and tired of being sick and tired."

I recalled that there had been a priest who had been in treatment. He had returned and basically said there is life after treatment. That was three or four years ago. I could have gone to him for help then if I knew then what I know now. But I thought that now it was too late. I don't know why I thought that. There was no good reason to think that way. But, as I heard a guy say recently, "I'm an alcoholic, I don't need a good reason."

How I survived Lent—I don't know. I was really happy when Lent was about over; I wouldn't have to face being a failure everyday. It was Tuesday of Holy Week. In our Diocese that is when we have the Chrism Mass. The Mass at which the Bishop blesses the oils for use throughout the year in the Diocese, and the time the priests renew their vows. After the Mass all the priests went to the Cathedral rectory for finger food and drinks. This year the only thing they had to drink was wine. I remember thinking: "They are trying to control my drinking." I had planned to have a glass, or two of wine and go home for some real stuff. That was when Peter Sartain told me that the Bishop would like to 'visit' with me tomorrow morning, at 9:00 a.m.

That is what it was like.

CHAPTER FIFTEEN
WHAT HAPPENED

"What happened" is really what this book is all about. I certainly won't go back over the intervention and treatment, but I would like to relate a graphic example of what happened as a result of the drinking, the treatment, and the recovery. Before I went into treatment I enjoyed photography as a hobby. I had been working on a "Book of Meditations." The book was to be composed of nature photographs that I took with each photo accompanied by a brief spiritual meditation and a scriptural quote. The meditation itself was to be about 500 words in length.

During the fifteen years that I worked on that book, I also worked on my addiction to alcohol. In those fifteen years I completed only a dozen or so meditations. That is less than one per year. During that time I proudly told people that I was working on a book.

As a result of the intervention, subsequent treatment, and continuing recovery, I have written and published five books—this one being the fifth. I am nearing completion of a novel based on events I have become aware of—genuine experiences of priestly ministry. I have also written a weekly column for our Catholic newspaper for over ten years.

To describe this briefly and succinctly, the Grace of God is "what happened." And I know that God's Grace is there for us all.

CHAPTER SIXTEEN
WHAT IT'S LIKE NOW

As you know from reading the earlier chapters I returned from my treatment at Guest House on Father's Day, June 18th, 1989. I was greeted at the airport by Victor and a small, but enthusiastic crowd. I was expecting a cookout on the Plaza, but the weather changed that. We had party food in the Narthex. The important thing was that I was greeted. I had been home on a therapeutic leave two weeks before so this was no surprise, but it was important. One of the first things I did was call Jim, my sponsor. He agreed to come over by 9:00 p.m. After the reception we talked until about 11:00 p.m. I knew that I needed Jim and I was assured that he would help me.

As I got to know my sponsor I was more and more comfortable with his instructions. I did balk, however, when he told me that he wanted me to go to 90 meetings in 90 days. I told him that I had just been in treatment for 90 days, and besides that I had a parish to run. I didn't see that I would have the time. Jim just looked at me and smiled. Jim had a special smile about him. It wasn't arrogant, it wasn't, "I know better." His smile told me, "We're in this together." He told me that the meeting only took one hour, and going and coming, another thirty or forty minutes. Then he asked, "How much time did you used to spend drinking every day?" I thought a bit, almost immediately saw his point, and quickly agreed. Besides that, Jim was my sponsor.

I balked again when Jim said he wanted me to do a Fifth Step with him. I said, "Jim I've already done a Fifth Step." He just smiled and said, "Well let's do it again, together." I agreed, and we did it. I'm glad I did because it enhanced our relationship. We did the Third Step prayer together also.

Jim taught me many things and introduced me to many new friends. That first year was the most different year I have ever lived. Confusion was a constant companion. A strange kind of fear, like a foreboding of danger, would take over my thinking now and then. There was nothing definite that I could put my finger on. Finally, although I felt foolish, I asked Jim about it. He said, "Oh, that's not unusual. Most everybody goes through that in the first year, or so." I felt better, except for the 'or so' part of his answer. I ask him what I should do about it. He said, "You're doing just what you should be doing." "What?" I asked. "Bill," he said with that smile of his, "You're talking about it." It was so simple. But it was true - talking about things really does help.

One time I told Jim I wasn't all that certain I was really an alcoholic, but that I always felt comfortable at meetings and around alcoholics. My real concern was something I had experienced while in treatment. Jim just looked at me, laughed that soft laugh of his and said, "Bill the only requirement for membership is a desire to stop drinking. You do want to stop drinking, don't you?" "Sure I do," I told him with a firm certainness. "Well, you belong, so stop worrying."

Jim never took over my thinking. He seldom gave me advice. He shared his experiences. He never laughed at me, but he frequently smiled and laughed with me. I guess the best way to put it is that he was a guide who lit my path and suggested that I take it.

We went to many meetings together. One time I was kidding with him and told him that since he was my sponsor I expected him to bail me out of jail if I got arrested. He turned serious immediately. He told me that if I got myself in jail, I would have to get myself out of jail.

I learned something very important from Jim about dreams. As I recall I had a dream some time after I had celebrated my first birthday in AA. I dreamed that I not only was drinking, but I got very drunk. I woke up in the middle of the night in my own bed. For a few minutes I could not remember how I got there. I was filled with shame, terror, guilt, despair, and many other emotions that I don't even have a name for. I finally realized that it was all a dream. My relief was total. Later that day I called Jim and told him about the dream. He assured me that many, if not most recovering alcoholics have this type of dream. I told him I had had drinking dreams while I was in treatment, but none of them were anything like this. Jim told me to frequently recall exactly how I felt, and how good it felt when I knew it was just a dream. This would serve as one good defense against that first drink. That memory has served me well. That was not the last drinking dream I had, but dreams no longer terrorized me.

Another strange thing happened shortly after I had celebrated my first birthday. The idea kept coming into my mind that now I had completed what I had set out to do. A question began to nag at me: "When are you going to go back to normal life?" When I say it began to nag me I mean that I seemed to be obsessed with that question. I talked this over with Jim. Jim always had a smile, and experiences from which I could learn. He told me that this too was not all that unusual. "Remember, alcohol is cunning, baffling, and powerful. It's always calling on you to let down your guard." I said, "Jim you're treating alcohol like it's a person." For a minute Jim lost his smile, and then he said, "Bill, alcohol might not be a person, but it is a monster. That's the way I treat it and it works for me." To this day I continue to look at alcohol as a monster that is cunning, baffling, and powerful."

Jim sponsored other people also. I met some of them. One was a young man, almost a boy. Without any experience I tried to help him. I thought we had a lot in common. We shared the same birth date, and we enjoyed writing. That was all we had in common. He was not ready for the program. In my eagerness and ignorance I wanted to help him, but I ended up enabling him to continue in his addiction. I learned some hard and painful lessons from that experience. One of the most painful of those lessons centered on codependency.

I have discovered that there are as many definitions for codependency as there are people who define it. The one most meaningful to me is: I am co-dependent when I seek, and accept an _inordinate_ amount of my self-worth from what others think of me. That is a lesson that I have to learn again and again. Some people tell me that priests, and other caregivers frequently fall victim to enabling addicts simply because they want to help. When codependency is part of this, it is real trouble. I found that paying attention to the principles of AA and Alanon can be very helpful in this regard. I am still willing to love. I am just more careful and realistic. As Jim told me, I had to become willing to accept life on life's terms. I still believe that love essentially involves a certain willingness to be vulnerable but not, necessarily, to be enabling.

I did encounter several people who wondered how a priest would benefit from the spirituality of AA. I have no difficulty with this. I have always found that the spirituality of AA was not in conflict with my faith and my Church. On the contrary, I find that it enhances the spirituality I have in my home - the Catholic Church.

About a year into my sobriety my Bishop asked me to consider accepting a new assignment. He told me that if it would endanger my sobriety, or even if I did not want to, I did not have to move. I told him I had to talk it over with my sponsor. The Bishop said he was happy to hear that. Jim and I discussed it. We prayed over it. I decided that this was good for me, that this was within the will of God, my Higher Power. This made it easier to leave Nativity, but still it was not without pain and difficulty.

The new parish was St. Joseph in a section of Memphis called Whitehaven. It was thought by some to be a dying parish. It was a racially mixed parish, but mostly African-American. I was flattered by the Bishop's trust, and overwhelmed by the welcome I received.

Jim told me of a good meeting called "The Hole." That was really a gut level meeting. It was also racially mixed. It was a noon meeting and really fit my schedule. I attended it almost every day for two, or three years, and then less frequently.

At St. Joseph I found a people who were willing to work and save their parish. I was very willing to lead, mostly by delegating and getting out of their way. We borrowed money to accomplish major reconstruction, and we repaid the money. We have paid off all our debts. With the guidance of Sister Mary Michael we established a Soup Kitchen three days each week, and a Sunday Dinner for the homeless on the fourth Sunday of each month. At the Soup Kitchen and the Sunday Dinner the people are our guests and they are treated that way. We built a beautiful Prayer Garden. Our school reopened in the Fall of 2001, thanks to our Bishop's Jubilee Fund.

In all of this I never lost contact with a sponsor. My first sponsor moved across the continent, so I got new sponsors. But I'll always remember Jim. I had so many doubts. I doubted I was a real alcoholic. One evening just before Jim picked me up to go to a meeting Bruce and Greg, and another seminarian were having a drink before dinner. When Jim arrived I told him about the incident. I told him I could smell the whiskey. I described the condensation on the glasses, the color, how slowly they were drinking, and how I was getting a little nervous. Jim looked at me, laughed a bit, and said, "Bill if you ever get the idea that you are not an alcoholic just remember this evening. A person who drinks normally would never have noticed as much."

I saw so many people slip time and time again. Jim said, "Learn from it." I told Jim, "I've never slipped." Jim said, "Yet, not yet. You haven't slipped yet." Whenever I thought I knew it all, or knew enough, Jim would say, "There's more to be revealed." Then there came the very painful time when I had to apply the lessons that Jim taught me. After he left Memphis, Jim slipped. He was over a thousand miles away. He stopped returning my phone calls. I talked to my sponsors and in the end the only, and the best, thing I could do was learn from it. It was, and is, a painful lesson.

When I was at Guest House, Len, my counselor, asked me to name some goals. One of the them was to finish writing the meditation book I had been working on for 15 years. That goal has been replaced by something more realistic. I told you about the letters that I wrote to Nativity. Those letters turned into a regular column in my weekly church bulletin. When I got to St. Joseph I continued to write this column. I then met a contact who wanted to publish those columns in a monthly recovery newspaper, called "Recovery Times." I wrote for them for a year or two. The same contact became my publisher.

My first book was a collection of columns on spirituality called, "Simply Spiritual." It was published in 1992 and followed very shortly by a workbook to be used with "Simply Spiritual." The book and workbook are utilized in rehabilitation counseling—focusing on offenders with substance abuse problems.

The Bishop visited the parish and saw a copy of my column for the bulletin. He liked it, and said it should be published in our Diocesan newspaper. So for the last 10 years "The West Tennessee Catholic" has carried my weekly column, known as *"From the Heart and Mind of Father Bill."*

A third book, "Spiritual Reflections on Everyday Living" was a collection of 54 of my columns and was published in 1998. In 2001 "YOU *CAN* GET THERE FROM HERE" was published. I saw it as: "A Road Map To Escape Addiction—My Story." While I was preparing that book I looked for—but could not find—the journal I kept at Guest House, and the letters I wrote and received. In the Spring of 2001, after the publication of "YOU *CAN* GET THERE FROM HERE," I found the journal and the letters. They form the basis of this book. I am also working on a collection of short stories about the daily experiences of a parish priest. Whether I ever publish the book of meditations is no longer important. The important thing is that writing is therapy for me, and it's working. I'm still sober, and I enjoy life, very much.

In recovery I am learning to deal with feelings that I never knew I had. I am recognizing that it is okay for me to make mistakes. It is not okay to deny them. I even know it's okay to be confused, to be sad, to be happy, to be me. I actually enjoy going out to eat without drinking. I watch the University of Memphis Tigers play basketball, and the Memphis Red Birds play baseball. I enjoy live theater. All

176

of these I enjoy without a drink. I know that a drink would only mess them—and me—up.

Remember that decision that I made that I might as well resign myself to dying drunk? Well now, HOPE is a reality for me. Remember how I used to hate those cute little saying in AA? Well now, I not only see the truth of them, I also enjoy those sayings. Especially, "This too shall pass" and, "Progress, not perfection, is my goal." A little bit of progress gives me a great deal of hope and joy.

I picked up something at a meeting recently and I thought I'd pass it on to you. What I picked up springs from one of those 'cute sayings.' The saying is: "Out There." Just two words—but they mean so much to people who take recovery seriously. The subject of the meeting that night was: "Celebrating Sobriety," and many of those who spoke referred to one of the blessings of sobriety as not being "Out There." "Out There" refers to the place, situation, the disaster of returning to drinking. One person said, "If I ever go 'Out There' it will be because I'm afraid to go in here." As he said 'in here' he pointed to his heart. Everyone knew what he meant.

I knew because, right then and there, I was experiencing a very difficult time. Someone had discovered one of my character defects that I was still working on. Sometimes I can go for great lengths of time and never be bothered by it. Then just when I think I'm done with it, I ease up, and you guessed it, that ugly monster rears its ugly head. I had discussed this particular defect with my confessor, my sponsor, and my counselor (while in treatment) so I was not afraid to go 'in here' and without difficulty, acknowledge, "Yep, this is one of mine." For me this is the importance of the fourth and fifth steps. I had made a searching and fearless inventory of myself.

What made it 'fearless' was a growing relationship with God, Who loves me unconditionally. I shared this with another human being, in fact, with several human beings. I knew what I was like, and I had no fear of looking inside of me. I'm seventy years old now, and I'm convinced that the truth will not hurt me. Even if it does, I know that "This too shall pass." The truth might embarrass me, but it will never again put me to shame. The way I see it, when I'm embarrassed it's because of what others think of me. When I'm ashamed it's because of what I think of me.

About Honesty: I no longer have to hide my drinking, because I no longer drink anything that would shame me. I no longer have to be dishonest about my character defects. I don't have to be, but sometimes I am. The worst thing about my drinking, and to a limited extent the pills, was that I was a slave to them. I don't like slavery. I want to be free. I'm convinced that everyone wants to be free. Remember, back in the first chapter (page 15) I was telling you about Marsalis, a man over seventy years old. I wondered why anyone would put him through a treatment program. Well the answer is that everyone wants to be free, even people over seventy. I am now seventy and I have a very strong desire to be free. God created me to be free. I want to grow. This requires honesty.

Honesty involves pain. The pain of being wrong, being embarrassed, being weak, being hurt by friends. Being honest sometimes includes admitting failure. It

177

also includes being right, being proud, and strong, and feeling good about myself. At times being honest includes rejoicing in success and a feeling of accomplishment. What I think it boils down to is that life is both good and bad, life is real. You've heard the saying, "I've been rich, and I've been poor, and rich is better." Well I like to say, "I've been rich and I've been poor, and real is better." When I'm free I don't have to hide from reality anymore.

Life's tough, and sometimes it's very tough, but it's also good, and sometimes very good. It's also a process, and I'm beginning to know how to work the process —12 steps in all my affairs. One day at a time. I recall that early in my recovery, in fact while I was in treatment, I was stunned that recovery might take one or two years. It will take the rest of my life, but this is not a burden to be borne. It is a life to be lived, a challenge to be accepted. I am convinced that all of us are recovering from something, even if it is just from the effects of original sin. Life is time for me to grab all the gusto I can, as a commercial for beer used to tell me.

For me, what's very important is meetings, and the attitude I can shape from them. I have enjoyed sobriety for over a dozen years now and I still go to meetings on a weekly basis. Sometimes more often, but I don't *have to go,* I want to go. I thank God for all his grace, and I thank God for you, and for every person I meet, because it is through you, and through them, that His grace comes to me. That's what it's like now, and I think it's getting better.

Rev. William F. Stelling

28 January, 2002

P.S. There are so many things that I could have written, perhaps should have written, but I fear my publisher will abandon me if I make one more change.

That's my story and I'm sticking to it.

Father Bill
1 February, 2002

CHAPTER SEVENTEEN
Austin (Rip) Ripley
March 3, 1896 - April 11, 1974

Who was Austin Ripley?

Austin Ripley had been dead for some fifteen years when I met him. Everything I know about him I learned, not simply from what others have written about him, but especially from the dedicated men and women who make up the staff of Guest House. The man was about life. He was about sharing life. There was an element about him, about his living, that even death could not kill.

Rip could be described in differing ways. He was a man of many talents, writing being one of them. People have resorted to portraying him as loving, determined, faith filled, saintly without being syrupy. He is described as a man of integrity, persistence, courage, and intelligence. And always coupled with any accolade was the virtue of gratitude. There are those who saw him as a visionary, a man ahead of his time, one who was intuitively knowledgeable about the disease of alcoholism. All, I think, would agree that he, and his wife, were dedicated. They were dedicated to what became known as Guest House.

As I said, Austin Ripley had been dead for some fifteen years when I met him. Perhaps you think that's just a neat—but God forbid—cute way of talking about the living memory of one who has died. But over and above the fact that God sustains life beyond death, I also believe that I met Austin Ripley when I was a guest at Guest House from March 22, 1989 to June 18, 1989. I met him as a living being in my counselor, Mr. Lynwood Buysse. I met him in the professional staff as well as in the cooks, the cleaning personnel, the drivers, the men and women in the various offices, and all the people who maintain the vision of Austin Ripley at Guest House. When I met him, he was a recovering alcoholic, and he convinced me that I, too, could be a recovering alcoholic. I met him as a living being, a living being beyond that which only God sustains.

I had not been a Guest at Guest House for more than two weeks when I became aware of the name Austin Ripley. Unfortunately there was little else that I knew about him. Oh, I knew that he had been the founder of Guest House but that was about it.

I associated the name Ripley with Robert Ripley. I guess every person my age had grown up being astounded by the items in Robert Ripley's *"Believe it or Not"* column in the newspaper.

As time passed and I became aware of the miracles wrought at Guest House, I thought it a happy coincidence that Austin and Robert had the same last name.

When I began to ready my journal for publication I felt obliged to put together a few facts about Austin Ripley.

Ripley was born on March 3, 1896 in Washington, D.C. It is his life after 1937 that I am interested in. His drinking had been a serious problem for some time and in 1937 he ended up in a hospital in Washington, D.C. where he was visited by members of Alcoholics Anonymous. This encounter turned his life around and effected the entire rest of his life.

He was on fire with energy to spread the good news about alcoholism that he had received and traveled around the country giving talks. He learned much about treatment centers that disturbed him. He was appalled by the total uninformed and, at times, punitive treatment he saw being given to alcoholic priests. It was at this point that Rip, a devout Catholic, decided that he would start a proper treatment facility for alcoholic priests.

Archbishop John Gregory Murray, of St. Paul, Minnesota, was his first, and for a while his only, ecclesiastical supporter. The Archbishop encouraged him to come to the aid of alcoholic priests. Ripley and his wife, Lee, made a retreat at a Trappist Monastery seeking guidance. The advice he received was, "Once you abandon all else to devote your life to this project expect violent continuous opposition of the devil. You now will be concerned intimately with his very choicest victims - priests. The devil has power, tremendous terrifying power. You will not bring this concept to reality if he (the devil) can help it, and should you succeed in doing so he will do his satanic best to bring it to ignominious failure. Your very strongest and heartbreaking opposition will come from those from whom you will expect help." All of this 'advice' came true. The monk also told him, "There is on earth only one body of men capable of successfully dealing with this most tragic problem - you men who have gone through the wringer of alcoholism and have recovered - you members of AA."

Ripley envisioned Guest House as a place where its clients were introduced to the principles of Alcoholics Anonymous and prepared to continue to use those principles. He also saw a treatment center that was owned and operated by laity, but of service to the Church. That vision continues to this day.

Guest House of today has grown far beyond the dream of Austin, but it has remained faithful to his vision. It continues to serve the Church by assisting priests, men and women religious, deacons, and seminarians to enter into recovery and with joy continue in the ministry to which they were called.

I close this section on Austin Ripley by including the eulogy for Austin Ripley delivered by Fr. Donnelly in April of 1974.

"In all my years of priestly experience and of life, I have never met a man who more embodied the program of our Lord and Savior Jesus Christ than Austin Ripley. What he did for all of us who are graduates of Guest House was, together with his deep penetrating knowledge of the disease, to show love and compassion such as most of us had never experienced in our lives.

What motivated him?

It was the spirit of being sent. It was a deep realization of faith expressed in his primary virtue which is gratitude, and he realized deeply that he had been gifted by God with all these natural talents, only to submerge them and let them be absorbed like the infinite love that had called him forth from the living slavery of alcoholism, to give to others what he had received."

A Tribute to Gratitude

I think it appropriate that I close this book with a definition of Gratitude written for Alcoholics. It is often attributed to Austin Ripley. It reflects the tenor of his times in as much as it is written in the masculine gender, but it is applicable to both male and female. It is also applicable to everyone who has a need to be grateful.

"Gratitude is the memory of the heart. That quality which enables a man to double his fortune by sharing it. It is the Golden Tray on which we give to another the things we have received from God. The measure of a good A.A., lies not in what he knows, but in what he does. Not in how he thinks, but in what he feels. The assessment of a good A.A. is made, not in the brilliance of his mind, but in the charity of his heart. His stature is not guaged by how high he will reach to receive, but how low he will stoop to serve. A good A.A. is thankful, not only for what he has got, but he is grateful for what he can give. He strives not for cleverness, but for wisdom. He would rather be right than popular. A good A.A. uses not the toughness of his mind, but the gentleness of his touch in bringing hope to the sick alcoholic. For he knows that if ever the lamp of his charity burns dim, the light of another alcoholic may go out forever. We, who when we came into A.A. were not trusted by man in the most trivial affairs of life, now are trusted by God in one of the most important missions on earth—trusted by Him to preserve and pass on this mighty miracle of sobriety to the alcoholic who still suffers."

The sign outside the Austin Ripley Memorial Research and Education Center at Guest House.

181